Antonio's Gun and Delfino's Dream

Antonio's Gun and Delfino's Dream

True Tales of Mexican Migration

SAM QUINONES

UNIVERSITY OF NEW MEXICO PRESS

ALBUQUERQUE

13 12 11 10 09 08 07   2 3 4 5 6 7

Library of Congress Cataloging-in-Publication Data

Quinones, Sam, 1958–

Antonio's gun and Delfino's dream : true tales of Mexican migration / Sam Quinones.

   p. cm.

   ISBN 978-0-8263-4254-6 (cloth : alk. paper)

1. Mexicans—United States—Social conditions.

2. Mexican Americans—United States—Social conditions.

3. Immigrants—United States—Social conditions.

4. Alien labor, Mexican—United States.

5. Return migration—Mexico.

6. Mexico—Emigration and immigration—Economic aspects.

7. United States—Emigration and immigration—Economic aspects.

I. Title.

   E184.M5Q56 2007

   305.868'72073—dc22

                          2006038078

Versions of some of these stories appeared in the *Los Angeles Times, Houston Chronicle, Baltimore Sun, San Francisco Chronicle, San Diego Union-Tribune, Chicago Tribune, Opera Now,* on NPR's *Weekend Edition,* and, in Mexico, in *Milenio* and *Día Siete.*

DESIGN AND COMPOSITION: *Mina Yamashita*

For Sheila

Contents

Antonio's Gun

T he stories in this book are about Mexican immigration to the United States—the largest movement of people from one country to another in our time.

If you are American or Mexican, this flow of humanity will touch your life and change your country for years to come.

I lived and worked as a reporter in Mexico between 1994 and 2004. I wrote often about Mexican immigration and continue to do so now that I live in the United States.

Mexican immigration differs from the waves of European and Asian immigrants that have come to America. It's now lasted more than sixty years and shows no sign of slowing. And unlike immigrants before them, Mexicans have moved to almost every region of the United States—from Alaska to Atlanta. Their arrival in the American South in huge numbers in the 1990s marked the largest influx of foreign-born workers to that region since slavery. Virtually every *municipio*—or county—in Mexico has sent people to the United States.

These stories are about the things Mexican immigrants seek in the United States.

I thought about this often while living in Mexico. Of course, immigrants were looking for work and the future for themselves and their kids that Mexico denied them.

But it was more complicated than that. For one thing, I noticed Mexican immigrants also sought to return home. Immigrants to the United States in other eras might have wanted to go home, too, but they faced arduous journeys. Mexicans' homeland is close, at peace; transportation is cheap and dollars buy a lot. Thus they send money home constantly and return often. Gardeners, drywall hangers, and factory workers spend lifetimes earning dollars in the United States while they build sparkling houses in their villages back home and dream of returning to them for good.

In time, I realized that this return home was partly why, in fact, Mexican immigration north hadn't stopped in sixty years. For one thing, immigrant wealth, on display in their home villages in the form of lavish houses and parties, has helped create conditions that keep people leaving. It entices people north. Furthermore, though immigrants have changed Mexico with the ideas they bring back from the United States, their return and their remittances have also kept Mexico from changing deeply enough. The billions of dollars Mexican immigrants send home resemble oil revenues in that they save the country from disaster. But they also help Mexico's political class postpone the painful reforms that are needed if the two-thirds of the country bogged in poverty is to rise above.

I also saw that while immigrants sought to return home, they just as fervently sought to escape Mexico—or at least the official Mexico that the world knows. This Mexico finds many ways to strangle the poor's aspirations, and therein is the cause of the country's poverty. Even as immigrants return in hopes of an embrace, this Mexico has extorted them, insulted them, and despised them as national turncoats. If that's less true today, it's a change that has come a tad late for many immigrants.

I'd spent several years in Mexico, thinking and writing about immigration, when I heard a story—the story of Antonio's Gun. It took place a long time ago in Jaripo, a village I often visited in a hilly northern part of the state of Michoacán. Over the years, I pieced the story together talking with older townsfolk. In time, I came to see it as a parable for what immigrants seek most.

When I first heard the story, Jaripo had long been an immigrant village, entirely dependent on dollars. But when the story took place in the late 1920s, Jaripo was a poor peasant village. Its plaza then was of dirt, not concrete, and its people lived in small adobe houses.

The story is about two men, Juan Muratalla and Antonio Carrillo.

Juan Muratalla, everyone agrees, was a twisted and merciless man. Before the Mexican Revolution of 1911, he was a member of the armed security force on a hacienda. The security officers protected the hacienda from bandits and controlled its peons. Muratalla was known to kill for no reason. One peon described him as an "evil dog."

After the Revolution, Muratalla settled in Jaripo, which had been part of the hacienda.

In time, he ingratiated himself with the town boss, or cacique, named don Juan, who owned a store on the plaza. Muratalla was one of the few people in town with a rifle. He kept it upright between his legs as he'd fall asleep, drunk, sitting in a chair on the plaza. He terrorized the villagers, as he'd done when they worked under him at the hacienda.

"He killed more than thirty people," says Jesús Díaz, a retired farmworker, sitting in Jaripo's plaza one night many decades after Muratalla had gone. "He'd kill for thirty pesos."

But don Juan's word was law. No one else had weapons or money, so villagers endured Juan Muratalla.

Eventually, don Juan's eye fell upon a girl from the village. This girl was the love of Jesús Carrillo, a poor ranchero. Jesús and his brother, Mauricio, were poor men. They had only one pistol between them, but they were known as men who didn't back down. Still, don Juan was used to getting what he wanted and gave Muratalla the job of ridding him of the Carrillo brothers.

One day, Muratalla heard Mauricio Carrillo would be coming through town. He climbed with his rifle into a tree in the plaza. As Mauricio walked across a street, Muratalla shot him in the chest.

By Mauricio's side that day was his son, Antonio. Antonio pleaded with his wounded father to give him his pistol to avenge the shooting. But Mauricio clutched the gun, fearing for his son's life. Antonio and townspeople carried Mauricio home. Mauricio gave his gun to his wife and bled to death.

Antonio begged his mother for his father's pistol. She hid it, fearing, as her husband had, that if Antonio used it, Muratalla would kill him, too.

So Antonio Carrillo left for the United States. He found work. With the dollars he earned, he bought a pistol.

One day Juan Muratalla received a card from the United States. On it, Antonio wrote that he was coming home to kill him. He ended with the words, "Mauricio Lives Again."

On the announced day, Muratalla and some gunmen rode to the train station. From the train, Antonio saw them and hid. The train left the station. Antonio was nowhere to be seen. Muratalla and his gunmen mounted their horses and returned to Jaripo, laughing that young Antonio was all talk.

A mile or two out of the station, the train slowed as it rounded a curve. Antonio Carrillo jumped off and walked over the hills and into Jaripo.

Juan Muratalla had been drinking at his usual spot outside a store on the plaza. His rifle was by his side. The day was sunny. He may have dozed off.

Suddenly, Antonio Carrillo appeared before him in the street.

"Defend yourself," he cried.

Juan Muratalla lunged for his rifle. Antonio pulled his pistol and fired. Some say he yelled, "Mauricio lives again," as he emptied his gun into Juan Muratalla.

Muratalla fell back. In his death grip his finger pulled the rifle's trigger, and a bullet went through the store's roof. He collapsed inside the store, his legs sprawling out the doorway.

Shops closed. Parents pulled their children indoors. Antonio walked home. The employees of the store shoved Muratalla's bloody corpse out of the shop and shut their doors, too.

Juan Muratalla lay there for a day, his rifle by his side. Only his sister, with a flickering gas lantern, stayed by his corpse that night. She buried him the next day with the help of some townspeople.

That gun was Antonio Carrillo's alternative to submission. He never returned to the United States. He'd found what he sought there.

* * *

I came to Mexico in 1994, intending to stay for three months. But a reporting job opened at a magazine in Mexico City. I jumped at it—though it paid poorly—so I could stay in the country. When the magazine closed, I became a freelance journalist.

As a reporter living in Mexico City, immigration stories became my refuge. They took me out of the capital, to villages in the major immigrant states of Michoacán, Jalisco, Guanajuato, Zacatecas, Oaxaca. I met with immigrants in their adopted U.S. towns. I went to border cities—Tijuana, Juárez, Reynosa. I visited the highway checkpoint in Sinaloa where Mexican federal police extorted from immigrants the gifts and money they brought home for Christmas. I toured often with Los Tigres del Norte, immigrants themselves, who are Mexico's greatest pop band, and whose songs are the best chronicle of Mexican immigration.

As it happened, the decade I spent in Mexico was momentous in the epic of immigration.

Americans were growing older, as well as wealthier and fatter, in the boom of the late 1990s. Demand for immigrant labor grew ravenously. Though the Border Patrol's budget quadrupled and the U.S. government invested huge amounts of money in steel walls in San Diego and El Paso, it had little effect, especially because an equal investment was not made in immigration enforcement inside the United States. Through the decade I lived in Mexico, the Mexico-born population in the United States rose steadily, roughly doubling to somewhere around eleven million people by 2004. The undocumented Mexico-born population also doubled—to six million, said the Pew Hispanic Center.

Mexican immigrants found new crossing points and new destinations. With Tijuana and El Paso walled off, immigrants took to paying smugglers huge sums to take them through the Arizona desert. Many perished. Large numbers of Mexicans moved into the American South and Midwest for the first time.

There were other upheavals. In 1994, Californians passed Proposition 187, which would have barred undocumented immigrants from receiving certain state services. It was overturned. Because of it, however, millions of Mexicans nationwide, fearing deportation, became U.S. citizens through the late 1990s and changed the calculus of local politics in several states.

New competition among banks and wiring services reduced the cost of sending money home. Immigrant remittances climbed—to $20 billion in 2005—and became Mexico's second largest source of foreign exchange, after oil.

During these years, I took a Mexican history class from Lorenzo Meyer, one of the country's great historians. Meyer said something I never forgot. It was about the meeting of the Spaniards and the Aztecs five hundred years ago. He said that this encounter so shook these two civilizations that the only event comparable to it today would be a visit to earth by space aliens.

The Aztecs, in particular, lived in ziplocked isolation, unaware of any earthly civilization that could upset the detailed cosmovision of their lake kingdom of Tenochtitlan. They had developed corn, astronomy, a calendar, and a civil service. But they'd never seen horses or steel. Tens of thousands of awed Indians in canoes packed the waterways to watch the arrival of five hundred trembling Spaniards, with horses, armor, and beards.

"There may or may not be flying saucers, but the [Aztecs] thought they were seeing something just as strange," wrote novelist Rebecca West in her memoir, *Survivors in Mexico*.

What seemed even stranger to me, however, was that these two utterly alien civilizations were so much alike. They fit together easily. Both had cultures of centralized governance, atop which sat an all-powerful king or emperor. Each civilization had rigid class structures, and revered power, pomp, ceremony, and submission to authority. To be happy, their upper classes required enormous numbers of servants. Both civilizations relied on religious images: saints, in the Spaniards' case, gods, in the Aztecs'. The Aztecs had human sacrifice; the Spaniards had the Inquisition, and it was this Roman Catholic Church, not that of St. Francis of Assisi, that crossed the ocean and found fertile soil in Aztec culture.

I bring this up because it seems relevant today to why Mexicans leave and what they seek. Though Mexico was called the "New World," it never was. In this New World flourished the Old World idea that the wealthy and powerful ought to be spared calloused hands. These were reserved for the poor man, who was despised for having them. Power was deposited in a long line of viceroys, emperors, caudillos, and dictators—and village caciques like don Juan. Those below them had little recourse but to submit.

In the 1920s, what became known as the Institutional Revolutionary Party—the PRI—replaced the dictators and emperors and ran the country for the rest of the century. The PRI gave access to power to anyone who joined it, ending Mexico's bloody power struggles. It was also a political Frankenstein—an amalgam of parts from Mexico's Old World authoritarian past.

Its philosophy through most of the twentieth century came from an unlikely source: the nineteenth-century dictator it reviled, Porfirio Díaz. "Poor Mexico," Díaz was famously supposed to have said, "so far from God, so close to the United States." Proximity to the United States, Díaz meant, kept Mexico poor.

This became PRI gospel, then its excuse. The PRI set itself up as the protector, the new emperor, of Mexico. Mexicans were encouraged to fear the United States and thus the world. Nationalist and anti-Yankee education in the schools was required. So, too, were high tariffs on foreign goods, for how could Mexicans be expected to compete abroad?

Mexico City became the symbol of what was supposedly most Mexican. The PRI drained revenue from the provinces and hoarded it in the capital. All that was important in government, academia, art, and business was gathered there.

Yet the longer I lived there, the more I viewed Mexico City as the depository of the country's pernicious Old World inheritance. Mexico City businessmen and bureaucrats remained ensconced in sinecures, insulated from economic upheaval. Government planners decided the fate of thousands of budget-starved towns and villages far beyond the capital.

As the decades wore on, PRI paternalism and the country's Old World culture, far from protecting Mexico, enfeebled it. Most damaged by this were the poor, the powerless, and the unconnected. They fled—for the United States, ironically enough.

The embarrassed PRI painted immigrants as traitors. It claimed Mexicans had to stomp and spit on the Mexican flag to become U.S. citizens. Mexicans, the party insisted, lost their souls the farther north they wandered from the Mexican center.

Never was the party more deluded. In the United States, far from losing their souls, Mexicans found themselves as they escaped the control of Old World elites back home. Certainly they struggled and suffered. Some failed. Like many immigrants before them, they endured racism, abuse, and the nastiest jobs. But a vast number rose above. Self-realization, not suffering, became the theme of their lives.

This liberation is what makes many immigrants' life stories so exhilarating. When I could bear no more of the pomp and frivolity of Mexico's elite, I found solace in immigrants' stories. They prove that PRI political gospel was wrong.

"Farther from Mexico City, closer to God" is a truer reflection of Mexican-immigrant philosophy.

I think the country's modern history has been one prolonged attempt to ditch the stacked deck that Mexico City symbolizes and escape the Old World for the New once and for all. Mexicans were doing this on July 2, 2000, when they ended the PRI's monopoly by electing Vicente Fox president. (Fox would leave behind a steadied economy and a new official attitude toward immigrants, welcoming them as "heroes" and "VIPs." Yet his own ineptitude and a petulant, divided Congress kept him from achieving the profound reforms Mexico needs in education, tax collection, energy, labor law, local governance, and much more.)

Many Mexicans had been making this escape for years by then. They'd left cloistered villages, where they were economic outcasts, and gone to America. They'd sought liberation, too, at the border—the Mexican region that is, not coincidentally, farthest from Mexico City and closest to the United States.

The United States became a poor Mexican's protection, his escape hatch, his alternative to the submission expected of him in the Old World. This may jar Americans who see the rough lives many immigrants lead. But a poor peasant with dollars in his hip pocket or a landscaping job in Fresno needn't bow to the Old World caciques who control his village. To the man who departs pesoless yet returns with cash to spend, the United States affords dignity, respect, and sweet vindication. Ignore the allure of that psychological boost and you miss a lot of the immigrant story.

Today it is houses, not guns, that immigrants seek. Yet the reasons they head north are much the same as Antonio Carrillo's. Like Antonio's gun, houses are protection, an alternative to submission and vulnerability. Like Antonio's gun in its time, houses are prestige, peace of mind, even revenge of a sort—a thumbing of the immigrant's nose at local elites. Houses are standing monuments to what a poor man can do when given a chance.

No, it was more than a job that sent Mexicans north. After years in Mexico, I came to believe that what immigrants seek in the United States is their own version of Antonio's Gun.

But because this epic is about the roiling human heart, there's even more to Mexican immigration than this escape from submission. This, too, I learned in Jaripo.

Juan Muratalla's death marked a turning point of sorts for the village. In 1942, Mexico signed the "Bracero" treaty with the United States, which was at war and needed men to harvest its crops. Huge numbers of poor rancheros left with contracts to work in U.S. fields, and back home people like Juan Muratalla no longer dominated things so easily. At least, other men had money for guns.

One village that joined this exodus in the 1940s was Jaripo, and after that people never stopped leaving. Over the decades, families settled in Chicago, some in Dallas, and a few in Orange County, California. But most Jaripeños landed in Stockton, California, where they picked tomatoes.

As a reporter for the *Stockton Record* from 1988 to 1992, I met several Jaripeños. Among them was Luis Magaña, a farm-labor activist who had taken on the quixotic task of organizing undocumented farmworkers.

In January 1994, I was going to Mexico to study. Luis told me that his village held its annual fiesta the last week of January. Thus the first place I visited in Mexico was tiny Jaripo just as its immigrants had returned for the fiesta.

The village was a party wonderland that week. Tuba-based *bandas* erupted in polkas about noon. Mariachis played each afternoon, serenading groups of men with ballads of unrequited love and of how *pistoleros* died. Pop bands played each evening, and hundreds of people packed the plaza until wee hours of the morning.

That week my life changed. It happened when Luis pointed out the houses of Jaripo. Every January, he said, immigrants returned and added to them, intending to retire to them one day. Two-story houses were now common. Many houses had satellite dishes and metal-framed windows. Some had curved driveways and winding staircases. One house even had a tiled, onion-domed roof. Because only the wealthy can afford home loans in Mexico, many one-story houses had rebar—the thin iron bars that reinforce concrete—sticking from the roofs, awaiting the day their owners would have enough dollars to add second floors.

As we walked Jaripo's streets, Luis also pointed out the remaining adobe shacks. They had dirt floors and latrines in back. They were what people had lived in before going north. The houses of Jaripo, Luis said, showed the difference between emigrating and staying put.

Yet, amazingly, despite the huge amounts of money invested in these houses, Luis said, few immigrants ever retired to them. Instead, they stayed in the United States, while their houses in Mexico stood empty.

When the party ended, and people went north again, I found Jaripo suddenly desolate. It would remain so for the next eleven months. Years before, Jaripeños were farmworkers and could return for six months at a time. Now, though, they had urban jobs in the United States. Their houses in the village were nicer than ever, but they came back less—only a few weeks a year. The more Jaripo developed, the more it was abandoned.

This is true of virtually every village in immigrant Mexico. Thousands of them are filling with empty houses that their owners see a month or two a year. Over the years, I walked many of their streets unmolested by traffic. My footsteps echoed down canyons of vacant two- and three-story houses with wrought-iron balconies, marble floors, patio fountains, and rebar that rose from roofs like tufts of electrified hair.

In time, I realized that immigrants' return home and their construction of these houses came at a huge cost. For immigrants, the trip home often consumed their savings. Jaripeño families pulled children out of school in Stockton so they could attend the fiesta back home. Some parents even urged their teenagers to leave school to make money for the family's return. Meanwhile, the dream of going home distracted them from absorbing the best of the United States. Many Jaripeños didn't learn English or become U.S. citizens. Instead of buying houses, they rented in Stockton's most dangerous neighborhoods, believing, sometimes for decades, that one day really soon they'd be back in Mexico for good.

The cost of this to Mexico was even greater. Enrique Anguiano helped me see this. Enrique was the principal of Francisco I. Madero Elementary School, which had nine teachers and two hundred students the first year I visited. Enrique had never been north, but he saw how the United States mesmerized his kids like television. Thus distracted, they expended little effort in class. At the January fiesta every year, they saw immigrants with no education return with fancy trucks, Nike tennis shoes, and dollars for parties. Immigrants added to their houses, which became year-round reminders to children of how little education mattered.

"They pass time here until they grow up so they can go to the United States," Enrique said. His kids entered the lowest levels of the U.S. economy, confident they'd do better than many professionals in Mexico, he told me. Jaripo's school, meanwhile, had only raggedy textbooks, and its teachers rationed chalk.

Immigration didn't create many solutions for Mexico, I realized. On the contrary, it stifled development and simply created more immigration. Through it, Mexico lost its most energetic young blood. Immigrant dollars were godsends to villages like Jaripo, but they also kept these villages from finding any economic alternative to leaving for the United States.

In time, this created a culture of departure that was tough to break. Teenage boys, above all, ached to leave. They'd heard stories about El Norte all their lives. They weren't starving. They just sought their own U.S. adventures and their own stories to tell. "Para que nadie me cuente" (So that no one can tell me about it any longer) was how many teenage boys responded when I asked why they wanted to go to the United States. Who, after all, wanted to be the only one not to go?

Able-bodied year-round residents, meanwhile, felt pressured to head north. Immigrant dollars inflated prices for goods and services beyond what they could afford earning pesos. In the end, the only people left in villages like Jaripo were the very young, the old, the infirm living from relatives' dollars, and the merchants who sold them their necessities.

This culture of departure, flourishing now in thousands of Mexican villages, defies attempts to change it. Job-creating industries usually avoid immigrant regions because so many people in these areas have worked up north and expect wages nearer those in the United States; either that, or they receive dollars from relatives up north and see no need to work.

In the late 1990s, a movement emerged among immigrants to invest remittances in businesses back home to create jobs and staunch the exodus. But the projects often failed. They couldn't pay U.S. wages, either. Plus they were doomed by all the reasons people left that were not economic, for a job was not the only thing a young man sought anymore. (A new attempt to fund businesses back home is now under way, led by federations of hometown clubs in Southern California; it's too early to tell whether they'll succeed.)

I visited a Oaxacan village whose immigrants in San Diego funded a greenhouse cooperative, hoping to create jobs. But the remaining villagers were too young, too old, too weak; they didn't know how to read, drive, type, or use a fax machine. Also, a political dispute years before had literally divided the town down one street. People from one side didn't talk to people from the other. The only phone in the village happened to be on the side opposite that of the cooperative. When people called asking for co-op members, they were told they'd moved to the United States. The greenhouse collapsed.

Today, after years of living from immigration, many villages are simply emptying out. Jaripo is one of these. Fewer immigrants return to Jaripo, and fewer still believe they will retire there. Only rare families keep their children out of school to attend the January fiesta in Jaripo, which nowadays ends about midnight. Remittances are falling. After renting in Stockton's worst neighborhoods for decades, hundreds of Jaripeño families have in the last five years finally bought houses elsewhere in Stockton and the surrounding county.

Jaripo, meanwhile, is left with no class of educated young people, no industry, despite sixty years of dollars cascading in from up north. The elementary school is down to sixty students and four teachers. Only the majestic houses remain.

Today the issue of Mexican immigration polarizes. U.S. ideologues on both sides tediously dissect it looking for heroes or villains. Mexico's elites, ignorant of immigrant reality, presume to lecture the United States on racism and protest how their people are treated up north—though poor Mexicans are treated better in the United States than in Mexico.

But I think nuance and complexity form the big beautiful heart of Mexican immigration, and they are what I seek. The stories of Mexican immigrants are about foibles, passion, love and envy, loss and courage, strength and weakness, cowardice and vindication—often roiling within the same person. I believe most Mexicans embody the spirit that founded the United States in that they are here to overcome as many obstacles as it takes to get ahead. I also know their presence in huge numbers carries costs that the United States has difficulty absorbing, and risks recreating here what they were trying to escape in Mexico.

I have wondered at how immigrants, treated so poorly by Mexico, could flee it while loving it so ardently, only to return to it and again be mistreated. I've wondered at how their return, motivated by such love, has both harmed and helped Mexico. Leaving Mexico is a logical choice for so many people, yet I love that it is sometimes so illogical.

Perhaps that's why immigrant houses mesmerize me. They embody the epic's quirks and nuances. The houses are immigrants' promise to return for good one day. Though few people keep this promise, the dream nevertheless lives on, and billions of dollars cascade every year into the most isolated villages, surreally filling Mexico with empty houses.

One immigrant in Los Angeles told me that houses in his impoverished village in Oaxaca have Jacuzzis—a bizarre fact, in his view. "First, water's scarce there," he said. "Second, no one goes home anymore." Those who remain behind use the abandoned two-story houses as warehouses for seed and fertilizer, he said, and the Jacuzzis are filled with corncobs.

All this is enough irony for a Chekhov story: a man labors most of his life in another country while dreaming of returning home for good. He prepares for that day by erecting a gorgeous house in his village for all his neighbors to see. When he's done, though, he finds his dream has changed, and he never settles in the structure that was the central point of his life.

A great opera, I believe, can be mined from each Mexican immigrant's story.

I hope the stories in this book reflect that. They are not a coherent whole of the immigration epic. They are tales that I loved telling that I hope also tell some of what I think is the essence of the greatest movement of human beings from one country to another in our time.

The first, middle, and last chapters are about the young construction worker, Delfino Juárez, whose dependence on Mexico City left him as unprotected as Antonio Carrillo was unarmed.

Atolingans in Chicago is about the distraction of returning home and how small-town envy was defeated. The complex motivations behind one immigrant's return are found in the Tomato King's story.

The saga of South Gate is about how America has changed Mexican immigrants. The 2003 season of the high-school soccer team in Garden City, Kansas, is about how Mexicans have changed America.

Velvet painting's emergence in Ciudad Juárez is the story of when the U.S.-Mexico border became a place where poor people could remake themselves. Opera's emergence in Tijuana is of how therapeutic can be the distance from Mexico City.

The epilogue is of my travels in the strange land of the German Mennonites, peasant farmers in northern Mexico, who stand with one foot in the Old World and the other in the New, succeeding at neither. That story, as it turned out, is also about how poking around their world required, suddenly, my leaving Mexico once and for all.

Chapter One

Delfino I

A Sunday Afternoon Dream in the Alameda

Most of every week during his teenage years, Delfino Juárez mixed concrete and laid brick at construction sites around Mexico City.

He was nineteen and had already been working construction for seven years in the capital. In that time he had built houses, apartments, and a Kentucky Fried Chicken. He began as a helper. He learned to lay tile and erect a wall that was straight. In time he acquired his own box of tools. It contained his planer, saw, and hammer, and in this he took great pride. When he returned home to his village 125 miles east of the capital, his mother would cook for him alone. As he ate, his little sister and three younger brothers would peer into the toolbox and take out its artifacts. Then they would replace everything, close the box, and return it to its place of honor in the family's only cabinet.

Delfino was a handsome guy. His cheekbones were high, his nose long and sharp. A broad smile lit his face and helped him flirt with girls. His body was lithe and sturdy and fortified with a grit that had formed within him as he'd left his village a tiny boy alone, and gone to Mexico City, and survived. For this reason, and for all he'd seen and done, Delfino carried himself with a brashness that Mexico doesn't always permit in its people who are poor, short, and dark-skinned, all of which he was. Indeed, his brashness belied his place, which was at the bottom of Mexico City's economy.

On Saturdays, he'd work a half-day and get his pay for the week. Then he'd run across town to the buses that took people back to his hometown and leave money with a driver he knew, who took the money to his mother. She and his siblings lived in a village named Xocotla. Xocotla was high on a mountain in the state of Veracruz. Up there, his family depended on him to survive. After delivering the money to the driver, Delfino would return to the job site, wash his clothes, and scrub the concrete dust from his skin.

But Sundays were different. Delfino had all of Sunday off. At whatever job site he was living, on Sunday he would fill a bucket with water and wash from head to toe. He would select his least wrinkled cotton shirt and his baggiest pants. He would put studs in his ears and his tongue and under his bottom lip. He would plow his hair with gel.

Then, about 2:00 PM, he and the crew of younger boys from Xocotla who had followed him to Mexico City would board the bus for downtown. On the way, hundreds of others would join them, tributaries to a river of rural youth that each Sunday swelled and flowed unstoppable to the center of the city and the park known as the Alameda.

Crisscrossed with tree-lined walkways, the Alameda occupies ten square blocks and is home to the Palace of Fine Arts and not far from the Zócalo, the city's main plaza. The park has been the center of Mexico City, and thus of Mexican history, since the Aztecs held markets there in the years before the Spaniards came. The Spanish Inquisition burned Aztecs in the Alameda and with that, colonization began. The invading U.S. Army camped there in 1847. In the mid-twentieth century, the middle classes took Sunday promenades in the Alameda, and for many years the park was a tourist highlight of the city.

Delfino looked forward to Sundays in the Alameda as nothing else in his life. For like a dream, for a few months and that was all, Delfino Juárez was one of the best break-dancers among the rural construction workers who spent their Sunday afternoons in the Alameda.

In 1947, Diego Rivera, Mexico's legendary muralist, was sixty years old, and his creative powers were fading. The Hotel Del Prado was about to open across the street from the Alameda. Its owner asked Rivera to paint a mural on its restaurant wall, so the artist mustered his energy for what would be his last great mural.

Delfino Juárez, third from the left, as a construction worker with
the younger Xocotla generation who followed him to Mexico City.

Rivera intended his mural as a walk through Mexican history, with
the Alameda as its stage. In riotous color, he crammed 140 figures from
Mexican history on the wall of the hotel's restaurant. Standing in the park
were Cortés and the Spanish inquisitor; a Revolutionary; an Indian peasant; a bullfighter; Santa Ana; U.S. Gen. Winfield Scott, who invaded
Mexico; a candy vendor; a president of Mexico counting money and fon-
dling a blonde woman as an archbishop looks on; a balloon seller; a newspaper boy; a policeman chasing an Indian from the park. On it went, the
park churning with the colors of Mexico's past.

Watching it all was little Diego, a frog-eyed boy in knickers and straw
hat, spending a Sunday afternoon in the Alameda.

Standing above the scene were the three great figures of Mexico's first
century of independence: Benito Juárez, the Oaxacan Indian president;

Porfirio Díaz, the dictator; and Francisco I. Madero, the liberal who deto-
nated the Mexican Revolution that overthrew Díaz.

By 1947, with World War II at an end, Mexico City bustled with
optimism. A one-party state had evolved over the previous decade
that incorporated much of Mexican society and put an end to bloody
battles for presidential succession. For the next thirty years, steady economic growth would create a sizable middle class. The new Hotel del
Prado itself was sign of the country's new promise, built to serve the new
European and American tourists who would come to Mexico now that
war was over.

The Alameda of Rivera's imagination cradled a Mexico of glowing
promise, a boy's warm and comforting paradise. He called his mural *A
Dream of a Sunday Afternoon in the Alameda.*

One place Mexico's national optimism infected was the faraway village of Xocotla, Veracruz.

Xocotla (pronounced Sho-COAT-la) means "Place of Bitter Fruit"
in Nahuatl, the language spoken by Aztec Indians. Villages near Xocotla
have similarly dour names: Chocamán (Tears), Tetla (Place of Stone), and
strangely, Huilotla (Place of the Penis).

Xocotla had, in fact, provided little to its people. It was far up a mountain, often hidden in rain clouds, and thus often foggy and muddy. Only
a steep footpath connected Xocotla with the world. People lived from the
corn and potatoes they grew on the mountainside. No one had schooling;
far from doctors, children died.

That, and eventually a lot more, began to change when, at about the
time World War II was ending and the Hotel Del Prado had Maestro
Rivera paint his mural, a grand idea also captivated the men of Xocotla:
they undertook to carve a five-mile road down their mountain.

Eleuterio Cruz remembers that the men intended the road to benefit their children. Eleuterio was born in 1933. He began working on the
road when he turned seventeen. For the next generation, every boy did
the same.

Today, Eleuterio is sixty-nine and has a sharp nose and jaw. His skin
is taut, dark, and calloused by years of hard farming. Raising corn and

potatoes all his life on a hilly patch of land made him spry. He'd played guitar in cantinas for many years; he drank a lot, then he turned to Jesus.

Eleuterio worked on the road as his twelve children were born, and as they grew up, and as they had the first of his thirty-five grandchildren. He served as mayor for a spell and organized roadwork crews.

Every man in Xocotla had to work on the road one day a week. On Tuesdays they would usually gather their tools and march down to chop, shovel, and pick at the mountain.

The Second World War ended with atom bombs. Then came the Cold War and an arms race. In Xocotla, the men had no explosives, so they hammered and chipped at solid rock, and at times clawed at it by hand, then dumped the debris down the mountain.

The world outside was changing quickly. The Cuban Revolution, the Vietnam War, the student rebellions of the 1960s, the hippie era, a man on the moon, the drugs and sex revolution, dictatorships and coups in Latin America, the Tlatelolco massacre, and the Olympic Games in Mexico City. Through it all, Xocotla's men remained steadfast to the idea of their road. Every Tuesday the mountainside rang with their picks and shovels glancing off the rocks.

"No one died," said Eleuterio.

One man's foot was crushed as he hammered at a massive boulder that stood in the road's path. No one touched that boulder for a generation after that, believing it hid the devil, who wanted to take people.

"I don't think so," Eleuterio said. "This person didn't know how to use a sledgehammer, which is why the rock hit him in the foot."

For a full thirty-one years the men of Xocotla pounded at that five-mile road. As they measured progress in centimeters, Mexico's population went from twenty million people to fifty-five million people. Six Mexican presidents, and twelve Xocotla mayors, came and went. A Mexican middle class emerged, though none of its members lived in Xocotla. Through it all, Xocotla's men kept at their colossal hand-carved public work. The government gave them no help until the end, when it provided a gas-powered jackhammer with which the men shattered the last obstacle in their way—that solid rock where the man had injured his foot.

Finally, in 1976, they finished. A red Jeep carried the priest from a town at the bottom of the mountain up the zigzagging, rocky five miles of one-lane road. Xocotla had a party. Eleuterio Cruz was forty-three; he'd worked on that road for twenty-six years.

As it happened, 1976 was the year Mexico's postwar promise began to fade. The government devalued the peso for the first time. Corruption lubricated the one-party state; lack of accountability made it arrogant. Two peso devaluations followed in the 1980s and a massive one again in 1994. Each crisis shuttered factories. Savings lost value; prices rose. The 1980s clobbered the middle class created by the previous thirty years. In each decade—the 1970s, 1980s, and 1990s—the numbers of Mexicans in the United States doubled.

Not one of them, however, was from Xocotla, Veracruz. The village seemed quarantined from any contact with the United States. Nobody in Xocotla knew anyone in the United States. Mexico City, though, was near. The road connected the men to the capital, just as the city was growing like mad with the people streaming in from Mexico's agonized country-side. Low-skilled construction jobs were plentiful.

A crew of Xocotla's men traveled to Mexico City for the first time in 1976 to work as construction helpers. For three months they helped build the Colegio de México, one of the country's premier private uni-versities. Then they returned home to harvest their corn and pota-toes. The next year, they worked on the Pemex Hospital. As time went on, peasants of Xocotla built the house of a nephew of then-Pres. Luis Echeverría and a state university in northern Mexico City. They built offices and apartment buildings. Each fall, they returned home to work on their fields.

Nearby villages, meanwhile, were discovering Mexico City as well. By 1990, thousands of men from western Veracruz provided the muscle and sinew that built Mexico City.

In 1996, the railroad line that connected Mexico City and Veracruz went bankrupt. The train trip one way lasted between eleven and fifteen hours—a torture so heinous that men spent months away from home and returned only at the end of the summer.

With the railroad's demise, workers found gypsy buses that could get them home in seven hours. Dozens of buses—chipped, battered and snorting like oxen—soon clogged the streets near the Mexico City railroad station on Saturday afternoons to take hundreds of construction workers home.

Villages in western Veracruz had emptied their men into Mexico City. Via gypsy buses, the capital now loaned them back every Saturday night for brief familial intimacy, though they had to return the next night so as not to miss work Monday morning in Mexico City. Men began returning home once or twice a month. They saw their wives and spent their money.

Xocotla's population exploded, though the town was high up a mountain, had no industry, no jobs, and its agriculture was wasting. Víctor Gutiérrez, the town doctor, was delivering twenty babies a month. He and a team of junior high school students set about counting people house to house. Xocotla had 3,200 people in 1990. Twelve years later, their census found 5,480 people—a 70 percent increase. Three thousand people were under fifteen. Of those, 1,500 people—more than a quarter of the village—were under six years old, born since gypsy buses replaced the railroad.

Xocotla now only masqueraded as a farming village. It was instead a factory producing low-wage workers for the capital. The elementary school had eight hundred students and denied entry to another three hundred first-graders a year. Children reached heights several inches below what a well-fed youngster could achieve. Any grass or vegetation died, overrun by people or by pigs or dogs wandering leisurely. The mountain was quilted into tiny parcels of farmland. Meanwhile, Mexico City sopped up each wave of youths, whose remittances sustained the town and postponed any reckoning.

So much of Mexico could be found in Xocotla. The government reported that almost two hundred thousand villages across Mexico had fewer than twenty-five hundred people each, yet never disappeared though their agriculture was nearly dead. They lived from the money sent by their migrants who lived in the cities. When these migrants returned home, they produced more children who, in time, would have no choice but to leave as well.

Thus the country's transition from rural to urban—begun more than half a century before—never seemed to end. Rural attitudes didn't die. Several Mexico City funeral homes were kept busy driving to remote hamlets with the bodies of people who'd resided in the capital for decades but had never completely left home.

Xocotla's relationship with the capital mirrored Mexico's with the United States. In villages where leaving for the United States took hold, migration became young men's only economic option. A generation after that road seemed to open Xocotla to the world's possibilities, one unavoidable fact bound its young men: their future lay in getting down that road and vying for a slot in the voracious Mexico City construction industry.

It was with this hope one bright day in 1993 that the grandson of Eleuterio Cruz, a thin boy who barely peeked above five feet tall struck out on his own down Xocotla's road and headed for Mexico City.

Delfino Juárez had nothing. His father, Lázaro, was a drunk, as his father had been before him. Lázaro Juárez began drinking aguardiente—sugar-cane hooch—when Delfino was eight and had been entranced by it ever since. He couldn't go two weeks without a few days of hard drinking that left him in a stupor on the bed or in the pig muck somewhere. His children often went from house to house looking for their father.

Delfino had spent his childhood hauling bags of flour at the bakery or picking corn for some farmer in an effort to earn money so the family could eat. Once, Lázaro Juárez signed up himself and Delfino to pick potatoes for a farmer on a plot of land up near the volcano. But the day came and Lázaro was drunk. Delfino went alone and dug potatoes for three days, with only a light sweater in a cold rain, as his fingers ached and his teeth clattered like drumsticks.

The family lived all but unprotected from the elements in an eight-by-twelve shack of wood slats and dirt floors well down the mountain, where rain runoff was torrential. Other families treated the Juárezes with disdain.

Delfino's mother, Adelina Cruz, remained nonetheless a cheerful woman, handsome and stout. Her greatest error was having believed that Lázaro Juárez would amount to anything. She cooked, raised pigs and chickens, and pieced together pants for her children from other families' discards, and did her best to blunt the harm her husband did the family.

"He's the kind of man," she would say, "who's so childish that when you scold him he uses it as a reason to rebel more. So now I just don't say anything to him."

Lázaro's drinking perplexed those around him. Some thought it the result of his mother giving birth to twenty-two children, only four of whom lived. This was a remarkable rate of infant mortality, even for Xocotla, and it was in due course attributed to witches who flew about and sucked the blood of children. Demons such as these, people reasoned, could also drive a man to drink later in life.

Delfino had another explanation. "Maybe it's because I'm not his child. They say I'm the child of another man called Raimundo. He lives four blocks from my house. He says he's my father. But I figure I'm alone, that I don't have a father."

The day Delfino graduated from junior high school, he cried. It was the end of his schooling and it hadn't been much. Years later, he still spoke bitterly of his meaningless junior high school diploma.

"They don't teach you anything there," he said.

One day shortly after graduating, Delfino told his mother he was going to the river. Instead, he put on two shirts and two pairs of homemade pants. He went to Fortino Tiburcio, the town baker and moneylender. Delfino asked for a two-hundred-peso loan. Tiburcio charged him 30 percent interest a month.

A little while later, Tiburcio's wife saw Delfino's mother in the street. "Why did you send the boy to borrow money?" she asked. Adelina had not. Alarmed, she caught up with her son.

"Mom, I can't stay anymore," he told her. "I'm going to see if I can give you what Papa doesn't."

Only men with families had ever left Xocotla to work in Mexico City. Still, she let him go. He was twelve.

That night, the train from Veracruz rolled slowly west into Mexico City. The tiny boy sat in third class. It was his first visit to the big city. He didn't sleep, but he wasn't scared; he was worried. Would the bosses give work to anyone who was so young and small? He wondered where he'd sleep.

Arriving Sunday morning, Delfino went to Chapultepec Park, where men from Xocotla spent their day off. The men thought they could find him work. That night he slept on their jobsite.

The next day, a cousin led him to find work. At two jobsites, he was rejected. As he feared, he was too young, the foremen told him, and he hadn't the body for construction work. Finally, though, a foreman on the crews building Televisión Azteca studios gave him a chance. If the architects come around, hide, he told Delfino. He worked in the supply depot, schlepping cement and bricks for the older workers from his village for 270 pesos a week. He slept for the next three months in the basement of what would become the studios of Mexico's second television network, then moved on to other jobs.

A prison ethic ruled Mexico City worksites, he soon discovered. At jobsites, kids would have their tools, shoes, and blankets stolen if they couldn't protect themselves. Xocotla's men, being peasants and innocent of city ways, had been always duped and beaten. They didn't know how much money they'd earned from a day's work. Delfino was small. Bosses cheated him. He had his shovel stolen.

He got used to fighting off gangs of Mexico City youths who saw the hillbilly workers as easy prey. While building a KFC restaurant, Delfino and other workers slept in the bathroom. One night, three guys broke in. They held knives to the necks of Delfino and his friends. One of the workers was able to slip away and up to the roof. He found a rope. Tying it to a fixture, he swung down the face of the building to the street

Delfino Juárez working construction in Mexico City.

and ran to a nearby convenience store, where clerks called the police. Officers arrested the robbers.

Delfino was later part of a crew of boys hired to demolish a three-story home. Atop the roof, they tied ropes around their waists and leaned over the edge of the building, whacking at it with enormous sledgehammers, shattering the concrete and leaving only the rebar protruding like cracked bones. One day, as Delfino worked, the rope that held him came loose. He fell. At the last moment, on his way down, he grabbed a piece of rebar. He hung there for a bit, then pulled himself back onto the roof and returned to work. It was the kind of event boys on Mexico City work crews knew to accept in silence if they valued their jobs. They knocked down that house in three weeks.

The other workers he knew from Xocotla were older men, so Delfino was often alone. With no land to till in the village, and his family needing his money, he returned to Xocotla for brief visits only every few months. As time went on, this suited him. He was away from the watchful eye of his mother, aunts, uncles, his grandfather, and the adults of the village.

Mexico City was a river promisingly polluted with money, danger, and adventure—enticing to a modern-day Huckleberry Finn who was eager to find freedom in it.

He discovered the Alameda not long after arriving in Mexico City. He'd been pestering older men from the village to take him. They told him he was too young. But he asked around and other men told him how to get there.

That Sunday, someone was playing music over a large sound system in the middle of the park. Delfino found the men from Xocotla there among the throngs of peasants and construction workers. Nearby, several *jotos*—transvestites—were dolled up and dancing by themselves, shooting wistful and haughty looks at the rough-hewn men watching them. The men from Xocotla marveled and joked among themselves, but didn't move.

Delfino hadn't danced before but wanted to learn. Dancing was the key, he sensed, to girls and good times in the capital. So on an impulse, the tiny boy took a joto's hand, and there, in front of everyone in the park, they danced. The men from Xocotla giggled.

"He was just happy that I took his hand," Delfino said. "After two songs, I let his hand go and stopped. But he taught me to dance the *cumbia*. You have to learn how to dance. If you just do these little steps like some Indian from the village the girls won't dance with you in Mexico City."

That first year, some older friends took him to a movie theater. His friends went in, but the cashier said Delfino was too young. So he bribed the cashier. The movie was in English. It was about two couples having sex. The screen filled with bodies and faces contorting in staged ecstasy. Later, two transvestites robbed his friends in the theater bathroom.

After a couple years in the city, he began hanging out at the Chopo market on Saturdays. Hippies, punks, goths, heavy-metal types come together in the Chopo, among stands selling blue hair dye, spiked dog collars, earrings, tattoos, CDs, and posters of the most obscure punk and heavy-metal bands. Delfino was fourteen when he got his eyebrow and bottom lip pierced in the Chopo. He shaved his hair into a towering mohawk, bought a leather jacket, tight, ripped pants, and Converse tennis shoes. Suddenly he was a punk.

In the Chopo, he first heard of Che Guevara, who was a revolutionary and died like a dog for advocating liberty for everyone. He learned that Doors' singer Jim Morrison, when high, could see things no one else could see.

"I wanted to see things no one could see," he said.

He began using whatever drugs he could find: marijuana, cocaine, glue, and paint thinner. While the older men returned to Xocotla, Delfino stayed in Mexico City and hung out in bars downtown. He began drinking and screwing, frolicking each weekend through the licentious muck, and sleeping on the street. Barmaids and prostitutes fell in love with the slight and handsome boy, even with his mohawk and pierced eyebrows. Each Monday he'd be broke and borrow money from the master bricklayer to eat.

After many months hanging out in Chopo market, Delfino decided to return home. He arrived in Xocotla with a mohawk, pierced eyebrows, and rings in his nose and tongue. Brashly he walked the village streets down to his family's shack. Seeing her sweet son like that, Adelina cried, "My fruit is rotten."

"Don't scold me," he told her, "or I might get more rebellious."

His brother, Florentino, mystified, asked him why he looked that way.

"It's the style in Mexico City," Delfino said.

Children gaped at him from their doorways. Some mothers were terrified. The men laughed, jeered him, and shook their heads. They had remained peasants, even in the city. Having their sons return as thugs was not what the men of Xocotla had in mind when they spent thirty-one years carving that road.

But Delfino awed a generation of Xocotla kids to whom his mohawk and earrings were the hippest things ever. They were ten and twelve years old and hadn't been off the mountain. He told them stories of transvestites and porno films, the older women he'd had. They would crowd around and listen.

Within a few years, these kids were in Mexico City training as apprentices under Delfino, working six days a week, smoking dope, sniffing glue, and having sex with as many girls from villages like theirs as they could convince. Their fathers vowed to whip any son who came back looking like Delfino, but that did no good at all.

To the adults in town, Delfino became a delinquent, drug-addled Pied Piper, leading their doe-eyed children over the urban precipice from which they would later climb back, their hair green, their bodies pierced, and unrecognizable to their mothers.

"That's not the way it should be," said Joel Lino Chávez, an older construction worker dressed in sandals and a straw hat, who worked on Xocotla's road for twenty years and even longer in Mexico City. "They're just screw-ups now. The way you see me now is the way we've always been. That's how our parents were."

Yet even during his most debauched, punked-out days, Delfino was the dutiful son and sent his mother money every week. As his salary grew along with his construction skills, his youngest brothers, Raúl and Zeferino, and his little sister, Abigail, would grow restless with excitement when Delfi was coming home, knowing he'd bring them clothes or shoes and buy them ice cream and soda. On Independence Day, he paid for Zeferino's toy sword and paper bandolier, then draw an Emiliano Zapata mustache on him with an ink pen, so his little brother could be like all the other kids and march in the town parade. He bought his family a color television, though their shack's roof leaked so badly during rainstorms that they wrapped it in a clear plastic bag so it wouldn't short-circuit while they watched it.

"The boy is the reason the family has anything at all," said Eleuterio of his grandson.

As Delfino took his place as the man of the family, Lázaro Juárez deteriorated. He hired himself out to farmers in Xocotla but spent most of what he earned on drink. Occasionally he went to work in Mexico City. Once, in the capital, he even hired on as a construction helper to his son, who had to tell him what to do—to the embarrassment of both. Then gradually, he stopped working altogether, and Delfino supported him along with the rest of the family.

"Look at you," Delfino would berate his drunken father when he'd return home. "You want to die so you won't have to work. I want to work so I won't die."

His father would shrink like a scolded puppy, then use his meek acceptance of his son's harsh words as dispensation to drink again.

Delfino's pluck, meanwhile, made him an alluring influence in Xocotla life. He relished the idea that he, one of the poorest kids in town, had such sway. He shaved the mohawk and became a cholo, inspiring kids in Xocotla to dress like L.A. gangbangers, with khaki pants and bandanas across their foreheads.

From there, his voyage led him back to the great park at the city's center.

The half-century that followed Diego Rivera's creation of his last great mural had been cruel to the Alameda.

The capital grew maniacally during the economic crises. Overuse withered the park. The 1985 earthquake crippled buildings nearby, as economics had crippled the country. Three hundred workers were hired to move Rivera's mural from the Hotel del Prado before the building was torn down. U.S.-style malls went up on the outskirts of the city through the 1990s and became the middle classes' preferred Sunday destination. The private sector, too, fled downtown. A decade after the tremor, condemned buildings still sagged like lopsided wedding cakes on the Alameda's perimeter. Vacant lots collected trash. As everyone else departed, into this jagged and abandoned landscape wandered legions of timid rural kids who'd come to Mexico City for jobs as maids and construction workers and needed fun to keep sane.

It was about this time that Samuel Shapiro, a drummer in a heavy-metal rock band, started a Sunday afternoon dance hall on the patio of a building next to the Alameda. The patio, as it turned out, was where the Spanish Inquisition had burned Aztecs and Jews five hundred years before. Shapiro's uncle, renowned soap-opera producer and writer Miguel Sabido, now owned the building.

Shapiro was an underground entrepreneur, as well as a musician. He'd opened a comic-book flea market in the space on Saturdays. Seeing rural kids in need of a place to have fun, he began holding dances on Sundays. He bought a sound system and hired a disc jockey, charged only fifteen pesos and sold only nonalcoholic drinks. Before long the patio throbbed with rural kids getting their groove on to cumbia, disco, and rock and roll for the few hours allotted them each week. Line dancing, to a Spanish version of country-western heartthrob Billy Ray Cyrus's hit "Achy Breaky Heart," was huge for a while.

"We have a DJ who is constantly urging them to dance," Shapiro said. "The kids arrive and stand around for the first hour, without moving. There'll be five couples dancing surrounded by three hundred people all standing around. After about an hour and a half, they start dancing."

What Shapiro created was part urban discotheque, part traditional dance on the rural village basketball court. But it turned Sundays in the Alameda into an open-air singles scene for rural kids. Merchants started erecting stands on Sundays selling food, clothing, and jewelry to these rural kids. A few industrious fellows set up minicasinos, based on Lotería, an old Mexican board game; vocational schools began offering Sunday-only classes; preachers offered the children the Gospel's protection. More dance halls opened. It irked Shapiro that they were often held in bars and sold the kids alcohol. He started a second dance hall in a nearby parking lot but kept the cover low and the drinks nonalcoholic.

Each Sunday torrents of kids flowed through the park and down Revillagígedo Street and Juárez Avenue. Some of them, still countrified, wore the bright yellow or white cotton button shirts, cowboy boots, and tight jeans that would have made their parents proud. Others shed their hillbilly look. The girls painted their faces, lubed their hair, wriggled into tight shirts their mothers would never permit in the villages back home. The boys rammed studs through their eyebrows and lips, dyed their hair red or green, mohawked it, scythed it, slicked it. Their T-shirts advertised Nike or anarchy. Their baggy pants fit someone twice their size. Yet few of these kids forgot their village manners. Under the urban façade, they remained country kids. They never made out in public. A mohawked punk construction worker in leather and chains still bowed and extended his hand when asking a maid to dance.

By 2002, nine dance halls operated on Sunday afternoons near the Alameda catering to thousands of rural working kids. One hall had a bus shuttling them from the park to its doors for free. The largest dance was El Rodeo, which packed fifteen hundred short, dark-skinned youths into a building that centuries before had been the palace of the viceroy of New Spain.

Like a Rivera mural come to life, the threadbare Alameda pulsed again on Sunday afternoons and witnessed another event in Mexican history: the country's unending rural-to-urban transformation. Watching it all was Delfino Juárez, the tiny youth from Xocotla with a stud in his lower lip.

But had Diego Rivera painted it again, the Alameda would have offered a grimmer glimpse of Mexico, for these kids were fodder. Provincial Mexico laid them before the capital like sacrificial virgins. Thousands of villages survived on their remittances; the capital's economy depended on their labor. Yet the girls endured the advances of the fathers in the houses where they worked as maids. The boys lived like gypsies, scorned as *macuaros*—dirty construction workers—and depended on foremen who sought out any fourteen-year-old too desperate to demand his rights. Across the street from the Alameda, two hundred of these kids were building the Sheraton Hotel—which city leaders planned as the centerpiece of downtown's renewal—and sleeping in its basement at night. While Mexico protested the treatment of its immigrants in the United States, in the shadows of its Congress, presidential palace, and a dozen human-rights agencies, thousands of migrant kids worked with no one on their side.

Construction work in Mexico City did pay more than these kids could earn back home, yet it offered far less future than the United States held out to young men crossing the Arizona desert. But saving for the trip to El Norte was exhausting on a construction worker's salary. A kid used all his energy to stay in one economic place. So workers met maids in the Alameda, married them, and had children. Thus few intrepid souls ever left Mexico City construction work for the United States.

❀

Over the years, Delfino had gone sporadically to the Alameda. But by 2001, as rap and hip-hop gained popularity, he rediscovered it, found the numbers of kids there had grown immensely, and that there were many more good-looking girls. He wandered amid its bustle, flirted with the girls, slept with a few.

He discovered Samuel Shapiro's open-air dance hall held on the parking lot near the Sheraton Hotel. One Sunday, Delfino and a few friends on a lark began imitating the kids they'd seen on television break dancing on the streets of New York. A few flips they tried didn't quite work. So they relied on spins and one-armed handstands, which looked better. It wasn't much, but kids stopped dancing to watch. From then on, each Sunday a few more guys would take turns entering the widening circle to display what they could do.

Within months, at jobsites across Mexico City, young workers spent their evenings practicing break-dancing moves. Then on Sunday, as hundreds of kids gathered to watch, they were backflipping, cartwheeling, and swinging their bodies inches off the ground, balancing on one hand, then the other, like gymnasts. They did handstands. They teamed up, backflipping two at a time. One would spin like a helicopter blade on the head of another. It became a madness for a while and started every Sunday when the DJ at Samuel Shapiro's dance hall switched the music to technofunk.

Delfino usually began with a semi-Charleston step. With a billowy shirt flapping like a flag, his legs flailed serpentine as he harmonized his body with the rhythm. Then he leaped in an arc. He landed on his right hand, kicked his legs in the air, twirled on his hand, and came down in a crouch. From this position, he placed his hands on the ground and locked his arms. Wrapping his legs around his arms, he walked on his hands, like a crab. Then he'd jump up and fade into the crowd, a sheepish grin on his face.

To Delfino, break dancing combined wild abandon with individual expression through athletic prowess. Construction work furnished him the muscles; the Alameda provided the spotlight. The younger boys from his village of Xocotla, who had followed him to Mexico City, again followed his lead. As break dancing at the Alameda grew, a large contingent of

Delfino Juárez break dancing near the Alameda in Mexico City.

dancers was made up of fourteen- and fifteen-year-old boys from Xocotla who'd learned construction work from Delfino. Break dancing quickly got back to Xocotla. Before long, eight- and ten-year-old boys were practicing backflips on the village plaza, preparing for the day when they'd go to Mexico City to work construction and break-dance.

Sunday became more than just Delfino's day off. It was the day he stood out. He unleashed his body's energy and ability not on behalf of KFC but in a bid for the smiles of cute girls and in advancement of his own reputation. The cheerful brashness that he knew to stifle on the work-site could receive full expression by throwing his body around the break-dancing circle every Sunday.

One Sunday, he asked a pretty, quiet girl to dance. She didn't know how, she said. I'll show you, he told her. He taught her to dance cumbia.

Her name was Edith Villanueva. She was a maid from the state of Puebla, the village of San Marcos Tlacotepec, where they spoke Popoloco, a Nahuatl dialect, as well as Spanish. She was demure, thin, light-skinned, with long black hair and large brown eyes. She wouldn't sleep with him at first. Then, she let him take her to a hotel. They spent the night at a hotel five times before she would make love. After they finally did, she started crying.

Delfino calmed her. "If you like, I'll go talk to your father, and we'll set a date to get married."

He went to San Marcos and lived with her family for a week. With her father, Delfino worked the fields, though he knew nothing of farming.

He and Edith were married on June 30, 2002. They held a ceremony in Delfino's family shack. Her parents came from Puebla. Delfino bought soda and beer.

"Love isn't something you put on and take off like a piece of clothing," her father told the newlyweds. Adelina told her son, "If you have a vice, drop it and dedicate yourself to your woman."

A couple months later Edith was pregnant.

Delfino had considered leaving Mexico City construction work for the United States ever since he'd been break dancing. Break dancing and emigrating had a lot in common. Both required the daring to step beyond life's limits and demonstrate one's abilities. Only three men from Xocotla had ever gone north, and then only for a short time. But since coming home with a mohawk years before, Delfino had prided himself on being in Xocotla's vanguard. Now he had a wife and a son on the way. They lived in the same shack he'd grown up in, and there was nothing protecting them from disaster should he be hurt and unable to work. He knew what it was like to grow up ashamed of one's father and didn't want his son doing so. For all these reasons, he made plans to leave Mexico.

His country would consider it a minor loss, the departure of this uneducated urchin, but this delusion crippled Mexico. His kind of gumption

Delfino in Xocotla.

was what Mexico continually lost in its people's northern exodus—and no amount of money they sent home made up for it.

On June 5, 2003, Delfino Juárez was among those who headed north for the United States. He'd come to Mexico City at twelve and survived. He'd learned two things: The unknown didn't scare him; and Mexico City, the heart of his country, had failed him. He wanted more from life than simply not to starve.

Thus almost a decade to the day after he walked down Xocotla's road for Mexico City, Delfino paid a young man named Diez to lead him out of the capital, through the desert, and into the promised land.

Andrés Bermúdez, the Tomato King.

Chapter Two

The Tomato King

At the foot of brown hills in the center of the sunburned state of Zacatecas is a two-lane highway. It meanders through the countryside for miles before it nears a village known as El Cargadero. Outside the village, two roads fork off the highway in different directions.

One road is a monument to the ineptitude of the Mexican government. It winds into the hills above the village. The state government budgeted this road to be built more than a decade ago. The governor inaugurated it to great fanfare while it was under construction. But then the money was spent, diverted, or wasted. The road should have provided people in the hills with access to El Cargadero, and therefore to doctors, schools, and markets. Instead, it never became more than a cranky strip of rocks and potholes that grinds cars into submission.

The second road is everything the first is not. Paved, painted, and forking south, it slides smoothly into the village of El Cargadero. Immigrants in the United States from El Cargadero built it with their dollars.

One of them is a portly man named Andrés Bermúdez, who lives near Sacramento, California, in a small town named Winters. One cloudy day in the spring of 2001, Bermúdez stood at the junction of these roads outside El Cargadero. He had been here before. Bermúdez had once been president of an immigrant club that raised some of the money for that sleek paved road leading into the village. And he'd been at this junction when the governor inaugurated the first road that never was finished. He remembered bulldozers and a large crowd and the unfulfilled promises of a state government.

Bermúdez was born on a tiny ranch far into the hills. Until he was ten he never owned more than one pair of pants. The Bermúdez family raised a few cows on a plot of arid mountain land. His father often had to make long trips to town to sell the family's cheese. The Bermúdezes couldn't afford soap. When picking lice from their hair, his mother would tie her children to a tree to prevent them from running off, so painful was the ordeal.

One night when he was eight, Bermúdez raced through the hills in a frantic dash to save the life of his sister, María. She was four and sick with flu and bronchitis. For poor Mexican rancheros, far from doctors and pharmacies, these illnesses could kill. Through the day her cough worsened. Their father was away in town. So Bermúdez, his mother, and his brother bundled up María and put her in a basket on a donkey. All night, they hurried down through the hills, accompanied by owls hooting and María coughing and gasping. An old wives' tale had it that hooting owls meant witches were nearby, and this terrified the girl.

They arrived in El Cargadero at dawn, meeting their father as he was heading for home. The trip had been too much for María.

"My sister began to cry when my father held her and then she died in his arms," Bermúdez said. "It was as if she were waiting to see him to die."

Holding his dead daughter, his father broke down and sobbed. The family abandoned its ranch in the hills that day and moved to Tijuana. From there, as a young man years later, Bermúdez entered the United States. Yet ever since his sister's death, Andrés Bermúdez had felt he'd been run out poor and unwanted from the region of his birth.

Now, decades later, on that cloudy spring day at the junction, Bermúdez looked into the hills and remembered. He had stopped at these roads because, to him, they proved that the humble immigrant could do things better than the Mexican government, that it was the immigrant who moved Zacatecas.

"If we don't do anything to change things, Mexicans here will never do anything," he said.

With these roads in mind—and with dreams of glory tinged with revenge—the immigrant Andrés Bermúdez had returned from California to run for mayor of Jerez. Jerez was the seat of the municipio—or county— that governed fifty-seven villages, his own El Cargardero among them.

Over the next several months, his campaign would unfold like a tragi-comedy starring a rough-hewn man with Rabelaisian appetites. Andrés Bermúdez was not some noble, doe-eyed ascetic who'd spent his life in self-abnegation, fighting on behalf of the humble; no César Chávez he. He had never thought of running for office until the opportunity improbably fell into his lap. He was a farmer and spoke most fondly not of public policy, but of "my tomatoes" and "my bell peppers." He never seemed more at peace than when driving around his farm in his adopted town of Winters, California.

"I like my life (in the United States)," he said. "Early in the morning I go check my fields. Noontime, I go back and eat, then watch the news. Then in the afternoon, I go check my fields. It's my life for so many years."

Bermúdez dressed in black: black cowboy hat, black shirt, black pants, black belt. He looked every bit the wizened ranchero, with a prosperous belly, sunburned skin, and snakeskin cowboy boots. He cursed, he ogled women, and he drank beer with infectious gusto. He had no education beyond what life had taught him. He spoke rough Spanish and English in a voice made raspy from going back and forth between one-hundred-degree tomato greenhouses and forty-degree predawn fields in California.

He was the antipolitician, particularly for Mexico, where politicians' well-coiffed hair and uncalloused hands contrasted so with those of the people they governed. Some people would see Bermúdez as a modern Don Quixote, though with his enormous paunch he resembled Sancho Panza.

He would rally the rabble to his side. Before the campaign was over, this simple man would be internationally known as El Rey del Tomate—the Tomato King—and would emerge as a symbol for his time. Returning ostensibly to change Mexico, he became a standard-bearer for immigrants the world over.

Jerez's middle classes would see him as a buffoon, another affliction to be endured from the United States. Immigrants, too, divided on his motivations and potential for success. But to many immigrants, he was at least one of them, and they figured he could do no worse as mayor than the political elite that for so long had run Jerez—or Mexico, for that matter.

What was undeniable was that the life of Andrés Bermúdez could not have prepared him more poorly to resist the narcotic of media attention or navigate the crafty Mexican political maze. He was a simple man without one political instinct. The first vote he cast in his life was for himself. As an illegal immigrant, then a farmer and businessman, he had learned directness and self-reliance. He depended on common sense and hard work. Life had taught him not to balance the interests of competing groups but to make quick decisions, alone, obeying only his gut. He was like his fellow immigrants. His interests were theirs: making money and a future for himself and his family, working out of poverty.

What motivated him, as much as the desire to govern a city, was an impulse common to immigrants the world over. He wanted to be noticed for what he'd achieved since he was forced to leave, as a poor urchin with one pair of pants, these hills above El Cargadero.

Andrés Bermúdez was born in Mexico, but his American experience formed him. At fifty-nine, after decades in the United States, he now thought in English and translated into Spanish. When he came to Jerez, he spoke of knowing how to make money produce, of turning Jerez "into a little United States." He had a gringo's optimism in his ability to extend life-learned knowledge to benighted Mexico, where the government promised roads it didn't finish.

"My thoughts, my ideas, all that are American," he said one day in Jerez, a few weeks before his campaign began. "Politicians have to know something of being an entrepreneur. I want to be entrepreneur and politician. I learned this in the United States. You need a good product to sell, and you need to convince people that it's good. It's the same in politics. Old Mexican politicians only wanted to know about politics—about convincing people. But they didn't have any idea what they were selling.

"Mexican immigrants [who come home] aren't contaminated by the political system here," he went on. "People here see a rock in the road, and it's been there for fifty years, and it seems to them natural that it's there. But those who come from outside say, 'Why don't you just remove the rock?'"

Bermúdez's life had been about removing the rock. In 1974, at twenty-two, the day after he married, he crossed the border into California in the trunk of a car, together with his wife, Irma. They moved to Winters. Over the next three decades, Bermúdez was a farm worker, a foreman, a farm-labor contractor, a tomato and peach grower, an employer of several hundred people, many of whom were from the Jerez area. When harvest began in Winters, Bermúdez paid *coyotes* to cross them illegally in large numbers.

For several years after he first arrived in Winters, Bermúdez ran the farm of a peach grower named Warren Tufts. The four Bermúdez children were born while the family lived in the Tufts labor camp.

The Immigration and Naturalization Service agents raided the area periodically. One cold morning, he swam through the frigid water of the ranch's large pond to reach an island where he could hide from INS officers. Chased by an officer on another occasion, he ran through the ranch. Days before, he'd dug a hole in the ranch's garage, thinking he might one day need it as a hiding place. He jumped in the hole and covered it with matting. He stayed there until he thought the agent was gone. When he emerged, the officer was waiting for him at the garage door. Bermúdez was deported but was back in Winters a few days later.

Bermúdez worked for Tufts for nine years, including five years as ranch foreman. Still, Tufts denied him the use of the foreman's house. The Bermúdez family remained in the labor camp. Finally, Tufts hired his son-in-law to run the ranch and gave him the house. Bermúdez quit in disgust.

"One day I'm going to build a better house than you," he told the grower.

Bermúdez became a labor contractor and eventually provided Tufts with workers. He bought sixty-nine acres next to Tufts's property. On his own farm, Bermúdez grew peaches, carrots, bell peppers, and tomatoes. He invented a machine that allowed tomato plants to be transplanted from the greenhouse to the field more cheaply and easily. He also built a sprawling four-bedroom house and put stone lions imported from Jerez at the entrance "to show those guys that I could do better than the son-in-law," he said. He added a swimming pool, though he couldn't swim, and the one time he used it he almost drowned.

"To be rich, you gotta have a swimming pool," he said.

And here Andrés Bermúdez and his family lived undisturbed until the end of the year 2000 when the governor of Zacatecas came to visit.

On a map, Zacatecas looks like an amoeba in the middle of Mexico. Its lines curve in and out of territories with the logic of a modern art painting. On the ground, the state is vast and beautifully rugged. In parts, mesquite trees pock forbidding deserts of beige dust. Elsewhere, the desolation gives way to dirt the color of cayenne pepper. But whatever its color, the land of Zacatecas never could hold people to it.

The Zacatecan upper classes owned large tracts of land, much of which they'd inherited, but were averse to investing in anything more than their houses.

"There are very few classic entrepreneurs in Zacatecas, in the strict sense of people who, with their own resources, create jobs," said Rodolfo García, a professor of immigration and development studies at the University of Zacatecas. "In Mexico, the capitalist class has mostly grown due to the support and money of the government. The capitalist class in Zacatecas, more than in any other state, has grown up on public money."

The extraction and export of raw materials began in the late 1800s, when mining ruled Zacatecas. The minerals from Zacatecas went elsewhere to be processed into something of greater value. When the mines gave out, they were replaced by ranching and agriculture but not by a new attitude toward risk. Zacatecas, the Mexican state that produces more beans and chiles than any other, still has few companies that process those products into, say, canned beans and canned chiles. Almost everything produced in Zacatecas leaves for places where it is transformed into something of greater profit.

This includes its people. Nothing has left Zacatecas like its people. Emigration to the United States began in the late 1800s, declined in the 1930s, then picked up a momentum in the 1940s that it hasn't lost. No Mexican state has a greater percentage of its people in the United States than craggy, red Zacatecas.

The folks who left were the state's real risk-takers. They risked their own capital—their lives—on the promise of a better return than Zacatecas offered. For most of them, the bet paid off. In time in the United States, they opened businesses, bought houses, and sent their kids to school.

One of the great centers of this exodus is the municipio of Jerez, which lies an hour west of the city of Zacatecas, the state capital. Its population of fifty-four thousand people is at least matched by the number of Jerezanos living in the United States. Jerez has no industry beyond the production of unskilled workers for the lowest rungs of the U.S. economy. The town itself has many stores but only one or two sewing factories. Tour Jerez and its surrounding villages and you will be struck by a feeling that there are too many merchants for the paucity of economic activity you've seen. The stores, like the families and the region, survive on dollars that funnel down from America. These dollars hike the cost of living to where no one can live without them.

"Here, either you're a pensioner and receive your dollars every month," said one merchant, "or you have a store and sell to those who have dollars."

In Jerez, children grew up hearing of the wonders of Denver or of Norwalk, California. Each year they saw uncles, brothers, or friends return home transformed, with new clothes, cars, stereos, and of course more stories of the great El Norte. Kids pined for stereos and stories of their own. What was the point of school and studying? A kid knew that at sixteen he was going to Los Angeles where he could get a job in a plastics factory or as a landscaper and make twice what an engineer earned in Jerez.

Strangely, immigrants' daring and risk-taking indirectly stymied what the state needed most—which was a daring, risk-taking state of mind. Instead of using immigrant dollars to jump-start an industrial economy, Zacatecas simply limped along, addicted to the dollar injections. Immigrants became the state's primary foreign investors and job creators. They hired local folks to build lavish homes in the villages they'd left as paupers.

Then came the Mexican presidential election of 1988. The ruling PRI faced real competition for the first time in its history. Cuauhtémoc Cárdenas—a PRI apostate who had left the party—formed a movement that would become the left-wing Party of the Democratic Revolution (PRD). Sinaloan businessman Manuel Clouthier rejuvenated the National Action Party (PAN) by swiveling it away from right-wing social morality and toward the issues of corruption and efficient government services.

Cárdenas and Clouthier were the first Mexican presidential candidates to visit the United States and avidly court immigrants. The PRI and its candidate, Carlos Salinas de Gortari, beat back their challenge through massive vote fraud. But the 1988 election showed the PRI that immigrants up north were a dangerously uncoopted source of dissent. Salinas set up an office of Attention to Mexicans Abroad.

Zacatecas Gov. Genaro Borrego tried another idea. Every dollar immigrants put up for public works projects in their villages, he announced, the government would match. It started as "1 for 1" and quickly expanded to "2 for 1"—with money from the state and federal governments. Immigrants could stretch their dollars, and Zacatecan villages could get the schools, wells, and clinics they needed.

For decades, the PRI had used budgets to buy off union leaders, businessmen, academics, and neighborhood groups. Zacatecas's "2 for 1" was the party's first try at buying off immigrants in the United States, and it grew largely from the PRI's 1988 election scare. Zacatecan immigrants were urged to form village clubs and raise money for projects back home.

But the PRI miscalculated. These immigrants were no longer the humble campesinos who went hat-in-hand to mayors across Mexico. They'd done well in the United States, and felt confident in their abilities.

They blamed the PRI for having to leave their villages. They weren't about to let the party push them around up in the United States, too.

The clubs they formed were not docile. On the contrary, as the party pushed, immigrants pushed back. They insisted on a say in how their money was spent. The PRI was adamantly secular, but when some clubs insisted that the money they put up be used to renovate village churches, the government relented.

Because of "2 for 1," Zacatecans became the best-organized Mexican immigrants in the United States. By the time Andrés Bermúdez ran for mayor of Jerez, there were some 240 of these clubs in the United States. No other Mexican state had even half that number. They invested millions of dollars in public works. Their money built the necessities for their people back home that the government hadn't provided. In time, immigrants nurtured a righteous sense of their economic importance to Zacatecas.

Yet they religiously avoided politics. Mexican politics had been the exclusive domain of lawyers, teachers, merchants. Every ranchero seemed to know some fool who'd gone into politics and lost everything, been jailed or killed, or gotten rich and turned on his friends. So while Zacatecan immigrant prosperity created a vast ranchero constituency in the United States with money, organization, and talent, it was oblivious to its own political potential. That's how things remained until the late 1990s, when a lot began to change back home.

* * *

The world dates Mexico's new political pluralism to July 2000 and the victory of Vicente Fox, who won the presidency and broke the PRI's hold on national power. But Fox's victory was only the culmination of many less-noticed events in states around the country. One place the breakdown of the PRI could be seen was in Zacatecas in the late 1990s.

Zacatecas had been a mighty fortress of PRI support. Its business class was weak, and anyone else who might have opposed the ruling party had left for the United States, or been bought off. All the interesting Zacatecan political battles were among PRI factions.

In 1998, the state prepared to elect another PRI governor. Ricardo Monreal, a party stalwart, was a congressman and had obeyed party discipline when the PRI needed folks in Congress to attack the opposition. By 1998, Monreal figured he was due. He had a large organization of supporters and a name that was nationally known.

But party leaders gave the candidacy to another, believing Monreal would submit in silence. That had been the PRI way. People joined the party only because it never lost power and thus could guarantee them a government job or an elected office. A politician who didn't get a coveted candidacy had no choice but to acquiesce and wait his turn. But in the 1990s, as the PRI crumbled, opposition parties began winning elections. Now PRI politicians could jump to other parties.

Ricardo Monreal jumped. He took his entire organization with him to the left-wing PRD. Overnight, he made the PRD a force in Zacatecas politics. Monreal made national news, and he was soon mentioned as a possible candidate for president.

Monreal understood immigrants' influence. They couldn't vote in Mexico, but their dollars supported hundreds of towns and villages, and thus they could tell folks back home whom to vote for. Monreal wasn't the first Zacatecan candidate to visit the United States, but he did so more often and with more zest. He went on Mexican radio in Los Angeles and met with immigrant clubs. He promised to govern for all Zacatecans, including those in the United States. He courted the important Zacatecan club leaders. He won handily.

Two years later, Vicente Fox won the presidency. Like Monreal, he visited immigrant communities in the United States several times. He promised to govern for all Mexicans and push to allow immigrants in the United States to vote absentee in Mexican presidential elections—a right they'd been denied.

Fox's promise encouraged Monreal's presidential ambitions. Monreal redoubled his efforts in the United States. He crowned the annual Queen of Zacatecas chosen by the Southern California Federation of Zacatecan Clubs. He came up with "3 for 1"; immigrants could now get three dollars for their villages' public works for every dollar they put up.

Most relevant to our story, Monreal also urged immigrants to run for office in Zacatecas. One of those who thought he was being encouraged to do so was Andrés Bermúdez.

In December 2000, Monreal visited the immigrant turned successful rancher in Winters, California. Bermúdez rolled out the red carpet, even paying for the Zacatecas state band to come play. Monreal urged him to bring his tomato-transplanting technology to Zacatecas. Bermúdez responded that he sure would—soon as he became mayor of Jerez. Monreal, in one of those magnanimous gestures that Mexican politicians are fond of, but which are hardly meant to be believed, said, "Run. I'll support you."

Zacatecan political observers doubt that Monreal wanted to associate himself with Bermúdez. "Monreal spoke like a Mexican politician, and Bermúdez responded like an American businessman" and took the governor at his word, said Rodolfo García, the University of Zacatecas professor.

By January, Andrés Bermúdez, the portly rancher dressed in black, was in Jerez preparing to run for mayor.

* * *

As all this was going on, a small class of young Jerez businessmen had been acquiring a collective conscience. They were merchants, travel agents, hotel owners, and distributors of farm and ranch supplies who felt the PRI elite had shut them out of local politics.

When Monreal broke with the PRI, "the business class woke up," said Ismael Solís, one of these entrepreneurs. "We realized we'd always let [the town's political elite] do whatever they wanted."

A thin fellow with a sharp crew cut, Solís had spent years chroming cars in San Diego. He returned to Jerez and used his savings to open three building-supply stores.

Up to that point, Solís had avoided politics. But with Fox's victory, he and the others saw change coming. They saw that Jerez lacked basic services, and they knew that a city governed by a party other than that of the governor must fight constantly for funding. Now that Monreal was governor, a PRD mayor was essential if they wanted money for their city. "I didn't care too much who it was," Solís said.

They looked for a candidate. One of these businessmen, Martín Sotelo, lobbied his associates to support Bermúdez. Bermúdez was a businessman, had joined the PRD, and he was not from the town's political class. He had left poor and made it in the United States. He had given work to people from the surrounding villages. His coarse speech was no drawback in salt-of-the-earth Jerez. He would campaign to transplant ideas like tomatoes from the United States to Mexico. This appealed to the local businessmen, who saw that things got done in the United States.

They threw their support to Bermúdez, and his campaign came to life. They didn't know Bermúdez, and he didn't know them. After so long in the United States, he was unknown and had no real supporters in Jerez. But the businessmen adopted him.

Their first hurdle was winning the PRD primary. Solís and his friends had employees and families show up at the polls at 5:00 AM. The PRD had limited the number of ballots for the primary to prevent ballot stuffing. Voting early, Bermúdez supporters used up enough ballots to make him the candidate.

But PRI city officials denied him the legally required residency card, saying he didn't live full-time in Jerez. Bermúdez went on radio to plead his case, then led hundreds of people to take over city hall; news photos showed his followers standing on the mayor's desk and Bermúdez shaking a fist at the mayor.

The obstacles Bermúdez faced "are another sign of the discrimination toward those Zacatecans who left the state so as not to die of hunger," wrote Ricardo Santoyo, a local dentist, on his website, www.jerez.com. mx, which had become a popular virtual meeting place for immigrants from Jerez.

Bermúdez was given his residency card, though the question of where he lived was left unresolved.

That year, three immigrants came down from the United States to run for PRD candidacies for mayor in Zacatecan towns. Andrés Bermúdez was the only victor among them. Ricardo Monreal's credibility as a politician and presidential contender was now wrapped inextricably in the campaign of one beer-drinking man. With no choice, Monreal proclaimed the Bermúdez candidacy an historic event.

"It's not fair that we only seek out (immigrants) to ask for their money," the governor said, "then we won't let them participate in politics when they want to."

He called the young businessmen in Jerez and promised to send professionals to run the campaign.

"No one thought we could put together a winning campaign," Solís said, "not even the governor."

They fired the professionals and ran the campaign themselves. They planned rallies and charted trips to the far-flung villages around Jerez. They gave movie tickets to kids. They paid for the daily bus tickets that students needed to travel to attend the University of Zacatecas, an hour away.

With Bermúdez in the mix, the race was probably going to be about the role of immigrants in Jerez life. But when the PRI chose Alma Ávila as its candidate, this became a certainty.

No one in Jerez better represented the town elite than Alma Ávila. Her father had been mayor, state legislator, and was the power behind the Jerez throne. A long-time PRI activist, Alma had been a city councilwoman and the town's director of economic development. She had a college education and had been a state legislator. She'd never lived in the United States and, amazingly, hadn't even any immediate family up there.

Ávila often pressed the point that she knew Jerez because she'd never left it. "I'm a candidate with roots here and a full knowledge of the problems here, since I've always lived here. This allows me a vision of what we have to do in Jerez," she said in the dining room of her spacious Jerez home one day. "[Bermúdez] has been living in the U.S. for thirty years. He isn't rooted here. He doesn't have any education. He doesn't know the municipio. He'd have a hard time understanding what the needs of the municipio are."

All this was true. But what Ávila counted among her advantages was not what was suddenly important as Bermúdez's star began to rise.

That she'd never left Jerez only meant she was out of step with most of the region's families. Further, a lot of people believed she'd never had to go north because her father had spent a lot of time feeding at the public trough.

Ávila made it easier for Bermúdez to run against the PRI, the town elite, the nonimmigrant. His Jerez campaign poster proclaimed: "If I did it up there . . . with your vote, I'll do it again here."

She suggested immigrants ought to contribute to Zacatecas's economic development but not its politics. Ávila followed that assertion with an uncharacteristically blunt expression of the view of immigrants that many Mexicans held.

"They're immersed in another kind of society that isn't adapted to the reality that is Zacatecas and Mexico," she said. "They don't have a concrete vision of what has to be done here. Our country is very different from the United States. They're not very clear on how to defend our customs, values, and traditions. They are 'deculturized.' I'd even say their values are less solid than ours."

Immigrants, whose dollars had kept Zacatecas from catastrophe, took this as more outrageous PRI ingratitude. Bermúdez's campaign was jolting a good many immigrants, particularly those in the clubs. They owned houses in the home villages, and their remittances kept the villages alive. At times, they could sound like American revolutionaries talking about "no taxation without representation." Among the most eloquent was Humberto Saldivar, president of El Cargadero Club in Anaheim, California.

"Every day I remember my El Cargadero, my Jerez," said Saldivar, a construction worker. "If I'd have had job opportunities in Jerez like there are here, I wouldn't have left. I think [Bermúdez's campaign] is a revolution of immigrants who are saying, 'We're tired of the government living off us.' The country depends on us in a lot of ways. But they've never let us vote. Many people in the government have said we shouldn't be involved in deciding the country's future. But they don't mind when we send money back. We're Mexicans, and we have family there. We send money back, and we have the right to be able to decide."

The race quickly spilled beyond Jerez. Fox had just made history. The eyes of the world were on Mexico. In the latter half of the twentieth century, no country had sent more people to another than Mexico had sent to the United States. Bermúdez's candidacy raised questions made relevant by the global economy: What, and where, is home? Can one be a citizen of two places at the same time? For immigrants, these questions were the marrow of everyday life. "As globalization advances, as telecommunications shortens distances, the requirement of being rooted in your community is less politically necessary," said Luis Medina, the PRD's state president.

Articles about Bermúdez appeared in the *San Francisco Chronicle*, the *Houston Chronicle*, and *San Diego Union-Tribune*. The Mexican newsweekly *Milenio* ran a story, too. With his magnificent beer belly, black outfits, and blunt talk, he made good copy. If the message of the day in Mexico was political change, then Andrés Bermúdez was an apt medium.

Those stories were followed by pieces in the *New York Times*, *Time*, the *Boston Globe*, the *Los Angeles Times*, CNN, Reuters, the Associated Press, and others. The Mexican media piled on. Mexico City dailies *Reforma* and *El Universal* ran long articles on Bermúdez and followed them with regular coverage of the campaign. It seemed that reporters who came to Zacatecas wanted only to talk about the immigrant who had returned to run for mayor.

The Mexican media dubbed him El Rey del Tomate—the Tomato King. Soon, Mexicans who didn't know Andrés Bermúdez knew that a man called the Tomato King was running for mayor of Jerez, Zacatecas.

For weeks the coverage was unrelenting. No one could remember a small-town mayor's race anywhere in Mexico receiving this kind of sustained attention. It sidelined Ricardo Monreal. He was quoted only inasmuch as he had something to say about Andrés Bermúdez. For three months in 2001, only Vicente Fox garnered more media attention than the Tomato King.

Bermúdez hadn't expected it. He was a barnacled man unused to public speaking. But the attention grew intoxicating, and he welcomed reporters to town.

"The eyes of both countries are going to be on me," he told them. "If this fails, the door will close to those in the United States who want to come down. So I can't fail."

The young businessmen who coalesced around him threw themselves into campaigning with an exuberance they didn't know they had. They brought in the romantic singer, Napoleón, for a concert. They staged a free rodeo and dance for eight thousand people. A week before the election, they held a Tomatón—a word they coined by combining tomato and telethon. Bands, singers, and comics entertained crowds for eleven hours in Jerez's plaza. The event raised fifty thousand pesos for a senior home and a drug rehabilitation center and promoted the campaign of the Tomatote—the Big Tomato, as Bermúdez was now called.

Behind the scenes, however, Bermúdez was emerging as a complicated man. The businessmen weren't sure if he was a clown or possessed an astute political mind in disguise. When reporters asked him what he thought of Ramón López Velarde, he said, "I don't know him, but if you bring him by I'll invite him to work on the campaign." Ramón López Velarde was a nationally renowned poet, the most famous person ever born in Jerez, and had died in 1929.

Monreal asked him about reports he'd been seen drunk firing a gun at a party. Bermúdez denied being at the party. He didn't deny having two wives—one in Winters and another in Watsonville, a town south of San Jose, California. In fact, by the time Zacatecan papers got hold of that, he'd acquired a woman in Jerez as well.

"I don't have two wives," he told reporters, "I have three."

He spoke of hiring only people from the outlying villages to work in city hall. His friends from the villages began to suggest policy. He should reserve a street lane for horses on Saturdays, they told him. "You know what you ought to do?" his friend Teodoro Orozco told Bermúdez one day over breakfast. "For queen of the fair, you ought to choose a girl who isn't all made up, the daughter of a doctor or lawyer, but a girl from the villages, who's got the sunburned color."

What Bermúdez's businessmen supporters saw clearly was that their candidate didn't have much enthusiasm for tedious campaign details. He loved interviews, but he often didn't show up to campaign until the late afternoon. Nor did he get along with the local media. Like gnats, they hovered about him, while foreign and national reporters came and went, content with general stories about his campaign.

"Bermúdez didn't want any contact with the local media," said Julio César Espinoza, a boot vendor who joined the Tomato King's campaign. "We'd say, 'Hey, let's have a press conference, treat them right.' He'd say, 'Forget them.' He only paid attention to the reporters from outside. When they'd come he'd put on his black suit, his hat, and pose for photographs."

Midway through the campaign, the businessmen had had enough. Martín Sotelo brought them all together, apologized for convincing them to join the team, and resigned.

"We were working without a candidate," Sotelo said later.

The others told Bermúdez that he had to get Sotelo back if he wanted their help. Three days later, they drove Bermúdez to Sotelo's house, where he apologized. The two men hugged, and the team continued on. The suspicion lingered that Bermúdez wasn't up to the job, but it was submerged in the furor surrounding the campaign.

The race turned into a political coming out for immigrants. The first debate was held not in Jerez, but at a restaurant in the Los Angeles suburb of Montebello, organized by the nine L.A. clubs that raise money for public works in Jerez and its nearby villages. No candidate missed it. Bermúdez apologized before he read an opening statement, saying he hadn't read in Spanish in many years.

Felipe Delgado, a Zacatecan leader in Los Angeles, went on local Jerez radio several times to urge people to vote for Bermúdez. Hundreds of immigrants called home to insist their relatives do the same.

Adding to the hoopla was Salvador Espinoza. Espinoza had gone to California years before and had made a lot of money growing lettuce. He now lived in the penthouse of the Hotel Leo, the nicest hotel in Jerez, which he had built. With too much time and money on his normally active hands, Espinoza joined the race for mayor on the ticket of the tiny Democratic Convergence Party. The local media dubbed him the Lettuce

King. His main contribution to the race was to fly over the town center one day and drop fliers and hundred-dollar bills to people below. It was all for naught. Espinoza finished fourth.

Ávila and the PRI, meanwhile, staked their campaign on the hope that Bermúdez's constituency was in the remote villages that had emptied into the United States. Jerez's middle class, Ávila's team felt, would cringe at a coarse ranchero running their town. They were half-right. The villages *had* depopulated, but many of these folks had moved to Jerez. So while Jerez looked middle class, its people were often poor ranchers at heart, and their income came in the form of dollars relatives sent them from up north.

Like Monreal and Fox before him, Bermúdez spoke of representing Jerez on both sides of the border. He noted that the educated folks who'd governed the town had done a poor job of it. "Now it's our turn," was his refrain. He vowed not to take a salary as mayor because he didn't need it. Folks surmised that he would thus be less likely to steal from the city treasury.

Immigration funded life in Jerez, and now it moved people to vote. Immigrants, and thus their relatives in Jerez, went for Bermúdez in a big way. A caravan of immigrants from the villages near Jerez drove down from Southern California to vote; many others flew.

And in the end, with all that media attention focused on one candidate, it wasn't really much of a contest. Ávila's problem was that, in the words of one man, "she doesn't know what it's like to spend three months in the United States paying off a coyote and not being able to send any money to the family back home."

On July 1, 2001, the immigrant Andrés Bermúdez was elected mayor of Jerez.

❋

Six days later, in a cavernous union hall in Santa Ana, California, the El Cargadero Club threw a big dance. Under large fluorescent lights, men in cowboy hats and boots whisked women in tight skirts across the dance floor. It was a warm and humid night. Foreheads glistened, and shirts and blouses stuck to the folks wearing them.

The dance was originally intended to raise money for public works back home. Now it had greater meaning: to hail the Tomato King, the conquering hero from El Cargadero.

Most of the people had left the village poor years ago. They had settled in Anaheim, but every one of them wanted to return a success to show the rich people back home what he could do. In the most visible way, Andrés Bermúdez was doing that for them. A thousand of them showed up at the dance to toast his victory.

Bermúdez had flown up from Zacatecas that morning. He was dressed in his signature black. He stood at a table and poured down can after can of Coors Light. A *norteño* band bounced through polkas. One song was a ballad Bermúdez had written about his brother, José, who died in a car accident years before. A banner proclaimed that the El Cargadero Club "welcomes the Tomato King."

Couples wandered up and congratulated him. Friends grabbed him around the neck and hugged him hard. "Put your heart into it," one man told him. Women asked him to dance. Younger women took his photograph. Spanish-language television stations interviewed him. He posed for a snapshot with a copy of a *Los Angeles Times* article about immigrant candidates in Mexico. When visitors to his table faded away, he meandered through the crowd to prime the pump of his people's love and be slapped on the back again. Walking by the bandstand, he grabbed the microphone and let out a yelp, and a "Viva El Cargadero!" Coors Light kept going down easy.

A year after the victory of Vicente Fox, the victory of Andrés Bermúdez seemed to consecrate the idea that a new Mexico was coming. Because of the Tomato King, other Mexican states were discussing allowing immigrant candidates. Mexican campaigns, it seemed, would finally have to include immigrants. Even Ricardo Monreal's future seemed to depend on Bermúdez now.

To one side of the dance stood Guadalupe Gómez, an accountant in Santa Ana and president of the Southern California Federation of

Zacatecan Clubs. Gómez was gushing. "I'm sure that in the near future—by 2010, say—we're going to have an immigrant governor [in Zacatecas]," he said. "By the next election we should have congressmen and senators."

Near the table sat Bermúdez's wife Irma, with whom he'd snuck across the border in the trunk of a car so many years before. During the campaign, Irma, too, had returned to Jerez to live for the first time in many years. She looked uneasy.

"It feels like we shouldn't even have the job," she said of her husband's newly won line of work. "We don't know how to speak well. We don't know anything about politics."

In fact, as Bermúdez was hailed as a harbinger of immigrant power in Mexico, politics seemed the last thing on his mind. He seemed to flee Jerez as soon as the election was over. Most other mayors-elect in Zacatecas had transition teams in place within days of July 1. Bermúdez waited more than a month to even reappear in town.

He was feted at fiestas in San Jose, in Texas, and at a Zacatecan immigrant-club convention in Chicago. He rode as grand marshal in a parade in East Los Angeles. At a rally of immigrants at a rodeo arena in Pico Rivera, near Los Angeles, he rode in on a horse. A band sang the "Corrido of Andrés Bermúdez," which recounted his life story in song.

"We didn't leave (Mexico); they ran us out," he told the crowd, and called for "more Andréses" to come down to Mexico to run for office.

All this prompted Ricardo Monreal to take him aside and only half-jokingly say, "Andrés, you're partying more than Fox," and urge him to get home—to Jerez, that is—and get to work.

"I'm trying to tell everybody, 'Thank you for your support,'" he explained later.

But it would be five weeks before Andrés Bermúdez would reappear in the town where he was now mayor-elect.

A strange coincidence in this tale is that in 1962, a movie was made in Mexico that was called *El Rey del Tomate—The Tomato King*. The story it told paralleled that of our Tomato King in several ways. Starring the comic Piporro, the film was about a man who made a lot of money growing tomatoes and was then duped into getting into things he knew nothing about. He lost everything and looked like a fool doing it. So while the term "El Rey de Tomate" literally means a captain of the tomato industry, in Mexico it can also refer to someone who blunders about in areas where he has no expertise.

In the weeks following his election, it was unclear to the people of Jerez which Tomato King they had elected. Once drunk on international headlines, Jerez awoke to a hangover and realized that, in fact, Bermúdez didn't know them or their town very well. He showed up in Jerez in early August, without having spoken a word in five weeks to the crew of young businessmen who had helped elect him. Worse yet, in their view, he could talk of little but his press notices.

He let everyone know that *People Magazine en Español* would soon run something on him. The *Washington Post* would attend his inauguration. Pres. Vicente Fox and George W. Bush wanted to meet him, he said. France's *Le Monde* had him on its front page. TVE from Spain and a Japanese film crew wanted to do documentaries about him. He had signed a deal with Warner Bros. to develop a film based on his life story.

His victory, he said, "will send messages to the world. The first message is to the immigrants, that living the American Dream you have to give up many Mexican dreams. You'll be making dollars and living better, but you'll leave your mother crying. The other message is to the government, that it's time to change the way they govern. If they don't see their errors, there'll be many more Andréses."

That sounded nice, but in Jerez a lot of folks just figured Andrés wanted to be a star.

Bermúdez did show some of the imagination and energy typical of immigrants who do well in the United States. He said he'd used his notoriety to line up a deal with the juice maker JUMEX to buy all the tomatoes, chiles, and guayabas that the Jerez area could produce. He urged club leaders in the states to change the focus of "3 for 1" away from unnecessary items like rodeo arenas used only when immigrants returned for annual fiestas. He lobbied them to buy police equipment, hospital beds, and fight the plagues rotting drought-weakened trees around Jerez. Bermúdez asked beer maker Carta Blanca to invest in a fairgrounds complex in which their products—Tecate, Dos Equis, and Superior—would be the only beer consumed. He magnanimously offered to star in their ads. "I figure people will drink whatever Andrés Bermúdez tells them to," he said.

Yet, even in those first few weeks in August, he rarely appeared in Jerez. Returning from the United States, he flew to Mexico City for a live television interview with Brozo the Clown, a political comic. Bermúdez told Brozo that he'd be charging foreign reporters for interviews: one computer apiece, to donate to the villages around Jerez. The PRD flew him to the state of Michoacán to campaign for their candidates there. He went to Tamaulipas to do the same. He told reporters that candidates in Mexicali and Tijuana had called asking if they could include portions of his speeches in their own.

"If the politician wants to use the speeches of a campesino, the campesino will be proud," he told them.

The Tomato King was nationwide.

Back in Jerez, rumors flew. One was that town residents would get jobs in the movie about his life. Another had it that the entire city hall staff would be fired. Who knew what the Tomato King would do as mayor? The once-humble ranchero was now a star, and to a lot of people he seemed much changed.

The people of Jerez are a down-to-earth lot. Bermúdez was letting the attention go to his head, they muttered. Soon some people were making the connection to that Piporro movie from years before. Bermúdez seemed to have an elevated idea of his role in Mexican political life. People marveled that he was now capable of statements such as, "Since Andrés Bermúdez crossed the border [to run for mayor], the politics in all Mexico is going to change."

Cartoonists showed him star-struck. Bermúdez "is more interested in appearing in movies and books about his life" than in getting to work at city hall, wrote a columnist in *El Alacrán*, a small local newspaper.

As Bermúdez basked in his stardom, none grumbled louder than the young businessmen. A month before his September swearing-in, they still knew none of his plans for city hall. They had to attend to campaign workers, some of whom were now expecting city jobs. What's more, many businessmen were left with political coitus interruptus, needing more of the action that they had lived with daily for three months.

"We were all left with the campaign bug," said Armando Carrillo, the current owner of Hotel Leo and of several travel agencies.

Andrés Bermúdez had won because of their efforts, they told themselves. They now realized how little they knew the man they'd helped make mayor. They sat together in the restaurant of the Hotel Leo and their resentment festered. They spoke of leaving Bermúdez with the bill for twenty thousand bus tickets that the campaign had given to students attending university in Zacatecas City. A radio station had sent over the bill for several campaign spots. Bermúdez refused to pay; so did the businessmen.

Armando Carrillo told of eating at a taco stand in the market one day. Bermúdez came in to eat at the same counter, he said. He turned his hat away, wouldn't talk to Carrillo. He talked instead with the waitress, then left.

In mid-August, fifty of these businessmen met at the Hotel Leo. They decided to have nothing more to do with the Tomato King.

"We're afraid that now that he's won he's forgotten the plan, which is to create a little United States here," said Carrillo at the time. "He's thinking about movies of his life, charging for interviews. But what about city hall? He thinks he's a big star. Well, hopefully he'll be one. We haven't had one since Ramón López Velarde."

"There's a feeling that he used people here in Jerez as a trampoline to gain stardom up there in the United States," said Julio César Espinoza. "So people ask what the hell is he doing on television with that clown in Mexico City? What does that have to do with Jerez? I think he's on the run. At city hall, there's nothing but problems."

"He has to learn that what he's won is not a prize, but a responsibility," said Ricardo Santoyo, the dentist who ran www.jerez.com.mx and still supported Bermúdez.

Meanwhile, some sectors of Jerez society were alarmed to see that what began as the Return of the Immigrant was becoming the Revenge of the Immigrant. The day after his election—on July 2—Bermúdez led a march through town. It was part victory celebration, part funeral for the PRI, which had lost the Mexican presidency exactly one year before. Jerez's middle classes glumly watched as Bermúdez led his rag-tag army of ranchero supporters through the streets. The King of Tomatoes was also the King of the Poor.

One function of Mexican mayors is to distribute city patronage jobs. Bermúdez promised that no one who worked in his administration would be rich—which meant, in the Jerez context, middle class. He vowed to hire only people from the villages.

"This will be a place for people from the villages who've never been taken into account because they weren't friends with the mayor or relative of a councilman," he said. "We're going to learn together. It's easier to teach new habits, than to correct old ones."

Nor was his the typical postelection rhetoric of inclusion. "If [the middle classes] feel ignored, they should think of how people from the villages felt for so many years," he said. "Now they're the ones who'll have to leave here as wetbacks—the merchant, the son of the politician."

He seemed convinced that he hadn't needed the young businessmen who coalesced around him. The victory seemed to be one more thing in life that he'd achieved alone.

Miguel Moctezuma, an immigration scholar at the University of Zacatecas and a Bermúdez advisor, used his isolation as proof that the Tomato King was not a typical Mexican politician. "He doesn't like alliances with powerful groups. He sees it as going back to the old way of doing politics." Others opined that Bermúdez simply didn't know what he was doing.

Whatever the case, Bermúdez, in his campaign, had done what any politician does: he'd promised a lot to a lot of people. But the backlog of needs and demands at city hall was already enormous. Alienating anyone in town seemed to be asking for trouble. Furthermore, the exodus north had so depleted the working-class talent pool in Jerez that people wondered where he'd find qualified administrators among those who stayed behind.

All of which was to say that the Tomato King faced monumental challenges in governing Jerez without those he was creating on his own.

But before he could face them, it all ended. Two months after his victory, the PRI brought a suit before Mexico's elections tribunal. The suit claimed that Bermúdez had forfeited his Mexican citizenship to become a U.S. citizen and thus couldn't run for office in Mexico.

The suit got to the very heart of the thing: could immigrants who lived abroad, but maintained a house and invested money in their villages back home, run for office in Mexico? Immigrants noted that many politicians lived in Mexico City full-time, yet ran for governor or Congress in the states of their birth, which they rarely visited.

The tribunal denied the PRI's claim. Bermúdez, it found, had indeed reinstated his Mexican citizenship under the country's new Law of Dual Nationality. But among the documents Bermúdez had filed to recover his Mexican citizenship was one that he'd signed in November 2000, on which he listed Winters, California as his principal residence. This meant that he had not lived in Jerez for a year before his July 1 election, as required by law. With that, the tribunal nullified his election.

Who found this document is unknown. Some people said it was a PRI functionary in the Ministry of Foreign Relations. Others said it was a member of the PRD, an ally of Ricardo Monreal, rankled that Bermúdez's star eclipsed his own. Everyone remembered that takeover of Jerez city hall months before the election when city officials had been pressured into giving him the residency card without resolving what country Bermúdez actually called home.

"Mexico remains so rotten that I don't think it'll ever move forward," said Bermúdez. "Ten thousand people voted for one person, and (a few) people in a room erase what the whole town decided."

Political observers noted that his permanent home was indeed Winters,

California—and that closed the case. But to many immigrants, this was quibbling in view of the fact that their dollars kept Zacatecas afloat. The treatment of Andrés Bermúdez confirmed their worst beliefs of the nastiness of Mexican politics. Some immigrants threatened to withhold money from "3 for 1," and boycott Mexican products.

Bermúdez fought on for a while, but Ismael Solís took his place as Jerez mayor. Solís had run along with Bermúdez as his *suplente*, or replacement. Suplentes are routine in Mexican politics; their job is to replace the officeholder if he can't finish his term. But in a rare move, the suplente split with the candidate. Solís had the young businessmen's backing. The poor supported Bermúdez. As Solís's swearing-in approached, Bermúdez supporters again took possession of Jerez city hall. State officials stepped in to broker a deal between the two sides. An accord was reached in which Solís would govern for three months. At the end of three months, a public-opinion poll would be taken to determine whether Jerez residents preferred Solís or Bermúdez as mayor. The winner would take office.

Solís governed until December. The poll was taken a week before Christmas. Bermúdez garnered 51 percent to Solís's 31 percent. Solís refused to leave office. The state legislature and Monreal supported him. With that, the Tomato King was out, just no one much noticed anymore. World attention had shifted elsewhere since the September 11 terrorist attacks. Andrés Bermúdez had grown used to the media's presence. Now they were occupied elsewhere.

He and his supporters staged another city hall takeover. That lasted a few days, but ended when some of the protesters were offered jobs in the Solís administration. Bermúdez returned to Winters.

"They didn't respect the vote of the people, nor did they respect a poll. I have my life here [in the United States]," he said. "I was just trying to change things, to help people."

Bermúdez broke with Monreal and the PRD. Bearing signs reading "Monreal betrayed Andrés," his supporters threw tomatoes at the governor during his state of the state speech.

The story of the Tomato King's rise to political stardom was a tale for the global economy. He traveled frequently between Winters and Jerez and supported both economies. He considered two countries his home.

But part of what Alma Ávila said also proved true. Immigrants were distanced from their places of birth. They lived in another world. In the end, when it came to local politics, maybe it did matter where you lived every day.

Still, the Bermúdez campaign changed the way immigrants saw themselves and their relation to Mexico. Immigrant leaders urged Fox to make good on his promise to push for their right to vote in Mexican elections. More than that, immigrants came to see a voice in Mexican affairs as their birthright. Leaders of the Southern California Federation of Zacatecan Clubs lobbied the Mexican government and Congress for more funds for "3 for 1." Academics and immigrants from Zacatecas drew up reforms to the state constitution that they called the "Bermúdez Law." The reforms would allow Zacatecan immigrants living in the United States to run for office back home. A good part of every Zacatecas governor's race, and perhaps some mayoral and legislative races, would likely now take place in the United States.

After the ordeal, Andrés Bermúdez returned to Winters and sought refuge among his tomatoes and his bell peppers. He vowed to retire from politics. He said he'd declined Monreal's offer to become state director of immigration. For a long time he had nothing good to say about Monreal.

"He never liked that I ran for mayor," Bermúdez said.

But months later Bermúdez was talking again with the governor. "It's better to have him as a friend than an enemy," he said, having apparently learned something about politics from his experience.

He hinted that he would run for governor of Zacatecas in 2004 or help found an immigrant political party. We'll see, is all he would tell reporters. He spoke of having lost the battle but not the war.

"I expected difficulties, betrayal," he said. "But I've never seen a movie in which the bad guy won. In this one, the bad guy won. We're going to have to make the second movie, in which the good guy wins."

Since I cannot prove a lover . . .

I am determined to prove a villain.

—*Richard III,* William Shakespeare

Chapter Three

The Saga
of South Gate

In March of 1999, just before local elections took place in South Gate, California, the town's registered voters received a political flier in the mail.

The mailer concerned a man named Joe Ruiz. Ruiz was a plumber in town who spent his free time coaching youth baseball and football. He was a tall, wide, and outgoing man. Ruiz had dropped out of junior high school to help support his family after his father died. He'd spent many years as a plumber at Roto-Rooter. Then Joe Ruiz founded his own plumbing business, Expert Rooter, which by now employed twelve people.

Ruiz had lived in South Gate for twenty-three years. He was active in the Chamber of Commerce and was one of those people newspapers and charity organizers tend to describe as a pillar of the community. His youth football team had just won the regional championship, the first time a South Gate squad had done so well. Now he was running for a seat on the city council.

About the only controversial thing Ruiz had done recently was to sue a man named Richard Mayer. Mayer lived in the town of Whittier, ten miles away, where he'd served on the water board. Now, however, Mayer was among the many candidates for South Gate City Council. He did not live in South Gate. He knew only one person in town. He claimed residence at a South Gate apartment, but neighbors said they'd never seen him. A police investigation showed that Mayer was registered to vote twice: in Whittier and in South Gate. What's more, Mayer was now calling himself Ricardo Ávalos Mayér, a name change that might presumably help him among South Gate's voters, who were predominantly Latino.

Ruiz sued to block Mayer's candidacy. A judge ruled in favor of Ruiz, but by then ballots had been printed with Mayer's new name on it. Citing Mayer's probable nonresidency, the judge said he'd disqualify him if he won.

Then, the weekend before that election, the mailer arrived at the homes of twelve thousand South Gate voters. Unlike the mailers that would come later, this one had a plain look, printed in black and white on thin cardboard. Its claim, however, was scandalous. The mailer announced that police had arrested Joe Ruiz for molesting two boys in his swimming pool during a birthday party in his backyard. It included what looked like a reprint of an article in the *South Gate Press* reporting the arrest. The story even quoted a South Gate police officer. The mailer urged people "not to vote for this molester."

As accusations go, this one was so bold that many residents thought it had to be true. Otherwise, who would say it? Yet as inflammatory as the claim was, it was just as false. Ruiz had a clean record. The *South Gate Press* hadn't published the story, and the quoted officer didn't exist. Ruiz didn't even own a swimming pool.

Ruiz asked for an investigation. The FBI and local police even opened their records on a Saturday and publicly vouched for Ruiz to the news media. No one ever figured out who sent the mailer, but the damage was done. Ruiz lost the race; Mayer came in fourth. And for weeks afterward, people called Joe Ruiz to ask if he'd really molested those boys.

Other anonymous mailers that election year made people queasy. One mailer accused Mayor Henry Gonzalez of becoming "one of the richest men in South Gate" through city kickbacks and bribes. Not everyone agreed with Henry Gonzalez on the issues, but no one could imagine him using public service to line his pockets. He and his wife lived in a modest house they'd owned for twenty years. Henry donated his six-hundred-dollar-a-month city salary to charity and didn't allow his son, an electrical contractor, to bid on city projects. Henry even forbade his grandkids from applying for city summer jobs because it looked bad.

Another anonymous mailer accused a city council candidate, Joe Gonzalez, no relation to Henry, of drunken driving. The mailer even reprinted a supposed police citation. Both the accusation and the citation were fabrications. Yet this libel, too, went out to thousands of homes in South Gate.

Later, people would debate what was the most notorious early symptom of the political virus that had spread through town. Some people would point to the night Henry Gonzalez was shot in the head coming home from a council meeting. Had Henry not turned at the sound of steps behind him, he'd be a dead man. The bullet glanced off the side of his head and the shooter ran off, never to be caught. Of course, no one could say it was a political crime. But the shooter sure didn't seem interested in robbing Henry, so what other motive was there?

Some people thought that the virus was encouraged when Richard Mayer—or Ricardo Ávalos Mayér or whatever his name was—hadn't been stopped from running for office and twice registering to vote.

However, most people came to see the mailers at election time as the most public sign of something rotting away inside the city's body politic. When the saga of South Gate was over, many of them would look back and remember that mailer attacking Joe Ruiz as the point where minimum standards of decency began to give way.

For the next few years at election time, anonymous mailers would grow into an incessant torrent of libel. Mailboxes would clog daily with thick wads of the thin cardboard. Each piece exploded in riotous color, loopy swirls, and loony babble of ever-more outrageous accusations. It jangled the nerves.

If the scurrilous fliers listed any sponsor at all, it was a fictitious association or neighborhood group at an address that didn't exist. California law doesn't require credible identification on political mailers. So the fliers remained anonymous. This, in turn, seemed to encourage whoever was churning them out to ever-greater flights of perverse creativity.

Collecting these mailers became a hobby in South Gate. Some people even sheathed them in plastic, like prized baseball cards. Ask for a copy of a specific mailer, and the response was likely to be, "I think I have that one. That's from '99, right?"

The mountain of mailers reached its pinnacle in March 2001, two years after the election in which Joe Ruiz was first attacked as a molester. The local post office reported one day receiving thirty mailers, each one going to twelve thousand addresses—which, postal officials said, was apart from the normal correspondence that each house received.

By then, South Gate had spawned a mutant strain of small-town democracy. It had spread and was now oozing out of control like some laboratory creation in a bad horror movie. Honesty stood in its path and was devoured and replaced by a thick slime of deceit. Meanwhile, wave after wave of poisonous mailers attacked like an invading pestilence.

"It's terrible," said Ali Moradi, a postman on the west side of town, who in March 2001 was developing muscle strain from carrying the load on his route. "It's only in South Gate. I don't know why."

The story I'm about to tell you is why indeed all that happened and what the people of South Gate finally did about it.

Southeast of Los Angeles, the town of South Gate spreads anonymously to the west of the 710 Freeway, an eight-lane vein of asphalt that feeds the main arteries in the Los Angeles automotive bloodstream: the 5, 10, and 405 freeways. South Gate contains no tall buildings or landmarks visible from the freeway. Were it not for a sign on the 710, you'd have no way of knowing you were passing within its city limits.

South Gate was among the first suburbs of Los Angeles when it formed in 1923, with a population of twenty-five hundred people. The area had been the southern gate on a large ranch and held an airfield where Amelia Earhart had learned to fly. It remained mostly farmland until the end of World War II. Factories moved there for the cheap land. Following the factories were housing developers, who built starter homes. That brought ex-GIs and their wives, who came on the Red Line—Los Angeles's metro system at the time—and bought houses for $135 down and $45 a month.

Jobs were plentiful. The men worked at the General Motors and Firestone factories that formed the economic heart of the town. South

Gate became a community of blue-collar homeowners. The small houses made them affordable. A lot of people would buy houses, stay for a few years, then move on to larger or nicer places in Downey next door, or in Orange County. But a core of long-timers remained. Amid the widening maw of L.A. suburbia, South Gate was a place where people still managed to know each other.

As it grew, South Gate created the institutions of white suburbia: Rotary and Optimist clubs, a women's club, Protestant churches, Little League, a Chamber of Commerce. An annual Christmas parade began in 1952. A Beautification Committee chose the azalea as the official flower. The committee organized the Azalea Festival each spring, at which the service clubs held dances to raise money for charity.

The *South Gate Press* was part of the McGiffin chain of newspapers that covered the cities southeast of Los Angeles. Twice weekly, in editions of thirty-six and forty-eight pages, the *South Gate Press* ran news about the clubs and the goings-on at city hall.

In the 1960s, television allowed Southern Californians everywhere to hear about South Gate. By then an energetic little city of fifty-five thousand people, South Gate had developed a strip of car lots grandly named the Firestone Boulevard of Cars. Owners of these lots would come on television to interrupt old Western movies or Dodger baseball games and— each salesman seemed to possess a hard Southern drawl—urge viewers to "c'mon on down" for some great deals. They'd sign off with "Firestone Boulevard, South Gate." Perhaps best-known of these was a boisterous old boy named Cal Worthington, who toured his lot in a ten-gallon cowboy hat with "his dog Spot"—which turned out to be a tiger, elephant, seal, or some other large, unfortunate mammal.

South Gate, which is separated from South-Central Los Angeles by the Alameda Street thoroughfare, developed the race discrimination typical of many white suburbs. The town's white parents fought fervently against school integration in the early 1960s. South Gate police were known to question any black person coming through town, and residents blocked the arrival of two department stores for fear they would attract black shoppers. By the 1970s, Latinos were moving into the west side, where the homes were smallest and most run down, so that soon car dealers on Firestone Boulevard were proclaiming "Se habla español" in their hard twangs. But Latinos couldn't buy homes in the better areas of South Gate. It wasn't until 1982 that South Gate elected its first Latino councilman: Henry Gonzalez, a United Auto Workers representative.

But then, 1982 was the year that everything changed in South Gate. GM, Firestone, and three other companies closed plants. The town lost 11,500 jobs in one year. Fleeing economic devastation, whites were now happy to sell to Latinos. Abruptly, South Gate and its neighbors with similarly WASPy names—Maywood, Huntington Park, Bell Gardens, Lynwood—morphed into a beltway of Latino suburbia southeast of Los Angeles. South Gate went from 80 percent Anglo in 1980 to 80 percent Latino in 1990. Moreover, the city grew from sixty-six thousand to eighty-six thousand people in that decade.

By 2000, 92 percent of the population was Latino, a mix of Mexican immigrants who spoke little English and fully assimilated Mexican Americans. About half the city was foreign-born.

The southerners on Firestone Boulevard sold their car lots to Arabs and Koreans, who translated everything to Spanish. If they advertised, their ads were now on Spanish radio. McGiffin newspapers' circulation plunged and the company sold out.

By the early 1990s, South Gate was a town with a Latino population, governed by a white city council, which a dwindling group of white seniors elected. Unlike Latinos, these white seniors voted religiously. They somehow kept alive the institutions of a bygone era: the Christmas Parade, the Azalea Festival, the Chamber of Commerce. Playing soccer was prohibited in South Gate parks, as were piñata parties.

Most Latino residents didn't vote or participate in civic affairs. Some could vote but didn't care to. Many others steadfastly remained Mexican citizens. South Gate wasn't their town; it was their way station. They weren't going to stay in the United States, they told themselves. They were going back to Mexico someday, so why bother getting involved?

Thus while everything was changing in South Gate, much remained the same, and in this awkward stasis the town spent the 1980s and early 1990s.

The jolt came in 1994 with Proposition 187. The proposition would have denied illegal immigrants education and health care, among other things. Californians passed Proposition 187 overwhelmingly, but the courts ruled it unconstitutional. Still, the initiative changed America. Millions of illegal immigrants had become legal residents under an amnesty that the U.S. Congress passed in 1986. By law, they had to wait at least seven years after amnesty to apply for citizenship. Just as those seven years expired, Proposition 187 came along. It terrified immigrants across the United States—even many who'd been legal residents for years. Through the late 1990s, millions of them rushed to become U.S. citizens. This transformed the politics of many states. None was changed more than California. And no place in California was affected more than the now heavily Latino suburbs southeast of Los Angeles, at the heart of which was the town of South Gate.

Labor and civil-rights groups held a prolonged voter-registration drive. South Gate's voter rolls jumped 40 percent in the six years following Prop. 187. The state assembly district that included South Gate was then the only district in California with a Latino majority of registered voters. South Gate, Lynwood, and other cities elected their first Latino council majorities in the late 1990s.

Increasingly, immigrants in South Gate began to feel at home. The number of contestants competing for Miss South Gate increased. So did South Gate Chamber of Commerce membership, particularly after the chamber hired bilingual staff and published a bilingual newsletter. Latino ladies formed the Multicultural Club—which was an adjunct to the white Women's Club of South Gate.

The new citizens and the boom years of the late 1990s blew air into South Gate's collapsed economic lungs. The empty GM plant became an industrial park. The city replaced an oil tank farm with El Paseo, a shopping mall geared to Latino shoppers, with a twenty-screen movie theater. The car lots on Firestone Boulevard got busier.

Home buying picked up. South Gate, in fact, made national news in

1999 because more new homeowners began painting their places. The colors they chose were pinks, purples, greens, and blues. The houses looked fine for Mexico, but clashed with the suburban white-and-beige tastes of the white seniors and Mexican Americans, who insisted the city council do something. This created a brief dustup that the ABC news magazine *20/20* found interesting enough to feature. The city resolved to offer homeowners free paint in more muted tones. The notoriety may not have pleased the Chamber of Commerce. But if people were painting their homes, it meant they were also buying them. That meant they were putting down roots in a town they'd once intended to pass through.

Politically, though, Mexican immigrants were still neophytes, and this was something new for America. Throughout U.S. history, new immigrants from Europe became the base for big-city political machines in Boston, Chicago, New York, and Philadelphia. In Southern California, however, many Mexicans' political assimilation began long after they arrived. By then, they'd found stable jobs and moved out of inner-city Los Angeles to the suburbs.

But while many of them were legal residents and had lived in the country for two or three decades, they hadn't become U.S. citizens. Instead, they dreamed of returning to Mexico. Nor had their U.S. years changed certain Mexican ranchero attitudes, one of which was that all politics are corrupt and better left alone. Often, too, both parents worked, sometimes at two or three jobs; that and raising a family left little free time. So while Mexican immigrants were crucial to Southern California's economy, they'd been absent from its politics.

Only after the Proposition 187 scare did large numbers of them naturalize as U.S. citizens and gain the vote. By then, they'd left Los Angeles for the suburbs and made up overwhelming majorities in suburbs like the towns southeast of Los Angeles.

These towns attracted little attention. The Los Angeles County District Attorney's office rarely investigated small-town political shenanigans. The news media, too, saw these suburbs as the placid communities they had been, instead of places where immigrants were just now learning

American civics. The *South Gate Press* had been sold twice and now had one page of local news. Television and radio never covered the politics of these towns. *La Opinión*, the nation's largest Spanish daily, rarely sent a reporter to the area. The *Los Angeles Times* and the *Long Beach Press-Telegram* devoted only one reporter apiece to all the suburbs southeast of Los Angeles.

Added to that, the population ballooned and with it came an anonymity South Gate hadn't known before. White seniors felt separated by age, culture, and language from their new neighbors. They shuttered themselves at home or played bingo at the senior-citizens club. Mexicans were working hard and busy raising families.

By the end of the 1990s, two thousand votes were still enough to win a local election, despite growing voter registration. Only a couple dozen people ever attended a council meeting. Even those who voted didn't pay much attention to the candidates.

All of which is to say that the rich roots of custom and connection that held the town in place had been severed. A vacuum existed, and in South Gate someone stepped in to exploit it.

His name was Albert Robles and he was a chubby, baby-faced, engaging fellow.

He came to South Gate in 1991 at the age of twenty-six. He'd worked as an aide to a state assemblywoman and had a UCLA political science degree. He was single and single-minded, articulate and talented. People in town remember him at Rotary meetings, as Henry Gonzalez introduced him around, beaming that he finally had a promising young Latino to mentor.

Many people remember Robles saying he was an orphan. Later he said he was a foster child, abused by his father. "He wanted a perfect son," Robles would say of his father, who was a Mexican immigrant. Robles had been shunted through foster homes and lived at times in friends' garages. He had joined the Mormon Church and gone on mission in Mississippi in the mid-1980s. He said he wanted to be governor one day. He could argue election-code minutiae like a Talmudic scholar. After a while, most folks in town simply called him Albert.

"I came to run for office," he said.

He won a seat on the five-member City Council in 1992. A few years later, he won a seat on the regional water district's board of directors, where he met Richard Mayer, who held the Whittier seat. Then he discovered that, legally, he couldn't serve on both the water board and city council. So in 1997, he resigned from the council, ran for city treasurer, and won. In 1998, Albert ran second in the state Democratic primary for treasurer of California. He didn't even campaign, but he was the only candidate with a Latino last name. Political analysts said his showing proved the potential of the newly naturalized immigrant voters.

But it didn't take people long to notice that Albert seemed poorly suited to local politics. Henry Gonzalez, his mentor, was probably the first to see it. Albert would grow enraged when his council colleagues didn't support him.

"He was complaining all the time. The council wouldn't go his way," said Henry. "He'd say, 'Some of my buddies come in for contracts and they won't give them to them.' I said, 'Albert, this ain't about giving contracts to your buddies.' He said, 'Goddamn, I scratch your back, you scratch my back.'"

In 1994, Albert, Henry, and two others made up the first Latino majority on the South Gate City Council. They made Albert mayor; Henry Gonzalez was vice mayor.

In California the job of small-town mayor is an honorary position. It has no power beyond one vote on the council and rotates yearly among council members. In 1995 in South Gate, the job was to go to Henry. But Albert wanted to remain mayor and found two votes on the council to support him. He stayed on, though his relationship with Henry Gonzalez soured.

"I told him, 'You got to start working with your colleagues,'" said Henry. "You need to compromise with people. He says, 'Ahhh, fuck them guys.' All the guys who were contributing big money to him were all of a sudden the guys who were getting contracts with the city: engineers, consultants, lawyers."

Several people in town began to feel uneasy about Albert after he became mayor. He voted to approve a city-funded loan program that lent money to first-time homebuyers. Then, he applied for and received a forty-thousand-dollar loan from the program, with which he bought a house. Albert took a speed-reading class and tried to get the city to pay for it. Henry, who was the auditor on the city council, refused to authorize payment. Albert also had city secretaries write letters to dozens of contacts he'd made at a financial seminar in Wyoming, which he'd attended as a private citizen. Henry put a stop to that.

In 1996, the council voted itself another mayor. Most people agree that it was about this time—in 1996 and 1997—that Albert's political style emerged. As treasurer in 1997, he would make faces and snide remarks at council members during council meetings. The council exiled him to the public seats. He was known to yell profanity across crowded rooms. City workers said he once screamed that he'd like to rip out the ovaries of Julie Butcher, president of their Service Employees International Union (SEIU). SEIU members complained that Albert would not sign their paychecks. They claimed he downloaded personal information about union workers from city-hall computers—hiring a temporary employee when a full-time employee refused to do it.

In time, he became almost the caricature of a villain. He was Richard III, the devious hunchbacked Shakespearean king, an enfant terrible, given to astounding tantrums and plotting. During these years, Albert apparently concluded two things: one, everyone in town politics was against him; two, that he therefore needed a council majority that didn't talk back. His efforts to achieve a rubber-stamp city council would turn South Gate into the tawdry melodrama it became for the next several years.

What puzzled many people about Albert was how he had such thin skin for a man bent on a life in politics. He hated compromise. Attacks and opposition were the nature of politics, yet he reacted virulently to them both.

"He figured everyone was going to be against him," said Martha Hernandez, his girlfriend during some of what followed. "That's what he said, 'No one likes me. Everyone's against me.'"

In his book, *The Powers That Be*, journalist David Halberstam analyzes why Richard Nixon wasn't weeded out of politics early in his career, despite his thin skin. Halberstam holds that in the late 1940s, the then right-wing *Los Angeles Times* and its powerful columnist, Kyle Palmer, coddled Nixon. They promoted his career and attacked his opponents. Shielded from scrutiny, says Halberstam, Nixon got used to soft media treatment and attacking people with impunity; his political skin never toughened. This caused him later to view anyone who opposed him as an enemy to be done away with—an attitude at the root of the Watergate scandal.

A similar analysis fit Albert Robles in South Gate. Instead of soft media coverage, though, Robles and South Gate received no coverage at all. He kept winning elections. He was free to do what he would.

I visited South Gate in late 2000. Albert was then the town's central figure—all politics revolved around him. By now, he basked in the hatred of others. He would genially greet these people in public, knowing they would recoil at his presence. Many folks around South Gate tell of Albert approaching them privately and detailing for them how he was going to do them dirty. Bill De Witt, then a city councilman, said Albert told him that he was old, white, and there was no longer a place for him in South Gate. Sam Echols, a retired factory worker, said Albert told him something similar. Former Police Chief George Troxcil remembers Albert telling him, "Many of the people in town don't speak English, and I can take advantage of them."

"He wanted people to know he was the one pushing the buttons," said Troxcil. "That was an important part of who he was. He didn't want to remain anonymous. Any publicity was good publicity, bad or good. He was very blatant and not bashful."

Several people in South Gate say Albert often privately insulted the town's Mexican immigrants, though he himself was the son of one.

"He told me, 'These people never change,'" said Martha Hernandez.

"'All they care about is going to work, coming home, and that's it. They're lazy Mexicans. They're burros and they'll believe whatever you tell them.'"

Many Latino politicians soon allied against him. At the mention of these enemies, I remember that his body tightened, and invective hissed from him like air from a balloon. State Sen. Martha Escutia was a "pig at the trough," he said. State Sen. Richard Polanco "can fuck himself, if I don't first . . . literally." He called Henry Gonzalez "a rabid dog." Later, amid the firestorm he would create, he was arrested and charged with making terrorist threats, promising to rape Escutia, and take state Assemblyman Marco Antonio Firebaugh to Tijuana in the trunk of a car and "blow his brains out." To a friend, he threatened to have a police lieutenant dragged into the street and shot between the eyes. Albert claimed that's how people talked in politics. A jury eventually deadlocked on those charges.

Albert had arrived in 1991 as a young Latino eager to get involved, someone people wanted to help. But by 2000, folks active in city politics saw him as a Latino Joe McCarthy, a bully unacquainted with scruples.

Running for reelection to the Central Basin Municipal Water District in 2000, Robles used Congresswoman Loretta Sanchez's official photo in a mailer and quoted her as endorsing him.

"That's not something she said or authorized," said a Sanchez's spokeswoman when the mailer appeared.

An anonymous mailer then appeared that had Loretta Sanchez attacking Robles's enemy, state Sen. Martha Escutia. Sanchez wrote a hurried letter denying the mailer, calling it "disgraceful and illegal." No one knew for sure who paid for the mailer, but a lot of people had an idea.

Meanwhile, Albert showed himself willing to fully use the perks of elected office. As treasurer, he hired a staff of four for what had always been a one-person job. He ran for the water-district job promising to abolish the district that "sucked money out of the pockets of people." Yet as board member, he charged the district more than sixteen thousand dollars for classes in acting, finance, flight simulation, and seminars by inspirational speaker Tony Robbins. Robbins held particular fascination for Albert, and he often attended the speaker's seminars, rising to hold a platinum membership in Robbins's business.

People routinely began to describe Albert as "evil," with no hyperbole intended. Later, Mexican immigrants would call him the *cucuy*—the boogeyman. People watched him with the same awe and horror as they might a passing hurricane. They spent hours thinking about him, analyzing his tactics and motives, sputtering at his audacity.

"He's the best villain ever," said Frank Rivera, a leader in South Gate's police union. "He's a short, fat little guy who gets all the money, all the women, all the cars, and he doesn't go away until the end of the movie. And even at the end of the movie there's still a chance for him to come back and grab you. That's Albert Robles. He is the cucuy. You can't even mention his name without fearing that he might have somebody listening. If he were a piñata, I could honestly get people to line up for some stick time on him."

Albert's life attracted bizarre rumors. It was hard to know what was true. Still I took the rumors as at least a sign of how people thought of him and, after a while, of what they were willing to believe. He was said to be a great follower of Sen. Huey Long, the populist from Louisiana. He was said to have photos of John F. Kennedy and Adolf Hitler on his wall. He was obsessed with guns and owned many. People said he ate bread and sweets to excess and that this was one reason his moods swung so wildly and why he never quite won the battle with his paunch. His mother was supposed to have cared for comedian Richard Pryor after Pryor lighted himself on fire smoking cocaine. Robles's father was supposed to have once been a Roman Catholic priest, leaving the priesthood to marry Robles's mother. His father had an affinity for great philosophers. Robles's brother was an ex-convict named Mahatma Gandhi Robles.

What was undeniable was that by 2000, Albert had assembled an impressive array of enemies: city unions and business owners, white seniors, and a good many Latino politicians; and soon, the editorial board of every newspaper in the area. Pastors at South Gate churches usually avoided politics. But Fr. John Provenza, the local Roman Catholic priest, eventually blessed a campaign kickoff of a Robles opponent. He noted in a bulletin to his congregation that three Robles opponents regularly attended mass. Provenza and Lutheran minister Chuck Brady spoke at a rally of Robles's opponents.

"We pray for Albert," said Brady.

Robles, in turn, called himself David confronting the establishment's Goliath. He was a friend of the little guy whom the political elite had ignored. "Competition in these small cities was nonexistent. Now there's competition," he told me. "That's why you see people trying to knock down the Albert Robleses of the world. Albert came to fill a need for leadership within the Latino community."

As I spent time in South Gate, it seemed to me that Albert was an essay in the contravention of small-town political customs. In most small towns, councilmen have lives and full-time jobs outside city hall. In California, they receive only $600 a month in salary to ensure that politics remain community service. Indeed, everyone in South Gate politics had outside jobs and families. Only Albert did not. He lived from income derived from his jobs as city treasurer ($75,000 a year, until a referendum reduced it to $600 a month) and water-district board member ($40,000 a year). Later, when he was running the entire city government, his council created the job of deputy city manager, at $111,000 a year, and hired Albert. Thus he had the time, desire, and eventually the money to devote to politics.

When he ran for his first council seat, he walked precincts tirelessly. But in time, he gave that up. He had been a member of the South Gate Rotary Club but quit, owing the organization money. Neither he nor the candidates he would gather around him belonged to community organizations or attend debates or candidate forums, which once had been the only way to get elected in South Gate.

Instead, his operation became so much more than small-town politics was used to. With no roots in South Gate, Albert used technology to reach voters, knowing that many residents didn't follow city affairs. He installed a thirty-line phone machine in his garage that continuously dialed registered voters at election time with messages urging them to vote for Robles or his allies.

"You have a community that's blue-collar," said his ex-girlfriend

Martha Hernandez. "They get home after a long day. They don't have time to follow what's going on in the city. All of a sudden the phone rings, and it's a short, recorded conversation saying this is Albert Robles, the treasurer, and so on. In less than three minutes, they get the full story. They learn to trust that, because he's going out of his way to communicate."

He had a computer program that sent birthday and Christmas cards to thousands of registered voters he didn't know. He hired immigrant day workers and paid them to leave fliers at homes on weekdays, when most people were at work, saying "Sorry I Missed You," as if a candidate had taken the time to drop by.

Another key to Albert's rise to power was his realization, beginning in about 1999, that Mexican political tactics would work in South Gate.

The Institutional Revolutionary Party (PRI) controlled Mexico for decades by associating elections with gifts and giveaways. Political machines in Chicago or Boston had done this, too, but those machines were local and often didn't last more than a generation. The PRI governed a nation for seventy-one years, training Mexicans to expect gifts at election time. A PRI hallmark was to send its candidates into a village or working-class neighborhood at election time to hand out bags of rice, T-shirts, caps, or sandwiches. South Gate's demographics resembled those Mexican villages and working-class neighborhoods. So in 1999, Albert went to the PRI playbook.

He had already managed to elect one ally to the city council: Raul Moriel, a local landlord. In 1999, looking for another, he supported Richard Mayer and Xochilt Ruvalcaba, a city-hall switchboard operator. The Robles slate gave away potted plants with their names emblazoned on the planter. That was the first example people give of Albert's use of PRI techniques.

During the campaign, Albert barged into Henry Gonzalez's office and took a photo of him while Henry was on the phone. That photo later turned up on the anonymous mailer, issued by a phony committee, accusing Gonzalez of becoming a millionaire at city expense.

The mailer accusing Joe Ruiz of child molestation came out during this campaign, as did the mailer accusing Joe Gonzalez of drunken driving.

So, too, did a mailer showing a doctored photo of Ruiz with a thick convict-style Fu Manchu mustache. The mailer questioned whether he hid a criminal past.

Remarkably, all this worked. Ruiz lost. Voters elected Ruvalcaba. With Raul Moriel and Xochilt Ruvalcaba on the council, Albert now needed only one vote to get his majority.

Over the next six months, he turned his attention to getting rid of South Gate's last white councilman. Bill De Witt owned a company that made doors for office buildings, factories, and airplanes. While most manufacturers left town, De Witt kept his company, and its union jobs, in South Gate. But you had to pay attention to local politics to know this. If you didn't, then the only obvious facts about Bill De Witt were that he was a white, Republican, business owner. This made him an easy mark in Latino, Democratic, working-class South Gate.

Albert qualified a petition to recall De Witt. A special election was scheduled for November 2000. During the campaign, anonymous mailers tied De Witt to a power plant proposed for the east side of town, though De Witt had never supported the idea. Other mailers harped on De Witt's race and business affiliations. They claimed that De Witt wanted to make English the state's official language, even though De Witt had pushed to have Spanish interpreters at South Gate city council meetings. "Bill De Witt doesn't want us to speak Spanish," blared one mailer, over a photo of a Latina with a white man's hand over her mouth and a baby in her arms.

Regional Latino politicians and local unions supported De Witt, but few others came to his aid. The city's police union had a policy of noninvolvement in elections. Media coverage of the campaign was scant. So for the special election in November 2000, mailers again made up most of the information available to voters.

The Robles slate sent out fliers inviting voters to a Seven-Eleven convenience store for free hot dogs and sodas on election day. The store was mobbed. De Witt was recalled. A beautician named Maria Benavides was elected to finish his term. Albert now had his three-vote council majority.

My introduction to Albert came a month later, as he was taking his Mexicanization of town politics to another level. It was just before

Christmas, and the March 2001 regular election loomed. So the Robles forces held a toy giveaway.

The giveaway was held in the parking lot of the Lido nightclub. Three thousand people eventually showed up for an awesome disgorging of free stuff. Hot dogs. Tacos. Polaroids with Santa Claus. Carnival rides. Balloons and clowns. Hundreds of expensive toys—dartboards, Baby Touch and Teach dolls, remote-control operated cars—came in by the truckload. All free. Amid the throngs was the Robles council slate of Xochilt Ruvalcaba, Raul Moriel, and Maria Benavides, shaking hands with parents and kids.

"Most toy giveaways give toys that are kind of cheap," said Albert, when we met on the Lido's parking lot. "When I was a kid, these were the kinds of toys I wanted."

By then, I'd spent seven years in Mexico as a reporter covering the country's politics. I was well acquainted with PRI election-time techniques and intrigued, therefore, to see them on display in suburban Los Angeles.

St. Helen's Catholic Church's youth group was listed as a sponsor of the giveaway. Fr. John Provenza, the priest of St. Helen's, said later that he'd assumed the event was nonpolitical. He was incensed that the church's name was associated with the giveaway, which was held in the Lido's parking lot across from South Gate's only strip club.

"This is not about votes," Robles said that day, as children and parents streamed by. "It's about doing good. How many of those people who were out there are registered voters? Maybe two out of ten. I really believe that if you do good, come hell or high water, you'll be compensated. It's that Protestant work ethic. If you do good, your good works will show through."

I wondered where the money for all this came from. A local businessman, he said. I asked him why the candidates were here pressing flesh, if doing good was the motive? Didn't it seem similar to what the PRI did in Mexico?

"The PRI were dictators. We're not," he said. "Given the opportunity, I would be a benevolent dictator. I wouldn't have to put up with a lot of BS, and I could get things done. But we're far from that."

As I watched him, it seemed to me that, just as the PRI knew Mexicans, Robles understood these immigrants. They may have blamed the PRI for having to leave Mexico, but they still responded to PRI political tactics. So while Albert's list of his enemies was long, he seemed supported by a sizable chunk of the town's new, Mexican-immigrant voters.

All that Albert had been building was at stake as March 2001 approached. The town was to hold its regularly scheduled election—the third election in twenty-four months. Maria Benavides had to run again because Bill De Witt's seat, which she'd won, was set to expire. Albert's ally, Raul Moriel, was up for reelection. Albert needed these two votes to secure his council majority.

The South Gate election in March of 2001 is today legend. It resembled more a pro-wrestling battle royale than any exercise in grassroots civic life. Even political veterans were awed at the load of lies and deception dumped on South Gate that year. The campaign seemed a supermarket tabloid come to life. Anonymous mailers asked South Gate voters to believe that running for office were boozers, deadbeat dads, PRI members, psychopaths, assassins, and Lexus owners.

One mailer falsely accused Carmen Avalos, running for city clerk, of drunken driving: "Carmen 'The Drunk' Avalos" it called her.

"We just CAN'T TRUST nor VOTE for the BOOZER Carmen Avalos," the mailer admonished voters.

It included a police drunken-driving citation that looked real but was fake. Avalos is a teetotaler, a high-school biology teacher, and single mother of two. The mailer reduced her to tears on election night. She won, but a few days later awoke to find a large teddy bear in her yard, its throat slit and body mutilated.

In 2001, Joe Ruiz ran for city treasurer against Albert. The phony child-molester charge had dogged him for two years by now. Ruiz still encountered people who wondered if he were a molester. This time around, another flier attacking Ruiz arrived in the mail. It asked the warped question: "Can You

Trust a Man who has been accused of child molestation, even though this has been found not to be True?"

Among the candidates for city treasurer was a fellow named Roberto Rivera. Rivera sent out three glossy mailers with a photo identifying himself as a middle-aged, white businessman. Rivera, in fact, was a twenty-two-year-old unemployed Latino man with a shaved head, known as Fuzzy. His mailers also claimed he had a master's degree in business administration from the University of Southern California. In fact, Fuzzy Rivera hadn't been to college. USC denied knowing him. I called Fuzzy Rivera's house several times to ask about the photos and USC and where he got the money for such expensive mailers if he was unemployed. He never got back to me. A theory gained currency that Albert had put up Fuzzy as a candidate to siphon white senior votes away from Joe Ruiz.

Councilman Hector De La Torre was a Robles foe now running for reelection. One mailer arrived proclaiming that De la Torre had fathered a "love child" named Irma with a "teenage Mexican girl named Guadalupe, whom Hector later left for a Norwegian bombshell named Tina." The mailer went on to claim that De la Torre was a Lexus owner, a member of the PRI in Mexico, and that he was a godson of the disgraced former president of Mexico, Carlos Salinas de Gortari. Needless to say, none of that was true.

Charges like these seemed too preposterous to believe. Still, said Henry Gonzalez, "if you're an immigrant and you leave a corrupted country and then you get this kind of propaganda, you say, 'I just left that. I'm not going to vote for this guy.' They basically believe it because they say, 'If it wasn't in print or didn't come through the mail, it wouldn't be true.'"

Hector De la Torre, meanwhile, found himself running against his doppelgänger. Another man named Hector De la Torre suddenly entered the race. This Hector De La Torre was an unknown in local politics. He worked at an L.A. printing shop. He told reporters that he'd dreamed of running for office, and 2001 was the year he'd decided to make this dream a reality.

Somehow, this Hector De la Torres was allowed to identify himself on the ballot that year as a "counselor." After the election, it was discovered

A flier attacking South Gate City Councilman Hector De la Torre for having an illegitimate child he doesn't support, belonging to the PRI, and being the godson of former Mexican president, Carlos Salinas de Gortari—all lies, of course.

that this second Hector De la Torre didn't live in South Gate anymore. He also told reporters that he'd never actually been a "counselor," though he allowed that sometimes his friends and family would seek his counsel.

Nevertheless, the first name that voters saw on the March ballot was of a man who didn't live in South Gate, and who was falsely identified as a "counselor." Below him was a man of the same name who was described, correctly, as a "city councilman." It was all pretty confusing, which was the whole point.

And so it went.

One mailer attacked Bill De Witt, who had decided to run again for council, despite his recall the previous November. The mailer accused him of not supporting a "love child"—a blond girl named Nancy, pictured in the ad, that he'd fathered with a woman who now lived on welfare in

Nevada. All lies. The mailer went on to call him "Bill De Wittless" and say he was so stingy "that he cut his own hair (When you see him, examine his bad, self-inflicted hair style)."

"That's the only part of it that's true," said De Witt. "I do cut my own hair."

No city in the area came close to South Gate in the sheer volume of mailers generated, or in the comic perversity of the lies leveled against candidates running for offices that paid a mere six hundred dollars a month.

No one knew for sure who sent these mailers, but many folks in town had an opinion. "The only people who would benefit from this," said Joe Ruiz, "would be Albert Robles or friends of Albert Robles."

The west side of town had the greatest concentration of new Mexican-immigrant voters. It was here that Albert found his most fertile base and here the mailers descended with greatest ferocity.

He issued a mailer with a photo of himself shaking hands with Mexican Pres. Vicente Fox at a meeting with immigrants in Los Angeles, implying Fox endorsed him. In similar fashion, Robles's ally Raul Moriel issued a mailer with photos of him together with rock guitarist Carlos Santana and actor Edward James Olmos, implying they supported him. The flier claimed Moriel was in favor of "entertainment."

Understanding that most of the new voters in South Gate watched television more than they read newspapers, Albert somehow arranged to appear on *Cristina*, the hugely popular Spanish-language afternoon talk show, to tell the story of his life: from foster child to rising young politician.

In Mexico, anti-PRI activists often resorted to public hunger strikes. The Robles crew tried this, too. They staged a hunger strike in a tent outside city hall, ostensibly to protest that power plant, which was by then a dead issue. It all looked quite noble, though people said they saw Raul Moriel eating at a restaurant in a nearby town while he was supposed to be fasting like Gandhi in that tent.

Albert's opponents went down in the dirt, too. One anonymous mailer showed photos of Albert, each stamped with a different label: "Assassin," "Psychopath," "Gangbanger," "Sexual Pervert," "Lexus Owner."

Albert Robles poses with Vicente Fox and uses the photo on his campaign flier suggesting they form an Alliance for Progress.

Perhaps the campaign's most collectible mailer hammered Robles and Moriel for holding a Christmas toy giveaway for children in the parking lot of a nightclub and near a strip club. "They take your children . . ." read the cover of the mailer, over a photo of a boy sucking his thumb. Inside it shrieked: "and carve out their hearts for play."

No one could say where the money came from for the rancid mailers and the thousands of campaign signs that papered South Gate. Few candidates on either side of South Gate politics filed the legally required campaign-finance forms. Yet again, neither the *South Gate Press*, nor the regional media covered much of this. Would South Gate residents have paid any attention? The city's police union again sat out the election. The city workers who were members of SEIU split on how far to stick their necks out, fearing retribution from Albert if he won a majority. Candidate forums were poorly attended. In the end, mailers and campaign signs were again about the only information voters had.

It would be nice to say that people saw through the lies. But in March 2001, many folks voted for a name they'd heard of or against someone they believed to be a molester, boozer, or godson of Carlos Salinas de Gortari. Many new voters felt justified in the feeling they'd brought from Mexico that all politicians were the same and didn't go to the polls.

Raul Moriel won, as expected. So did Albert, as treasurer. But most astonishing was the election of Maria Benavides to a full term as city councilwoman. Since she'd taken Bill De Witt's seat in November, it had become clear to anyone who paid attention that Maria del Refugio Benavides was utterly unsuited for public office.

First, Benavides had grown up in South Gate, but no longer lived in the city. In fact, she'd sworn in two government documents that she lived in the town of El Monte, ten miles away. Neighbors of a house in El Monte assured reporters that she lived at that house.

Nevertheless, in filing to run for office, she had listed a South Gate apartment complex as her address. Apartment residents told visitors that she didn't live there. "How people do ask about her," said a woman who lived in the South Gate apartment Benavides claimed to occupy. Benavides was registered to vote at that address, but then so had Robles's brother, Mahatma Gandhi Robles, and there was no evidence he lived there, either. Within two days of reporters inquiring about Benavides at the address, a white mailbox on a post was installed in fresh concrete by the side of the house with "Benavides" emblazoned on it in black letters for all to see.

Curiously, too, Benavides seemed incapable of speaking in public. She hadn't campaigned nor attended civic events. By March 2001, Maria Benavides had been in office for five months, yet had never spoken during a council meeting. She never explained her votes. She didn't ask questions of city staff. She never answered the public's questions during council meetings. She sat mute through it all. City employees were forbidden contact with her by Councilwoman Xochilt Ruvalcaba, who turned out to be her cousin. When members of the public phoned city hall to talk to her, secretaries were instructed to pass the messages to Ruvalcaba, who said Benavides preferred not to speak.

The campaign mailers issued in the name of Maria Benavides showed the kind of deception the Robles crew had mastered. One, for instance, had Maria smiling with her daughters and husband, Miguel—a glowing family portrait—though Miguel had deserted the family and Maria had filed for divorce months before. In another mailer, a photo of a stiff Maria was superimposed over a photograph of gang members and insisted Maria cared about combating gangs and graffiti.

That same mailer also showed a closely cropped photo of a construction worker identified as Oscar Carrillo. He had a mustache, a yellow safety vest, and a hard hat. He was quoted as saying that Maria Benavides wanted to create jobs. But it turned out that the same photo had been used two years before in a mailer for Xochilt Ruvalcaba. Only that time the photo was reversed, the man was identified as Michael Estevez, and the picture had been doctored to where he sported a goatee and an orange safety vest. The mystery was resolved when a third mailer was procured, this one supporting Richard Mayer's candidacy for city council. It showed a photo of Mayer with several construction workers. One of these was the man Ruvalcaba had called Michael Estevez and Benavides had called Oscar Carrillo. No one ever knew who the man was or if he ever knew he'd been used in mailers for three South Gate candidates, all of whom touted their own honesty and integrity.

Yet voters elected Maria Benavides as their councilwoman in March 2001. She added the crucial third vote, with those of Moriel and Ruvalcaba, that gave Albert Robles his council majority. The Robles crew did best on the city's west side, where most newly registered Mexican immigrants lived. The four of them were now free to do as they pleased.

The town emerged from the March 2001 elections having learned some malignant civics lessons: libelous mailers could be sent with impunity; people could register to vote twice; those who didn't live in town could run for council; giveaways worked; and it didn't matter what you did while campaigning or in office because neither the media nor law enforcement had the resources to pay attention.

When the March election was over, I wrote a story about South Gate for the *Los Angeles Times Sunday Magazine*. It detailed the mailers, the giveaways, Maria Benavides's residency, while profiling Albert Robles and the withering of political discourse in town since his rise to power. They headlined it, "The Savage Politics of South Gate."

One day not long after the election, I sat down with Hector De la Torre—the city councilman—at a Mexican restaurant in town called Casa Jimenez.

De la Torre was born in Los Angeles, of parents from the Mexican state of Jalisco, and attended high school in South Gate. He studied international relations at Occidental College. He'd taught for two years at a local junior high. He had a master's degree from George Washington University and had worked for the U.S. Labor Department. Now De la Torre worked for the region's electrical company. He'd been a South Gate city councilman since 1997. He was tall, thin, and articulate, a young Latino politician on the rise.

He had just beaten back the challenge from the other Hector De la Torre, whose lifelong interest in running for office apparently did not extend to actually campaigning, walking precincts, debating, or putting out material explaining his positions on anything.

Over the next two years, De la Torre and Henry Gonzalez would oppose the Robles majority again and again.

Our conversation at the restaurant that day had a lot to do with Albert Robles. Like many folks in town, De la Torre suspected Albert was behind the scurrilous mailers.

"He's accused somebody of being a child molester. He's accused somebody of having two DUIs who didn't," De la Torre said. "The bigger the lie, the more attention you're going to get. We have a working-class community that has a whole lot on their plates. It's hard to get through to those people who are very, very busy and get them to understand what's going on in the city. When they're told so-and-so's a crook, or a racist, the burden of proof is on that person to defend himself. How do you defend yourself from that? How do you say I'm not a child molester? Why should you have to defend yourself from something like that?"

De la Torre felt these were symptoms of South Gate's weak social girdings. Economic and demographic change, like a hurricane, had razed the traditions and institutions that maintained community life. These had not had time to grow back. White seniors, Mexican Americans, and Mexican immigrants now lived together without knowing much about each other.

A lot of Mexican immigrants had become citizens after Proposition 187. But they didn't yet understand how city hall affected them. Too many people remained wedded to political apathy acquired in Mexico. Local politics was well down their list of priorities, De la Torre said.

"Latinos moved in as residents not as community members. The institutions that Anglos had created, most of them have faltered or have died," he said. He wondered what Latinos would create in place of the Kiwanis Club, the Women's Club, and the Optimists that would make South Gate a community. He also wondered when they'd do it.

What especially bothered De la Torre was the image South Gate was sending to the rest of Southern California. "(Latinos) are ready to lead everybody," he said. "But if we take that next step, it's not going to be on raw numbers, because we're not going to have the raw numbers to make it happen. So we need to build coalitions. We need to be addressing issues that are broad and not just ethnic issues.

"But some Latino politicians, certainly at the local level where you can get away with it, are playing the race card. They're appealing solely to ethnic issues, like you see in these mailers. That creates distrust and that sets us back in the broader goal, which is to be accepted in the mainstream like the Irish, the Germans, the Jews were elsewhere.

"We cannot be seen as not being fair, that we're incapable of doing the job, that we have recalls and fights and nasty hit pieces. We need to have some model cities being run by Latinos and I don't see enough of them."

For the next two years, anyone hoping for signs of Latino political maturity watched South Gate in horror. Buttressed by his unquestioning council majority, Albert's tantrums now took the form of public policy, aimed at bankrupting South Gate as fast as possible. The words of Richard III—

"If I cannot prove a lover . . . I am determined to prove a villain"—seemed his motto.

The new council majority had come to office claiming their opponents enriched themselves at city expense. Those were lies, playing on Mexican immigrants' suspicions that all politicians take the public's money. Having used the votes of those immigrants to gain power, however, the new council majority set about doing that very thing.

First, it engineered itself a 500-percent raise. To get around the $600 monthly limit on small city-council salaries, the Robles crew created something called the Community Development Corporation. They made themselves its directors and voted themselves a monthly salary of $1,600 to run it. They formed a Financial Authority and a Finance Committee and made themselves the members of each, paying themselves $150 every time they met, which was for five minutes before each council meeting. They gave themselves a communications allowance of $150 a month, though the city already paid for their cellular phones. They tripled their travel budget and gave themselves new laptop computers. Positions that had paid $7,200 a year, now paid $36,000 annually.

They defunded the South Gate Chamber of Commerce, where Joe Ruiz was now president. The city usually gave the chamber $30,000 a year, which the chamber leveraged with volunteers and donations, to produce the Miss South Gate Beauty Pageant and the Christmas parade. The Robles allies now took over these events. But with few connections to the community, they found no volunteers or donations and had to pay for everything. The pageant and parade in 2001 wound up costing the city $235,000.

The Robles council began firing city department heads and replacing them with notably unqualified people. These replacements received contracts unheard of in California city government. For example, South Gate agreed to pay eighteen months of each manager's salary if he were fired, twelve months of his salary were he to quit. To expedite matters, the council did away with written civil service exams. People were hired based entirely on oral interviews.

Jesse Marez, a young man who'd worked for the nearby city of La Puente for only a few months, was hired as city manager at a salary of

$137,000 a year. The council hired Lou Moret, a boxing referee and po-
litical operative, as a consultant for $12,000 a month. One of Moret's
jobs was to create an entirely new department: the Community Services
Department. This department came on line with a hundred employees at
a cost of $3.2 million. Many of these new employees were just out of high
school and were paid $14 an hour to do nothing anyone could figure out.
Maria Benavides's brother was made a manager in the new department at
a salary of $53,000 a year.

The council went on a lawyer-hiring binge. City Attorney Salvador
Alva received $1.5 million over eighteen months, plus his monthly salary.
This made Alva the state's highest paid city attorney. The council hired at-
torney Clifford Albright, as well, to write legal interpretations for Albert.
His firm would receive $3.8 million in fees from the city of South Gate in
less than two years.

The council forced out Parks Director Paula Grimes, a thirty-three-
year city employee, and in her place hired a paralegal from Albright's
firm with no experience, at a salary of $100,000 a year. Another Albright
"paralegal," Cristeta Klaparda, was hired as the city's litigation specialist
at $200 an hour. Later, it came out that she had been a lawyer, but had
been disbarred after a conviction for embezzlement and forgery in 1997.

Other law firms were hired for obscure reasons. A bewildering string
of lawyers began to move through South Gate. At some council meetings, there'd be three, four, or five attorneys, each billing the city $350 an
hour. Normally, the city's legal bill was about $500,000 a year. The new
council majority paid twenty-eight law firms $10.6 million in legal fees in
eighteen months.

On it went.

"With their bloc of three votes, they can give away the bank and have
been doing so routinely," Hector De la Torre told reporters.

In the spring of 2002, Albert was arrested and charged with threatening to kill state legislators Martha Escutia and Marco Antonio Firebaugh. His
city council majority responded by creating the job of deputy city manager and hiring him for it, at $111,000 a year, though he'd never managed
a city before. His contract gave him a $180,000 severance package, even

if he were convicted of making the threats. The council hired Sheppard Mullin and Richter, a downtown L.A. firm, to defend Albert and paid his legal bills of nearly $1 million.

The council also erased the rule that prohibited the city from paying for hotel bills for employee junkets within a fifty-mile radius of South Gate. This allowed Albert to require all city bureaucrats to attend a Tony Robbins seminar in Orange County at city expense, where they, along with hundreds of others, were asked to walk across hot coals in the parking lot of a hotel—part of the Robbins regime.

The city council sold an eleven-acre property for $1.9 million to a man named George Garrido. Garrido had been Albert's business partner. His nursery had provided the potted plants that Albert and his allies had given away to voters a few years before. The council was about to quietly sell Garrido the property for $200,000. Word of the sale leaked. Others in the community quickly offered five times that. Garrido countered with an offer of $1.9 million. Problem was, Garrido had only $400,000 in hand. So the Robles majority gave Garrido $4 million in city grants and loans to buy the property from the city.

All in all, it amounted to a two-year fleecing of city government that was awesome in scope and audacity.

For decades, issues in South Gate had rarely been controversial enough to fill the city council chambers. But as the fleecing became more obvious, public outrage grew. People would ask their neighbors: Did you hear what they're doing down at city hall? Curious, the neighbors would attend and discover that it was, in fact, even worse than they'd been told. They'd tell their friends and family.

By mid-2002, each meeting was a standing-room-only war. The council majority allowed people to speak for three minutes. When speakers ran over time, Xochilt Ruvalcaba, mayor that year, would pound her gavel.

The Robles council majority further enraged citizens by not answering questions or explaining its votes. Maria Benavides became the symbol of the council's unwillingness to explain itself as it hired lawyers and people with no government experience. People would try to get her to say something, anything. They would direct questions to her. Ruvalcaba, her cousin, would answer for her. Benavides never said a word. Furious, people took to saying "Meow" every time Benavides voted "yes" or "no" because her voice resembled a feline purr. When ordered to be silent on the threat of expulsion, they took to waving signs saying "Meow" each time she spoke. Remarkably, in her tenure on the council, Maria Benavides would never say more than four words from the dais: "present," "yes," "no," and "second."

Amid all this bedlam, though, a few important changes were taking place outside South Gate. First, a new district attorney, Steve Cooley, formed a public integrity task force to investigate corruption in small cities. One place the task force went was South Gate.

California Sec. of State Bill Jones announced his office would be overseeing South Gate elections, the way elections in the Third World are often observed.

"The voters of South Gate confront some of the most serious allegations of official misconduct and voter intimidation that I have ever seen," Jones told the *Los Angeles Times*. When the city council refused to cede control of the elections, the state legislature got involved. It voted to put the county registrar of voters in charge of South Gate elections.

Regional newspapers began covering South Gate. The *Long Beach Press-Telegram*, in fact, stopped pretending there were two sides to what was going on and simply editorialized on South Gate, usually under the headline "Throw the Bums Out."

"We do not have the space to list every bizarre, maddening or wasteful example of the council majority's Tammany Hall approach to politics; rest assured it is long," the *Press-Telegram* wrote in one editorial.

Meanwhile, *Los Angeles Times* reporter Richard Marosi was assigned to cover seven of the cities southeast of Los Angeles. Faced with this massive beat, Marosi picked his spots. He began dedicating virtually all his time to story after story on South Gate.

This was a turning point. "In our democratic system, it's the newspaper that's the thing," said Bill De Witt. "Go back to the Federalist papers, Benjamin Franklin and those guys. We'd still be an English crown colony if it hadn't been for the guys in the newspaper industry spreading the word."

South Gate's profile rose. Out of that came the most important change: Mexican immigrants awoke and began getting involved in city affairs. They were new U.S. citizens. Many of them had cast their first votes for Albert and Raul Moriel, Benavides and Xochilt Ruvalcaba. As time went on, more immigrants attended council meetings. What they saw made them apoplectic, realizing they'd voted these people into office. By 2002, immigrants made up half of those in attendance. They would stand at the podium for their three minutes and in halting but furious English, they'd say that they'd left this kind of thing in Mexico and weren't about to tolerate it here in the United States.

As the council wantonly spent taxpayer money, it faced a raging crowd each Monday night. Years had passed since a member of the public had been thrown out of a South Gate City Council meeting. But as citizens stormed the ramparts, Mayor Xochilt Ruvalcaba began ejecting two, three, four people a night. Eventually she ordered the ejectees to leave not only council chambers, but city hall entirely. Sam Echols was thrown out twelve times.

Never had more than one police officer been needed at the council. Now there were six.

Joe Ruiz, meanwhile, was circulating a petition to recall Robles and his allies. Ruiz turned over the petition, signed by eight thousand residents, to City Attorney Salvador Alva. The petition disappeared. Undaunted, Ruíz circulated another petition, got another eight thousand signatures, made a copy, and again delivered them to the city council. A few nights after that, someone firebombed Ruiz's plumbing business with five Molotov cocktails, destroying three trucks; police found five more unused gasoline cocktails in a bucket near the business. No one has ever been charged in that crime, nor in the drive-by shooting of Ruiz's house one night not long after that.

Given South Gate's demographics, the fleecing of the town might have continued for years. The beginning of the end came over what seemed a small matter. That matter was this: Albert Robles had his heart set on becoming a reserve police officer. It seemed a sweet, plaintive yearning that may have grown, who knows, from blows and abuse suffered as a boy years before. Other people said Albert wanted to avoid paying speeding tickets.

Whatever the case, once he had a council majority, Albert pushed new Police Chief Doug Christ to send him to a police academy at city expense. Christ acceded and promptly retired. Albert, still chubby, flunked the physical exam and never attended the academy. But the idea of Albert with a gun and badge nonetheless alarmed the police. Furthermore, if he became a police reserve, by law he could also be made chief.

Albert met with police union leaders. "He actually comes to you and tells you his intent," said Frank Rivera, the police union leader. "He said, 'I'm going to be city manager and I want criminal immunity.' He said that to me personally. He said, 'If you're smart, you'll get in line with me and you'll get whatever you want for your guys. If not, I will bankrupt the city.' Well, we didn't want to play."

Albert denied saying this, though it rings true. Whatever the case, the battle for South Gate now entered its final stage.

To punish the police, the council hired Rick Lopez, chief of the nearby town of Maywood. Lopez was awarded a five-year deal, under which he couldn't be fired unless convicted of a crime. Nor could Lopez be fired within six months of an election. And were he ever fired, his contract read, the city would have to pay him eighteen months of salary; twelve months if he decided to quit.

Chief Lopez took the extraordinary step of disbanding the department's gang and narcotics divisions. The department's tan and green uniforms, which officers had worn since 1923, were scrapped and blue uniforms were bought, costing one hundred thousand dollars. In defiance, officers wore their tan-and-green emblem on their bulletproof vests beneath their new blues.

The department had existed for years with a chief and three captains. The council also hired an additional four assistant chiefs—giving tiny South Gate a command structure similar to that of the massive Los Angeles Police Department.

The council paid a firm $150,000 for a telephone survey of police conduct. The firm set up on the Garrido property, and for several months its employees called South Gate residents—some people as many as ten times—asking if police had ever been abusive, rude, or had made them feel unwelcome in the country. The survey came up with only two people alleging police misconduct.

Then someone high in city government began giving away South Gate police badges to friends and allies. These were real police badges—two dozen of them—given to secretaries, tow-truck operators, and lawyers, like Clifford Albright, who used his badge to plead for leniency when a Whittier police officer stopped him for speeding one day.

Amid all this, Police Officers Standards and Training—the state board that certifies police agencies—wrote to say that South Gate's department risked being decertified. POST hadn't decertified a department before, and doing so would have left the department ineligible for state and federal grants.

Finally, Albert moved to do away with the seventy-nine-year-old department entirely and hire the L.A. County Sheriff's Department to provide police services. South Gate came very close to losing the police force it had had since 1923. Sheriff's deputies began an equipment inventory, preparing to replace the cops.

As this was going on, Joe Ruiz's proposed recall of Robles and his majority was moving forward. The council spent $2 million on lawyers to fight the recall up through the courts, losing every step of the way. They succeeded only in postponing the recall election. But eventually a date for the recall election was set. And for the first time, South Gate's police union decided to get involved in a local election. It threw its support behind the recall of Robles and his crew.

Albert apparently believed that a town with so many Mexican immigrants would not support its police. Perhaps he was pumped with the hubris of one whose opponents seemed powerless before him. Whatever the case, it was his great miscalculation. In the 1950s, Sen. Joe McCarthy's undoing began with his attack on the U.S. Army. Albert's came when he took on the South Gate Police Department. In 2003, South Gate's

Mexican community rose to stand by its cops. The reason for that had to do with the department's recent history.

In April 1992, Los Angeles and its surrounding cities burned. A Simi Valley jury had returned not-guilty verdicts of four Los Angeles police officers charged in the beating of motorist Rodney King, which had been videotaped and shown the world over. Black and Latino neighborhoods erupted at the verdict. Motorists were beaten at stoplights. Television cameras in helicopters captured youths looting stores. Pockets of South Central Los Angeles, as well as nearby Lynwood, Maywood, Huntington Park, and Compton, exploded in flames. Clouds of smoke ushered from the L.A. basin.

Through it all, South Gate was untouched. Police effectively walled off the city, using officers and railroad cars at train crossings. During the L.A. riots, kids in South Gate played at the park as the air filled with smoke from the horseshoe of towns burning around them. South Gate emerged from the ordeal to find only one business looted, with five thousand dollars in damages. That began a change in residents' view of their police.

Before the riot, LAPD had always kept officers separate from the community. Cops stayed in their cars. Contact with citizens might breed corruption. Police solved crimes, and it was best if citizens just stayed out of their way. Suburban departments, like South Gate's, had similar attitudes.

But the riots showed that that separation had become a dangerous chasm. Many communities were made up of blacks or Latinos who viewed officers as invading soldiers.

"Even the children were afraid of the police," said Araceli Dominguez, a South Gate resident. "I would never say the police are bad. But their demeanor didn't make anyone warm up to them."

After the riots, a new concept—community-oriented policing—gained popularity in Southern California. Community-oriented policing was intended to forge the bonds between residents and police departments that would have existed had officers spent more time out of their cars.

One town that adopted it was South Gate. Building on the goodwill established by the department's defense of the city during the riots, then-Chief George Troxcil formed a group called Community In Action in 1997. Community In Action attempted to bring the police and neighbors together to address crime problems.

At first, "no one wanted to hear about it because . . . people were always afraid of getting together with the police," said Señorina Rendón, a Mexican immigrant and a CIA founder.

Police officers, too, were used to keeping the community at a distance. Moreover, when cops got to know residents, they learned that residents weren't concerned about crime as much as about abandoned sofas and broken streetlights.

"We're trained to protect people from burglars, robbers, and rapists," said Robert Todd, then a captain in the department. "But when you get into the community, the first thing you hear from them is, 'I've got this graffiti painted on my wall, and this ice cream truck was speeding down my street.'"

Officers soon found they had to rethink their jobs. Policing, it now appeared, also involved introducing residents to other city departments: public works, streets, parks. Community In Action became about neighborhood cleanups. The city provided the dumpsters. Cops and residents spent Saturdays ridding alleys of junk, painting over the graffiti, and fixing torn chain-link fences. At CIA's urging, police opened a substation on the west side of town. The substation held after-school tutoring and recreation, as well.

Neither officers nor the community was used to this new relationship. "In what town in Mexico have you seen any kind of relationship between the police and the community?" said Araceli Dominguez, another CIA founder. "It doesn't happen very often in the United States, either."

But it worked. After a while, things got so cozy that police commanders gave out their telephone and pager numbers to CIA leaders. Soon, it was normal for a captain or lieutenant to get a call on his day off or late at night from a resident asking the police to do something about a downed tree branch or a dumped mattress. He would call the appropriate city department.

"We were trying to create an environment where folks would take responsibility for their own neighborhoods and bring us their needs," said Troxcil. "There was a downturn in crime. The city took on a different appearance. It was looking much better all the time. I think services for the community improved. Support for law enforcement grew tenfold."

Slowly, the residents of South Gate, and particularly those newly naturalized Mexican immigrants, got to know the police and the city workers who fixed potholes, too. Immigrants began to see human beings where they'd once seen only uniforms and impregnable bureaucracy. Community In Action was many Mexican immigrants' introduction into American civic life.

Community In Action started marching a lot. Neighbors and officers, business owners and politicians marched together down thoroughfares and along quiet streets, urging others to join the group. Within a year the marches ballooned from a few dozen people to four and five hundred people. More and more of the marchers were Mexican immigrants.

One of them was Waldo Perez. Perez had come to the United States from the village of Tumbiscatío, in the state of Michoacán, in 1974. He had lived in South Gate since 1985, yet had never entered city hall. He became an American citizen, but steered clear of the police. He went from home to work to home and thus passed his years in America.

But on a whim, as a CIA march passed his house, Perez joined up. To Perez, Community In Action was a revelation, a new way of understanding his adopted country. In time, he became a CIA leader. He organized neighborhood cleanups and took ride-alongs with police officers; he got to know city workers.

"The most important thing was that they taught us how the police department works, and how city hall works. We didn't know," said Perez, sitting one afternoon in the living room of his home. "It opened our eyes, showed us who to go to. We got to know the police department from the chief down. We know the officers. They know me. I know most of the folks in public works. Our police department is the best around.

Our department came together with us, and we did so with them."

A key moment in all this came on October 30, 1997. Deputy Sheriff Michael Hoenig was shot and killed in South Gate by a man on a bike. Police eventually caught the killer. Still, Community In Action rose up in outrage at Hoenig's killing. For eight days, the group kept a shrine and prayer vigil at the spot where the deputy died. It marched through neighborhoods. On the last night, in wind and rain, Community In Action members held a candlelight march, huddling around their candles.

"That was a turning point for us," said South Gate police Capt. Andy Key. "That's when I knew the community here was with us. Community members were praying and crying over a police officer, and he wasn't even one of ours."

Community In Action created a core of neighborhood activists, like Waldo Perez, Señorina Rendón, and Araceli Dominguez. They learned organizing and the workings of city hall. With friends now among city workers and cops, the folks of Community in Action naturally paid more attention to goings-on at city hall. So while CIA wasn't formed to do politics, it lent itself to that.

Something similar took place with a group called Padres Unidos—Parents United. In the late 1990s, South Gate's schools had become unbearably overcrowded. South Gate Middle School had the highest enrollment—forty-three hundred kids—of any junior high school in the country. So mothers, most of them Mexican immigrants, formed Padres Unidos. With the help of local politicians, Padres Unidos brought school district board members to meetings. Hundreds of angry parents demanded more schools. Soon the board was seeing it their way, and in time, funding loosened up for five new schools in South Gate.

"The success of dealing with L.A. Unified School District emboldened them to think, 'We can do this. We can take anybody on,'" said Hector De la Torre, who had helped form Padres Unidos.

Padres Unidos and Community In Action marked a radical change of mind for South Gate residents from Mexico. In Mexico, working with the police had been unthinkable. Cops were corrupt ruffians, exploiters of the vulnerable. Supporting them, even when an officer died, was a bizarre idea.

Equally bizarre was expecting anything from city hall. Cities had almost no taxing power, meager budgets, and no civil service. So paving streets and building water-treatment plants were monumental tasks. Poor people came to city hall with needs government couldn't meet. They waited for hours in city hall for the privilege of seeing the official they'd elected or one of his employees. Coyotes—influence peddlers—came to lurk in city hall lobbies. For a price, they would get a common citizen in to see, say, the public-works director, who would take a cut of the coyote's fee. Whether public works would resolve the citizen's issue was another matter.

So when Mexican immigrants marched with the police or called city workers to have an abandoned mattress removed, these were huge civic moments. Years after coming here, immigrants in South Gate were warming to a fuller participation in American life.

This was the subtlety that Albert Robles missed as he took on the South Gate police. Neither he nor his allies attended Community In Action meetings. They missed the depth of support for the police. Nor, for some reason, could they see how their behavior in office was energizing a population that they'd assumed would take anything lying down. A town where separate groups had lived apart for years was coming together in startling ways.

After months of court battles, the recall election was set for January 2003. A coalition of white seniors, business owners, and Mexican immigrants organized to oust the Robles crew. Community In Action's bylaws barred it from participating in politics. So CIA disbanded temporarily, allowing its members to join the recall fight. Solidifying the coalition were the police officers' union and pastors from several churches.

"The union started to get involved because the people needed the actual structure and organization skills to effectively go against the beast," said Frank Rivera. After the firebombing of Ruiz's business, officers spent nights sleeping outside the homes of prominent people who'd signed the anti-Robles recall petition.

Meanwhile, recall organizers had to confront the reality of a town made up largely of working-class Mexican immigrants. Many immigrants still didn't know city government enough to follow it. Too many of them didn't go to council meetings or read newspapers or attend CIA marches. Reaching them would have to be done one-on-one, after work and in their neighborhoods.

So the coalition resorted to that time-honored institution of white suburbia: the coffee klatch. Five nights a week for four months, residents gathered at homes across South Gate. Frank Rivera led the meetings. He'd explain how things are supposed to work in a U.S. city hall: bidding on contracts, open government, accountability, and budgetary oversight. Then he'd explain how things were in South Gate.

"It was Government 101, right in their living room," said Rivera. "It felt really good to know citizens actually had an interest, including these immigrants that just became U.S. citizens. They felt the responsibility to know how to vote. They realized they'd sometimes taken it for granted. Before they'd sometimes just vote on party, or last name. There was no sense of responsibility of finding out who the candidates are."

The coffee klatches were intended to outrage the citizenry. They succeeded. Soon so many folks wanted to host coffee klatches that Rivera and the other officers couldn't attend them all. More people were swept up in the crusade—for that's how it came to feel. In a town that had grown used to the arms-length politics of mailers and phone machines, the recall of Albert Robles and his allies became vibrantly grassroots.

After a while, those involved took joy in taking part. Outside a Monday night council meeting, Jesus and Sonia Miranda, owners of a *taquería* in town, brought a grill to city hall and cooked tacos for the multitudes. The Mirandas had been active in Community in Action and Padres Unidos. Their daughter had been a police cadet. Jesus Miranda, mortified that he'd voted for the Robles slate in 1999 and 2001, threw himself into the recall.

"When they began trying to get the department, that was when I got mad," he said. "I don't want corruption here. Mexico is the most beautiful country in the world. The reason it's poor is corruption. If Mexico were like the U.S., I wouldn't be here. For me, it's gone very well here. Where else am I going to go live? Great Britain or France?"

To raise money, Señorina Rendón made pozole and tostadas and had neighborhood feeds at her home. "The old Americans, the white people, were the first in line to come buy the food. At 10:00 PM, the cops showed up," she said. "It was white seniors, Mexicans, and cops, all eating together."

Rudy Navarro, a young man who was running for treasurer against Albert, wore out two pairs of shoes walking precincts. Frank Rivera put everything else in his life on hold. "If it didn't have to do with police work or saving the city, it didn't matter," said Rivera. The police softball team took a hiatus. Every night, volunteers walked precincts, talked to neighbors, and handed out fliers.

"Albert would never have been able to accomplish this no matter how much he paid people to do it," said Rivera. "He hired guys—day workers in front of Home Depot—to do this, but [they didn't] have the passion."

As expected, nasty mailers cascaded into mailboxes. One claimed that Rudy Navarro had bounced a check because he'd spent all his money partying with a girl. The mailer called Navarro "a horny dumb crook," and said a neighbor had heard Rudy shout, "Baby, let's keep on partying, and make me write another bad check!"

This time, however, the district attorney's office entered the fray. It tried Angel Gonzalez, who ran the printing company where Albert did his printing. Gonzalez was convicted of printing fraudulent campaign mailers. In a raid on the firm, D.A. investigators found originals of that mailer in 2001 that claimed Bill De Witt had a love child in Nevada.

Kevin Shelley, California's new secretary of state, came down from Sacramento to hold a press conference outside South Gate City Hall. He was placing observers at South Gate polling places. As he spoke, Albert ordered city workers to hydroblast the sidewalks, drowning out Shelley.

Another classic mailer appeared, attacking Henry Gonzalez. It showed a photograph of Gonzalez on a milk carton. It read: "LOST! Have you seen this senile, dirty old man?

"Henry Gonzalez," the mailer went on, "was recently seen wandering in a vacant parking lot near his home at 3 AM, unaware of his whereabouts, and mumbling 'Where did that sexy lady go?'"

That's really what it said.

Raul Moriel sent out a mailer with a photograph of himself standing with an old white man, a volunteer crossing guard, at a stop sign, reading "Seniors STOP Recall." The man's wife was outraged, as her husband had died months before the campaign.

The Robles crew's election-time giveaways had gone from plants to sodas and hot dogs to toys. Now they went to the extreme.

First, the council majority announced that the city's new garbage company, Klistoff and Sons, would offer residents free trash pickup in January. Months before, Klistoff had taken over the city garbage contract from Waste Management. Waste Management executives later told reporters that Albert had tried to extort money from them for his campaign. When they refused to pay up, they said, Albert gave the contract to Klistoff and Sons. City garbage contracts typically run for three or four years. Klistoff got a ten-year deal from Albert's city council and then another six years in exchange for free residential trash pickup in January, the month the recall election was scheduled.

Yet free trash pickup was only prelude to the greatest giveaway of all. As the recall loomed, the Robles council announced it would be giving away a three-bedroom, two-bathroom house. Not only that, the city would pay to build the house for the lucky winner on land it owned that had once been a park.

A week before the recall election, with hundreds of people and Spanish television stations watching, the council raffled off the house. Maria Guadalupe Fitz, a Mexican immigrant and a divorced mother active at St. Helen's Catholic Church, had the winning ticket. Because Fitz didn't have money to pay the taxes on the house, the council voted to give her one hundred thousand dollars as well. All told, the city's gift of public money to Ms. Fitz was close to five hundred thousand dollars.

Moriel followed the raffle with a last-minute mailer with a photograph of Ms. Fitz proclaiming, "God and Vice Mayor Raul Moriel changed my life." She denied saying anything of the kind.

"(Albert) thought that with a soda or a hot dog he could get the Hispanic vote," said Waldo Perez later. "I'm ashamed that early on it was true. When Benavides was elected, the Seven-Eleven was full with people getting free sodas and hot dogs. He knew that we were like that and that's why he did it. It worked for him."

But it didn't work anymore. Enough immigrants believed the Robles crew was playing them for fools. Bedlam erupted at the council meeting before the recall. Angry South Gate—white seniors, Mexican Americans, Mexican immigrants—packed the chambers and spilled out into the corridors. Araceli Dominguez was ejected to a roar from the crowd that drowned out Xochilt Ruvalcaba's banging gavel. Police Chief Rick Lopez flipped off Henry Gonzalez. When the meeting adjourned, several members of the crowd went after Ruvalcaba, Moriel, and Benavides, yelling "You're out of here!" and "One more day!"

Like the PRI in Mexico, Albert and his allies had seemed invincible. But in the end, like the PRI, they folded because there wasn't much left to hold them up. South Gate voted by an eight to one margin to recall Albert Robles and his allies. Some eight thousand voters turned out—small compared to the twenty-six thousand registered voters in town, but four times more than usual. People formed lines twenty deep to vote.

Albert Robles was recalled, along with Moriel, Ruvalcaba and silent Maria Benavides. Elected in their places were Steve Gutierrez, Greg Martinez, and Maria Davila. Rudy Navarro was elected treasurer.

Remarkably, though, the battle still wasn't over. Albert and his allies had succeeded in postponing the recall so that it was held only a few weeks before the regularly scheduled election in March 2003. Six weeks after the January recall, everyone had to run again. It was the fifth South Gate election in five years.

By now, though, Albert Robles's name stained anyone near it. The coffee klatches, Community In Action, the press coverage, and the D.A. investigations combined to arouse the people of South Gate. Neither Albert nor his allies campaigned.

Instead, in their last week in office, Robles and his managers wrote city checks for $2.1 million, mostly to lawyers. South Gate's assistant finance director told the *Los Angeles Times* that he was forced to take much of the money from the city's rainy-day reserve fund, while Albert, City Manager Jesse Marez, and several attorneys stood over him.

"I was basically under duress to sign the checks," he said.

One final mailer of the campaign arrived in voters' mailboxes. It claimed that Albert was endorsing Greg Martinez and Maria Davila. "Albert Robles is endorsing no one else for city council," it read. Who knew who wrote it? But trying to confuse voters by associating himself with those trying to oust him felt like classic Albert. People expected nothing less from him by now.

By 10:00 PM on election night, March 4, South Gate's American Legion Hall overflowed with the people who'd fought Albert Robles.

Though Albert was absent, he was everywhere. People talked about him. He was the butt of jokes. Others remembered some moment from the campaign, what they said to Albert, what he had said in response. People ate and talked and laughed. Burly cops and city workers hugged each other.

"I have only two words for Albert Robles: 'tar' and 'feathers,'" Greg Martinez, a hardware store owner and newly elected councilman, told the crowd.

To one side stood Rev. Chuck Brady, of Redeemer Lutheran Church. Brady had founded Churches In Action, a coalition of clergy that had come together for other reasons but had joined the fight to depose Albert. They were particularly upset that the Robles council had approved the permit for a massage parlor.

Brady had watched the rise and now the fall of Albert Robles. "The question was, 'Are we going to import PRI-style Mexican politics here, or are we going to reject it?' So far, it seems the Hispanic people have said we don't want that style of politics here. The strength of the American system is being perceived by the people who are coming in."

At a microphone, Hector De la Torre read the returns. The Robles crew, he read, had polled only a few hundred votes apiece. The tallies drew loud applause and pounding on tables. Albert Robles received 182 votes.

Also defeated was a measure Albert's council had placed on the ballot—a final raspberry to the people of South Gate—that proposed raising local property taxes by 1,000 percent. It was cynicism's last gasp, inspired perhaps by the belief that immigrant voters wouldn't pay attention to what they were voting for.

Henry Gonzalez took the microphone. "It's a great day in my life and in my family's life. We're going to restore integrity."

Hector De la Torre stood again. He began by mentioning all the groups that had made up the campaign: seniors, Padres Unidos, Community In Action, young people, the city workers, the Chamber of Commerce, Jesus and Sonia Miranda, the Junior Athletic Association. The Police Officers' Association got a standing ovation. The night ended with the crowd singing, "Na-na-NA-na, Na-na-NA-na, hey, hey, hey, goodbye."

In the weeks that followed the March 2003 election, South Gate showed signs of returning to normalcy. At the first council meeting, Fr. John Provenza declared the first council meeting after the recall to be "a great day for the city of South Gate, a day when we can rejoice in the hope for democracy." Community In Action started up again. The new city council addressed issues like street-sweeping fees and declared one week to be "Always Buckle Children in the Back Seat Week." People who got up to speak at council meetings were not ejected. The council chambers were packed. The high attendance probably wouldn't last long, but I thought it was nice to see nonetheless.

After the election, I dropped by the office of Rudy Navarro, who'd just been elected city treasurer. Rudy was twenty-three. He said he'd just graduated from San Diego State University with degrees in finance and political science. He wanted to go to law school, but for the moment he was the treasurer of a nearly bankrupt city. State auditors were coming to inspect South Gate's books.

"We gave away a house!" he began, still incredulous. "The day after they left office, we stopped a half a million dollars from going out."

The city's payroll had risen from 340 employees to 570 in two years, he said. Contractual landmines were everywhere, and the city would be paying for them for years. The new police uniforms. The attorneys. The police badges. The loans to George Garrido. The $3.2-million Community Services Department that did nothing. South Gate looked like a dictatorship after the dictator had fled.

Still, Navarro had a healthy attitude toward it all. "To me, it's a golden opportunity," he said. "It's tough on six hundred dollars a month, but . . . I have this opportunity to do something great, and you can't beat that."

I went across town to see Joe Ruiz. Ruiz had been spending more time at his plumbing business. He had emerged from the child-molester mailer, then the firebombing of his trucks and the drive-by shooting at his house. He'd started the recall, but then had to withdraw from the campaign to tend to his business. He was now coaching a junior varsity football team that had just won the league championship. Now Albert was defeated. Joe Ruiz was feeling good.

"I'm happy. My kids are happy. We're trying to get back into regular life," he said. "It's a whole different city now."

A few days later, I met again with Hector De la Torre at Casa Jimenez. He was now the mayor. The council had to lay off at least 224 workers. The city's redevelopment agency was $5 million in the red. The rainy-day fund was down to nothing. Yet De la Torre was euphoric. New social girdings in South Gate had been created and had sustained the recall. A community had formed.

"You had the white organizations that had faded, and nothing had replaced them. We didn't take over theirs, and we didn't create our own. Two years ago I didn't know what was going to replace them. Now I do. Community In Action is one. Padres Unidos is another. The Women's Multicultural Club, which is an adjunct to the Women's Club of South Gate. The sports leagues at the park.

"Before, we had a vacuum of community organizations. We had these different groups: the whites, the second- and third-generation Latinos, and the Mexican immigrants. There were lots of ethnic barriers between them. Albert was able to divide and conquer. But what happened was what I said would have to happen: those barriers between them would have to come down. He succeeded in doing that, because then the one thing all those people ended up having in common was a strong willingness to get rid of him.

"That got them all in the same room. What they then discovered was, 'Hey, we're not that different after all.' 'Hey, I really like that guy even though his English isn't very good.' Or 'Hey, I really like that old white guy who I thought was cantankerous.' You've got some real bonds now, forged in battle."

It took Albert—the cucuy—for South Gate to sprout a community, for Mexican immigrants to learn U.S. civics, and for Mexicans and white seniors to get to know each other. Residents came together against mailers about boozers and deadbeat dads, against Ricardo Ávalos Mayér and Hector De la Torre 2, against silent Maria Benavides and Xochilt Ruvalcaba's banging gavel, against toy giveaways and house giveaways and city-enriched lawyers. They'd come together against police badges and city land handed out like candy.

South Gate hadn't entirely lost its anonymity. But people now knew more of their neighbors. South Gate had become an unashamedly teary-eyed, heartwarming Norman Rockwell painting, updated to the twenty-first century. Young shaved-head Latinos and blue-haired ladies stood shoulder to shoulder during the campaigns and ate from the same box of donuts.

"Outside of my family, this is the best experience I've ever had," De la Torre said. "There was a real feeling of something bigger than just an election. It was a community coming together, a willingness to work together. All the things you want to see as a person involved in public life. I don't imagine I'm going to see something like that the rest of my life."

Over the next few days, I called Albert a few times to see if he wanted to talk about the turmoil he and his cronies had caused. He sounded willing. "History has yet to be made," he said, in his typically epic style.

Finally, we met at a restaurant in South Gate. Albert said he saw himself as Winston Churchill or Jimmy Carter, rejected but looking to rebound. "Jimmy Carter rose above it. Winston Churchill rose above it. The question is, will Albert Robles rise above? My Creator knows the answer."

He told me of people stopping on the street or in stores to tell him he'd been mistreated. He quoted an old Mexican proverb: "There's nothing bad from which something good doesn't come." Before, he'd had a distant relationship with his mother, and no relationship with his father, "the man who wanted to pummel his kid into perfection." Now the Robleses had grown closer. He no longer feared his father. He said he looked forward to the day when he could take care of him.

He'd read, too, that the county had closed its feared home for juveniles, McClaren Hall. "Every time I'd run away from my foster home, they'd threaten me with putting me there: 'Albert, you need to turn yourself in or you're going back to Mac!' Back to Mac."

He said he was thinking of getting his master's degree and teaching political science. "Who better to teach political science than someone who lived it at warp speed?" he said.

He vowed to run for office again. "I forgot what my winning formula was," he said. "I ran campaigns from a distance. There was a huge disconnect."

I told him I thought his rise and fall was about Mexican immigrants, who finally realized that he represented what they'd left in Mexico. They'd risen to throw him out the way I'd seen Mexicans throw out the PRI three years before. I thought he was a Latino Joe McCarthy, lacking in scruples. No, he said, he liked McCarthy's attorney better. What was that lawyer's name? he asked. Roy Cohn? I ventured, referring to McCarthy's amoral legal hatchetman, and the only person in Washington DC at the time more despised than McCarthy himself. Right. Roy Cohn, he said, I liked that guy. This was typical Albert, aiming to be as dastardly as he could be.

Albert said his politics evolved from his understanding of what people want. "People want to know what's in it for them. Nobody's going to vote for you unless you let them know what's in it for them. What is it? Your brand of leadership? Your vision? Determination? There's people who still appreciate the fact that I was a determined pit bull fighter, that I was an SOB."

He grew more animated. He said I'd done him a disservice writing about him in the *Los Angeles Times Sunday Magazine* two years before. It had lost him part of his constituency, he said, and claimed he'd received hate mail after the story appeared. He said it also started an avalanche of media coverage of South Gate. That caused his downfall, he said. Nonsense, I said. His downfall was the result of what he and his allies did in office. Why didn't I write about his enemies, he asked me. He gulped down a handful of vitamins, saying he wanted to outlive these enemies.

"Justice in America is not blind," he said. "It goes to he who has the greatest resources. The criminal justice system is as bad here as it is in Iraq or Mexico. It's who you know, how many resources you have. . . .

"You think you understand Albert Robles," he went on. "You will never understand Albert Robles. You live in the box that says, 'This is what I know.' In order to understand me you have to go to a box that you don't even know that you don't know about.

"History and our Creator and life itself will either reward us or punish us for our shortcomings. Your Creator will either reward you because you helped to uncover a bad guy, or your Creator will say, 'You know what? You derailed one of my emissaries.'"

With that, we parted company. I found that, indeed, I had no special understanding of what motivated Albert Robles. Still, his acts spoke for themselves. Maybe as a journalist I could only hope for that. I believe that there is more to a person than his actions. But when that person is in public service, it's his actions that count. Albert Robles came to a working-class city and within a few years brought it to the edge of bankruptcy. He and his crew enriched lawyers at working people's expense and left a police department in shambles. They had defiled a decent tradition—of treating small-town politics as public service. Above all, they had created simple meanness.

Albert's personal story started as the kind of touching tale Hollywood favors: a poor kid rises from foster homes and against all odds gets a degree from a top university and goes into politics. But the tale had no Hollywood ending. Albert turned out to be a rogue, the cucuy. Maybe his tough childhood had not made him more compassionate but haunted him instead. Years in a foster home made his skin thin. He'd learned to lash out when things didn't go his way. He was the last person who should have been in public office.

As a reporter, I'd grown used to seeing gray in every story. People have complicated motives for what they do; human beings aren't characters in soap operas. Judging who was right and wrong was something I'd given up long before. But South Gate had been different. I'd never covered a story where who was good and who was bad was so clear. The saga of South Gate was a soap opera, a melodrama, a *telenovela*. Sometimes a reporter has to say, based on the evidence, that a source is no longer credible. Reporters finally did that with Joe McCarthy back in the 1950s. I had reached that point with Albert Robles and his crew.

Within two years, Albert was tried and convicted of thirty federal counts of bribery, money laundering, and depriving the electorate of honest public service. During the trial, evidence showed he'd solicited $1.8 million in bribes from companies bidding on city contracts. A lot of the money went to lawyers, Albert's friends and family, and to running campaigns. He used $165,000 of the funds to buy a house in Rosarito Beach, south of Tijuana, and another $65,000 to buy a platinum membership in Tony Robbins's organization—which allowed him to take trips to Fiji and the Czech Republic.

Ironically, though, South Gate had melted together because of him.

"You got to know people you'd never had much contact with, and you became friends," Marilyn Echols said of the campaign after it was over. "In a roundabout way, Albert may have been the best thing that ever happened to us."

On the Thursday after the election that finally ousted Albert and his gang, South Gate opened its thirty-eighth annual Azalea Festival. It was held on the smooth green grass of the baseball field at South Gate Park. I got there as the sun was slowly setting through the trees. The festival would run for four days. But with this day's work now done, parents had brought their children early. They stood in line on the grass to buy tickets to the rides.

Near the infield were food stands—Tortas de Jalisco and Tacos Acapulco. One vendor sold *pupusas*, the Salvadoran dish. Young girls in tank tops drank sodas. Overweight fathers in sports jerseys and buzz-cut hair pushed their infants in strollers.

Awaiting them all were the Zipper, the Gee Whiz, and the Yo-Yo Swings. Each ride sparkled in neon and carnival colors—yellow, blue, soft purple, and light pink—that looked lifted from the houses of South Gate. An aquarium was filled with goldfish, which anyone could win by tossing a ping-pong ball in dozens of small-mouthed jars of blue and red water.

The Azalea Festival mirrored the town's transformation. The festival had started in 1965. Through the 1980s and 1990s, as South Gate became Latino, the festival remained what its white organizers had created: a parade followed by service-club dinners. But attendance dropped along with the white population.

Instead of shuttering the festival, city officials turned to an entrepreneur named Ted Holcomb. Holcomb brought in mariachis and bandas and Spanish radio stations as sponsors. The Azalea Festival became a small carnival, a virtual replica, in fact, of the traditional fiesta each Mexican village holds every year to celebrate its saint. It now attracted twenty thousand people a year.

"These aren't folks that will go often to Disneyland or Knott's Berry Farm, where they have to pay forty or fifty dollars per person," Holcomb said, as we stood on the grass, near the food vendors and the aquarium. "They want what they're used to in Mexico. You have to give Latinos what they're used to."

Maybe in carnivals. But it seemed to me that when it came to politics, in South Gate at least, Mexican immigrants opted for something much different than they were used to. I wondered how other cities would do it, absent a cucuy to unite against. Still, in the aftermath of Albert, this festival had a lot in common with the town: whites had created them both; Mexicans had now rejuvenated them by making them their own.

Holcomb walked off to attend to business. I stood on the outfield grass. The rides hadn't started up yet. The families waited quietly in line. The setting sun shone through the large aquarium, and its rays refracted through the water and reflected off the motionless fish.

After so much nastiness, this felt an especially peaceful moment. It was time, finally, for turning away from noxious cynicism and the poisonous lies of anonymous mailers. It was time for carnivals, for the innocence of children, for bare feet on green grass, and for the return of decency to small-town American democracy.

Chapter Four

Doyle and Chuy Wrap Juárez in Velvet

By the time Chuy Morán returned to Ciudad Juárez at the age of fifty-four, he had been away from his hometown for what had not been his best years.

He had lost a lot over the previous two decades. This included, in order of importance, his wife, his businesses, his land, most of his money, and his cars. His kids still talked to him, and he had his health. But he didn't see his brothers much. Back in Juárez now, he hadn't much but stories to show for his first fifty-four years.

Chuy was a sweet-hearted fellow, quick and alert, and his smile was feisty and infectious. The years had engraved on him the leathery look of an old boxer. He was short and had a thick neck. His nose was slightly bent and under it, a thick mustache curled around his mouth. His voice was coarse, adding to the boxer effect. His brown hair swept across a wide forehead, and he tossed it back frequently. He carried himself deferentially, as though in constant apology.

Chuy Morán had been to the velvet mountaintop. Back when velvet paintings were what Juárez made most, Chuy Morán was the king of Juárez velvet painters. Before he was thirty, velvet had made Chuy a wealthy man.

He and three of his brothers were the first family of Juárez velvet painting. The Morán boys—nine in all—were known as tough brothers who raced old cars in the streets and shrank from no fight. To neighbors, they were thugs. But several of them became velvet painters; they opened painting studios and made a ton of money. Neighborhood mothers began sending their teenage sons to ask for work.

Chuy's velvet studio was the largest in Juárez. It may be that no painter anywhere put his name on more velvet paintings than Chuy Morán. The livelihoods of more than forty families had once depended on him, and he drove the streets of Juárez in a cherry red Corvette bought with velvet dollars.

But those days, and the money, were long gone. When he returned to town this time, no one noticed. He'd found a tiny house for himself, miles south of the center of things. It had three rooms. The living room had a few sticks of furniture from a business he'd owned that had failed. He laid a mattress on the living room floor, and there he slept. In the corner was an old air conditioner. His curtains were moving-van blankets, and his cable television came via a pirate connection, for a one-time payment of two hundred pesos to a couple kids who could jury-rig such things.

Since returning to Juárez six months before, he'd tried working for his son-in-law, who sold used cars on vacant lots around town. The salesmen didn't report sales tax on the cars they sold. So apart from spending hours in the Juárez heat working for someone half his age, Chuy had to dodge tax inspectors. When they arrived, Chuy and the other salesmen would jump in the cars and speed off. Chuy quit that job, but nothing else presented itself.

So it was that, in the fall of 2003, Chuy Morán turned again to velvet painting. Twenty-three years had passed since he'd painted on velvet. It had been almost that long since velvet painting had provided anyone on the border with a decent living. But it was what he'd done well. So he went to it once again, steeling himself with an optimism that he could again make money at his art, and fearing any negativity that might weaken his resolve.

"I'm not afraid. I feel really good about starting again," he said. "I don't think it'll return to the boom there was before. But if you make paintings that are well done, fewer but well done, there could be a market for it."

Chuy Morán in his makeshift Juárez studio.

In the back room of his house, a room with no air conditioning, he fashioned a studio. He propped a velvet canvas on a crate and against the wall. To the right he placed a palette of goopy paints, small tin cans of thinner, chemicals to cut the paint, and brushes of varying widths.

He crouched on an upside-down bucket. Then tentatively, he hunched toward the velvet canvas, waved his brush like a wand over the canvas, and attacked, spreading strokes of white paint across the black fabric.

After a few minutes of getting his feel, he crowed, "I'm back."

He stared intently at the velvet as he brushed it.

"It's like seeing an old girlfriend after many years who hasn't gotten married," he said. "She's waiting for me. She hasn't found anyone like me yet."

Within an hour, a snowcapped mountain, a waterfall, and a stream running through a stand of pine trees materialized on the velvet canvas before Chuy Morán.

✳

Almost forty years before that, during the summer of 1964, a young man from Georgia was vacationing in the Southwest, and, while visiting El Paso, he crossed into Ciudad Juárez for the day.

He lived in Columbus, Georgia—a burg run by an upper class that the young man figured had been intact since the days of slavery. He was a short and gregarious fellow, uneducated, but with a fertile mind that brimmed with a million ideas for how to get ahead.

Up to that point, his life had been something out of a southern novel. He was the son of a poor cotton farmer in Aramis, Alabama, a hamlet far from paved roads and anything that smelled of a future. In 1953, at the age of eighteen, he left home penniless and hitchhiked to wherever he could get a ride. A car dropped him in Columbus, a sweltering town of about fifty thousand people at the time, located in the South's black belt on the Chattahoochee River in southwest Georgia and not far from the U.S. Army base of Fort Benning. He slept that night behind some park hedges.

In time, he found work driving trucks in Columbus, delivering first ice cream, then bread, then potato chips to local markets. Things went well, and after a while he bought a few of the small markets on his route.

Like many Southern towns at the time, Columbus was socially and economically cloistered. Carson McCullers's 1940 novel of Southern isolation, *The Heart is a Lonely Hunter*, was set in Columbus. By the 1950s, the town had run for decades on the economic power of textile mills. The families who owned the mills formed a blue-blooded gentry that prized lineage and the social graces. "There's a group of elite families, and you're either in or you're not," one historian said about the Columbus of those years.

To this elite, the sweat and rough hustle of a self-made man appeared, perhaps, unseemly. So it was a matter of some consternation in Columbus's highest social circles when this son of a poor cotton farmer fell in love with the daughter of one of the town's most influential businessmen. The woman's father never thought the young man worthy. Unable to gain her father's consent to their marriage, the couple eloped. Upon their return, his new father-in-law presented the young man with a deed to a house, stating that his daughter required a certain style of life that he doubted the young man capable of providing. The young man refused the deed. He'd buy his own house, he said. The test of wills escalated until the young man tore up the deed.

His life in Columbus now became about limitations. It wasn't something he could touch or prove, but it was definitely there, these obstacles to an unconnected man's advance. He believed his father-in-law had something to do with local banks' reticence in dealing with him, despite his perfect credit. He'd come to town destitute and still spoke like it. Nor had he conformed to Columbus society's idea of how a successful businessman should act. He didn't join the country club. He cared nothing for pedigree, and his elopement hardly endeared him to the ladies and gentlemen of Columbus society. Meanwhile, the dominance of a supermarket chain hemmed in his markets.

So it was that, as he vacationed in the Southwest in 1964, Doyle B. Harden was a young man looking for a way out of Columbus, Georgia. The Juárez he visited that day was a small, hot town catering to gringo tourists. Along the strip known as Avenida Juárez were restaurants and cantinas and shoeshine boys and beggars. Lawyers offered quickie divorces. Cabbies hailed him at street corners.

Curio shops along the strip were crammed with sarapes and ceramic bulls. But what caught Harden's eye were the paintings these shops sold. They were of landscapes and villages, painted on black velvet. The colors seemed to leap off the fabric. Enchanted, he bought seven paintings and took them back to Georgia.

It was a decision made with scarcely a thought. Yet it would ignite one of the border's strangest careers, create a nationwide velvet-painting craze, and make painted velvet an icon of American pop culture and the U.S.-Mexico border. An epic would unfold across the next two decades through which passed Palestinians and Eskimos, drunkards and three-wheelers, five-and-dimes and discount retailers, Scientologists, legions of immigrant street-corner vendors, and Chuy Morán. At the center of it was Doyle Harden, the country boy from Alabama by way of Georgia, who had to come to El Paso/Juárez and found his life's work.

Doyle Harden never could paint a lick. Yet he would become the Henry Ford of velvet painting, mass-producing oceans of hand-painted velvets. The velvet boom he ignited began the transformation of the border from a dusty outpost of sin into a land of opportunity, however unsightly. Velvet painting was Juárez's first attempt at industry. Harden would create a prototype for the hundreds of border *maquiladoras*—assembly plants—that now put together televisions, computers, car parts, and appliances and export them to the United States.

Long before anyone envisioned intra-American trade, Doyle Harden's velvet paintings blazed a trail from El Paso/Juárez across the United States, through Canada and Mexico and into Central America.

In the office of his gift company, Chico Arts, near the El Paso airport, forty years after first coming to town, Harden had this to say about the medium:

"People find it distasteful to call velvet paintings art. I never met many people who would even admit they would have them in their homes. But I've sold more than $100 million worth of velvets and to me it's beautiful art."

As it happened, velvet painting shared a lot with the border that produced it. Despised and artless though it may have been, velvet, like the border, wasn't controlled by elites. Only the law of supply and demand governed it, as it fed on the voracious U.S. market nearby.

Economic outcasts found a refuge in both velvet and the border. Hundreds of poor and working-class people learned to paint velvet, though they'd never imagined themselves artists. Even educated Mexicans would grab velvet like a life raft amid the churning waves of economic crises that made jobs scarce in their professions. Painting velvet earned dollars for all these folks, insulating them from periodic peso devaluations. It afforded them houses and cars, a good life, and a good time for many years.

The 1970s made all this possible. In the United States, the 1970s were years that worked hard so that social critics could look back and proclaim them "The Most Embarrassing Decade of the Twentieth Century." The drug revolution mated with the sex revolution. Their offspring were lava lamps, black lights, waterbeds in Dodge vans, and freebased cocaine. Rock

Doyle Harden, with a velvet painting of the *Last Supper*,
in his Chico Arts warehouse in El Paso.

bands felt they couldn't fully express their souls without their drummer
having a Chinese gong and their guitarists stacks of Marshall amplifiers
and rows of pre-CBS Fender Stratocasters. Armed with this loot, their
souls turned out to be full of rock operas about wizards and mountain
gnomes or bluesy lamentations on the demands of sex-starved groupies
and big record deals.

Velvet was the 1970s' official fabric. Velvet paintings looked bitchen
under black lights. Within a few years of Harden's visit to Juárez, Americans
could not get enough black velvets of unicorns or Aztec warriors. They
had to have paintings of *Dogs Playing Poker*, or boys piddling in puddles,

or Jimi Hendrix, or John Wayne. Mexican velvet painters feverishly interpreted the dead pop icons of America: James Dean, Marilyn, the Kennedys, Jim Morrison. When Elvis passed, Juárez velvet painters almost dropped dead themselves from painting the King around the clock.

Every day, caravans of velvet-filled eighteen-wheelers headed north out of Juárez. The town became the Florence on steroids to America's hyperventilating renaissance of kitsch. This was largely because of Doyle B. Harden. And it began when he strolled down Avenida Juárez that day in 1964 and those landscapes on velvet beamed out at him from inside those curio shops.

But before we hear that tale, it bears mentioning that no one alive today seems to have the faintest idea how the art Doyle Harden industrialized came to Juárez in the first place.

Those who might know are dead, gone and forgotten. Velvet's cheap *odeur* has convinced art historians that investigating the medium's story is better left to scuffling freelance journalists and others equally oblivious to the artistic differences between, say, a Toulouse Lautrec and a Smiley Clown/Crying Clown.

This gaping hole in our history is strange, inasmuch as velvet painting's paternity is in no doubt whatsoever.

The father of modern velvet painting was, in fact, a debauched American sign painter who lived with his mother in Tahiti, admired Hitler, and went on tirades against "chinks," "longhairs," and "queers," and built the largest outhouse in the Tahitian islands.

This man's name was Edgar Leeteg. He was a short, gruff, not terribly handsome fellow. He was born in 1904 in East St. Louis, Illinois. As a young man, he made a living painting signs and billboards. When the Depression made work scarce, he took an offer from a theater in Tahiti to paint its lobby signs. He moved with his mother, Bertha, to the island of Moorea, Tahiti. The theater went bankrupt, but Leeteg remained. He subsisted on odd jobs, while painting portraits on canvas of Tahitian old men and naked girls, but mainly naked girls, and occasionally trading the portraits to bartenders for booze.

According to a profile of him by James Michener and A. Grove Day in their book, *Rascals in Paradise*, Leeteg began painting velvet one day when his art supplier ran out of canvas. As a billboard painter, he had learned to paint faces well. These faces, Leeteg found, glowed off velvet.

Rascals in Paradise reports that some time later, fate hooked Leeteg with a gallery owner in Hawaii by the name of Aloha Barney Davis. Davis was a former submariner and traveled the South Pacific looking for art-work he could sell in his gallery. He just loved Leeteg's velvets. Davis could also perform "Over the Waves" on the accordion, while accom-panying himself on a mouth organ and simultaneously drinking a beer and eating a ham sandwich. Leeteg is reported to have deemed this feat "a pinnacle of human achievement." Both men, moreover, were given to rants about the art world's snootiness. Leeteg forbade Davis from send-ing his work to museums. They remained friends and business associates until Leeteg's death.

Davis began promoting Leeteg as a South Seas Rembrandt, an American Gauguin. Leeteg's paintings began to sell, eventually fetching thousands of dollars apiece. Commercial success lifted Leeteg from penury and provided him the funds he required to go crazy.

As demand for Leetegs heated up, every Tuesday a boat from Hawaii would arrive at the dock in Morea. On it were cash and whiskey for the painter; it returned to Hawaii that day with batches of Leeteg velvets for Davis to sell. Leeteg generally spent Tuesdays drunk, fighting with whoever presented himself, and pawing young Tahitians for sex. After a while, Davis's weekly cash infusions also supported not just Leeteg's visits to island bordellos, but a number of Leeteg children, mistresses, and two wives, according to *Rascals in Paradise*. Police got used to fishing Leeteg from the harbor on Tuesdays.

The money let the painter indulge his other obsession, which was building. He built an estate, called it Villa Velour, and added to it through his life, to the chagrin of the colony of American expatriates on the island with whom Leeteg often feuded. At the end of his life, Villa Velour had five houses, a prim lawn, and the aforementioned outhouse, the largest in the South Seas. The structure was itself as big as a house, had ten seats, was decorated with coral and Italian marble, and from the toilet offered the lucky occupant an incomparable sunset view.

A sharp marketer, Leeteg buffed his own image as a top-flight philanderer. He once wrote: "I have boozed more, fought more, laid more girls and thrown more wild parties than anyone else on the island, but it's all good publicity and gets me talked about plenty, and that's what sells pictures." As it happened, he also painted like a madman, was serious about his art, and possessed both an elegant touch and few scruples about copying the photographs and paintings of others.

Diagnosed with then-untreatable venereal disease, Leeteg died in a motorcycle accident on a drunken spree in 1953, at the age of forty-nine. *Rascals in Paradise* reports that he left behind several Tahitian children, Villa Velour, his outhouse, and hundreds of velvet paintings in bars, restaurants, and whorehouses in Hawaii that formed the foundation of an art form that would sweep the world like a hurricane two decades later.

Perhaps sailors stationed in Hawaii saw Leeteg's work in bars and restaurants. When they were reassigned to San Diego, according to one version, they asked Tijuana painters if they could do similar work. From there, velvet painting spread east along the U.S.-Mexico border. That's one version. Maybe it's true. But whatever the case, within a decade of Leeteg's death, painters in Juárez knew how to paint velvet, and a few of them sold their wares to Doyle B. Harden, vacationing from Columbus, Georgia in 1964.

Returning home, Harden displayed the paintings in his markets. Customers snatched them up. The money he made paid for his entire vacation. He returned to Juárez with a truck and bought every velvet painting on the tourist drag. These, too, sold quickly.

Before long, Harden was sending two trucks a week to Juárez for velvet paintings, which were now flying out his markets in Columbus. Soon Doyle Harden was making more selling paintings than he was selling groceries.

In the history of velvet painting's U.S. boom, it is the unlikely state of Georgia that got everything rolling. By 1965, the state was sopping up every painting Juárez could manage. Harden rented a warehouse in Juárez and hired a velvet buyer. Mobile-home builders were his first big clients. They used his paintings to decorate the living rooms of their trailers. From there, he sold to the Eight Days Inn motel chain, which was building motels along Interstate 75 and used Juárez velvets to decorate its rooms.

His father-in-law hated the velvets, thus enhancing their value in Harden's eyes. "He thought they were the most degrading thing," Harden said, who was coming to see his future as clad in Juárez velvet. It was an unexpected yet appropriate match: Doyle Harden, the shunned working-class Southerner, and velvet painting, the low-class semiart, coming together in this dusty border outpost where anything was possible.

Demand for velvets began to rage. To boost output, Harden provided materials to painters in Juárez, who provided only their labor. Yet even this proved inadequate. More painters were needed. Harden started paying established painters to teach neophytes—promising to buy the product of anyone who completed the course.

"Teachers," he said, "went and come like raindrops."

So did students. Hundreds of people took these classes, and through them velvet painting spread and became a border handcraft.

"When Doyle came was when the boom came. A lot of people became velvet painters: housewives, students, unemployed men, everyone," said Juan Manuel Reyna, a painter whom Harden hired as an instructor and who still has a studio in Juárez. "Doyle wanted all my product. Sometimes I was so busy that I'd show up at class and write the tips on the blackboard on how to begin, then leave. My brothers and I were always working. They called us the Zombie Brothers. We were always working overtime."

As fast as Juárez painters could pump them out, the paintings were on a truck to a Georgia warehouse. Harden, meanwhile, sent salesmen to scout the Southeast, selling velvets to five-and-dimes, gift shops, and motels.

Soon Harden was traveling the border looking for more supply. Tijuana had painters, too, but it was so far from Georgia. Juárez was a centrally located door to the entire United States, and only Juárez had enough painters to produce the volume Harden required.

At the dawn of the 1970s, Harden did what he'd seen coming all along. He sold his grocery stores, divorced his wife, and left Columbus for the wilds of El Paso and Ciudad Juárez. Competitors were starting up—Fletcher Imports, High-End Traders, Aztec Imports. They bid up both the wholesale price for velvet paintings and the wages painters could demand. Velvet studios began popping up all over downtown Juárez, which had easy truck access to El Paso.

About this time Doyle Harden met Leon Korol. Korol was from Chicago, the son of Russian Jewish immigrants. He was a blunt fellow, given to good-natured railing about "gentiles." Korol bought discontinued merchandise—cat food, diapers, brooms, shoes—then sold it to discount retailers around the country.

One day, Korol noticed vendors on the streets of Chicago doing brisk business selling velvet paintings. He did some research and flew to El Paso with his accountant. The two men spent a fruitless day at the library and the Chamber of Commerce asking where to buy velvet paintings.

That afternoon, Korol and his accountant sat in an El Paso café and discussed options. As they sipped coffee, a truck pulled up outside. Velvet paintings filled every corner of the truck. Clasped to the truck's roof were velvets. They jutted out the window. They were crammed into where the spare tire usually goes. Climbing from the truck was Doyle Harden.

Harden and Korol—a Georgia country boy and a blunt Chicago Jew—would become fast friends, business partners, and would transform the marketing of velvet painting in America.

"He changed my life in the velvets," Harden said of Korol, who died in 2004 at the age of seventy-seven.

Harden had been sending a semi truck a week back to his Georgia warehouse. But Korol believed velvet had national potential. He was the first customer to buy an entire truckload of Harden velvets from Juárez. Within a month, he had ordered five trucks of paintings delivered to Chicago. He kept this up for years. Velvet paintings filled the cavernous warehouse at the Leon Korol Company in Chicago, exuding a smell of oil paint and fabric that years later Korol's sons still remembered.

"We kind of grew up with velvet paintings," said his oldest son, Steve. "There'd almost be a mountain of these things in our warehouse. Workers would climb up and have to pull a certain size or color. When we were kids we'd go through them and try to find all the nudes. That's as close as we got to a subscription to *Playboy*."

Korol pushed velvets across America, to flea market vendors, carnivals, five-and-dimes, and discount retailers. The more he pushed, the better they sold. He once sent a truckload of paintings to a Walgreen's in Washington DC. The manager called to complain that there were too many nudes in the load. Korol told him to throw them out and he'd refund the man's money. But a half hour later the manager called back: he'd sold all the nudes in fifteen minutes and wanted to know if Korol could get him a truckload of nudes only.

Meanwhile, Korol pestered Harden endlessly for volumes of paintings that Doyle had never considered possible.

It was to meet this demand that, in 1972, Korol fronted the money with which Harden built a block-long velvet-painting factory on a Juárez vacant lot belonging to a Mexican customs commandant. The factory soon hummed with three shifts a day.

Harden's velvet-painting factory is legendary among Juárez old-timers. It was really a cluster of about two dozen studios of different sizes—each with a master painter and team of assistants. Harden provided the materials and paid dollars for everything the master and his crew could churn out.

Harden tested the painters to see who could paint the best trees, or waterfalls, or clouds. Then he set up production lines. Each studio had a wooden shelf along which the artists would slide the paintings. One man would paint the clouds, slide the canvas to the next fellow, who'd paint the sun. The third guy would paint the mountains and slide it to the guy who'd paint the stream. And so it went until the painting was finished. A crew of framers cut the velvet, stapled it to frames, and fed blank canvases into the maw of it all.

An assembly line for handmade art, the factory was one of the first maquiladoras in a town now dominated by them. Each studio was designed so no painter used more than one color and thus avoided wasting time by switching or cleaning his brushes.

Each day, after reviewing sales orders, the master painters chose the subjects to be painted: a landscape, an eagle, a wolf, an Aztec warrior, a pachuco by his car. An assistant forged the master's name on each painting. As soon as it was done, the artwork was in a truck and on its way to some far-off part of the United States, sometimes arriving still wet.

Two big rigs would leave Harden's factory for the United States every day. Urged on by Leon Korol, who bought from no one else, Harden reached awesome heights in velvet production. A dozen or more competitors followed his lead into mass production. A man named Molina had a studio of twenty or more of Juárez's best artists to whom he paid cash every day; it was accessible off a downtown back street with security guards vetting each person who wanted to enter. But no one equaled Harden's volume.

By the mid-1970s, when Juárez was a town of half a million people—a third its current size—thousands of people painted, framed, moved, and sold velvet. At the zenith of Harden's velvet-painting empire, he held a Christmas party for employees and their families, and twelve hundred people showed up.

It was through these years that Chuy Morán ascended to become Juárez's most prolific velvet painter.

His father owned one of those curio shops that Doyle Harden visited during the summer of 1964. His father and brother, José, painted watercolors. Other painters had studios on the strip. As a boy, Chuy began to copy the painters around him and pester them for tips on technique. Soon, he was a painter, too.

He loved art, but it hardly paid. So in 1969, when he turned twenty, Chuy left for Los Angeles to look for work. He found only low-paying jobs. After a year, his brother called. Come home, he said. Velvet paintings were the rage. A man named Doyle was buying every painting

he could find. Chuy returned and got to work along with his brothers
—José, Nacho, and Miguel—who were painting velvet as fast as they
could.

When Doyle built his factory, the four Morán brothers moved into it.
There were other groups of brothers painting velvet in Doyle's factory—
the Reynas, the Morenos—but none had the Moráns' capacity. Miguel
had six assistant painters. José and Nacho each had ten.

Chuy's studio came to employ thirty-six assistant painters. On the
side, he taught his wife's four sisters and set them up painting sixteen-
by-twenties in his home. No other painter in Juárez had an operation
near that size through the 1970s. Most of what it produced were sunny
landscapes of snowcapped mountains, waterfalls, streams running through
the pines.

Chuy found painters among the youngsters in his neighborhood.
When a kid showed talent, Chuy had him bring his brother along, too,
since painting talent seemed to run in families. He was careful to teach
each boy only one thing—trees, say—so that none knew enough to form
a competing studio.

One week, Chuy's studios worked round the clock to put out twenty
thousand hand-painted velvets to satisfy an order Doyle had with the
McCrory's chain of five-and-dimes. Each painting bore Chuy Morán's
name. Chuy didn't sleep for three days.

"I concluded that each American family must put up a velvet painting
in the living room," he said, "then the next month they'd throw it away
and put up another."

By the early 1970s, a velvet art scene had emerged in Juárez. Harden's
classes notwithstanding, a good many master painters jealously guarded
their secrets. But by the 1970s, the scene's effervescence was such that they
couldn't conceal what they knew forever. As with the very act of painting
velvet, "little by little you start bringing the light from the darkness," said
Daniel Ponce Márquez, who was a teenager in Juárez in the early 1970s
when he began painting velvet.

Determined boys found ways to borrow, steal, or learn techniques
as they wedged their way into the trade. Márquez was one of these. He

followed a painter to an art store to learn where velvet was purchased because no one would tell him. His first painting was of a blue-green Jimi Hendrix. He went on to paint at several studios, earning the typical three-dollar fee per painting, though he earned ten dollars apiece for the complicated pictures. Soon he was making thirty dollars a day, every day, and inviting his friends to the movies or rock clubs.

An informal apprenticeship emerged at some studios. Young painters like Márquez started by painting cartoons: an Indian boy pulling a donkey or the Roadrunner chased by Wile E. Coyote. These were painted separately, so that tourists had to buy, say, a painting of the Roadrunner and another of the Coyote chasing him. Youngsters learned to paint the Roadrunner's thin legs by using the edge of the paintbrush. They learned that Tigre—a black dye for leather—blended perfectly with black velvet and could cover their errant lines.

"But you had to be careful, because it would get you high," said Márquez. "It's for leather, really strong. Probably that's why half the velvet painters were crazy."

From cartoons, young painters moved on to desert scenes, learning to paint clouds and use knife blades to paint cactus spines; from there, they proceeded to still lifes of fruit and vegetables, then to portraits of stars, and finally to landscapes or almost anything anyone wanted copied.

Velvet painters invented new branches of kitsch in the process: dripping tar on velvet in the shape of Don Quixote or ships at sea; they painted on onyx and on leather.

Velvet trained and supported a generation of Juárez artists. Efraín Mendoza, patriarch of the Mendoza painter clan, had a talent for Mexican landscapes. Noel Espinoza painted expressive peasants. A man named Santos painted only nudes, starting always by painting the woman's nose. One of the best painters was Antonio Arellanes, renowned for his bulls and landscapes. Arellanes trained many youths who became first velvet painters, then fine artists. Mario Parra, an Arellanes pupil, and other velvet painters who wanted more from their art formed the city's first art school—the Arts and Trades Workshops at the Autonomous University of Juárez—in the 1970s.

As a youth, Chuy Morán, too, had visions of creating great art. He yearned to explore the Mexican themes and colors of muralists Diego Rivera or David Siquieros. Then velvet came. Chuy was grateful to it; through it, he could live from painting. But he also watched velvet replace his artistic dreams with relentless, deadening commerce. As the 1970s progressed, he let those dreams go.

Ironically, it was an innovation of Chuy's that helped rescue Juárez velvet painting when it could have died. It had to do with white and yellow paint, which were especially luminous against the black velvet, but also horribly expensive. The Juárez velvet style is heavier than the style that took hold in Tijuana—which is light, with semidry brush strokes. White oil paint emphasized the sun and the reflections and brought the scene to life.

For this, thick oil paint from tubes was needed. But tube paint cost too much. Chuy's studios, known for their landscapes, relied on white and yellow. Early on, the quantities of whites and yellows that painters needed kept their costs high.

One day, he noticed his wife's votive candles to the Virgin of Guadalupe as they burned. The wax would melt, then congeal. He wondered what would happen by mixing candle wax with cheap latex paint.

He struggled to find the proper combination. Finally, though, he hit upon the formula of boiling enamel paint with candle wax and linseed oil. The concoction thickened to the consistency of tube paint, at a small fraction of the cost. Chuy began buying a thousand candles a week from a religious candle distributor and boiling big vats of whites and yellows for his painters. He taught the technique to others. Daniel Ponce Márquez remembers another artist coming up with a similar concoction for paint that included linseed oil, coloring, and soap.

Using these cheaper alternatives, painters could now use as much white and yellow as necessary to highlight the sun's rays on mountains and streams. They could now paint Tweety Bird or the soft skin of Marilyn Monroe. Cheap paint allowed the cost of Juárez velvets to drop to between five and ten dollars—where the medium found its place as Everyman's art form.

Painting velvet made Chuy and his brothers rich, and this allowed them to go as crazy as Edgar Leeteg. Chuy had his Corvette and his wife had a Ford Bronco. Brother Miguel had a three-wheeled motorcycle that he rode through Juárez, his long hair blowing in the wind. José Morán had a bouncing Chevy lowrider.

With money no object, velvet painters became notorious drunks. The Morán brothers, in particular, took to partying through the weekend and waking up on Mondays too hung over to work.

"When you're young," Chuy said, "you don't know how to use money, and it does you more harm than good."

❋

Doyle Harden, meanwhile, grew into a velvet tycoon. He forever sought new markets to tap. Sales of velvet boomed across the United States, but he noticed that North Americans weren't the only clients for his paintings. Vendors were coming from southern Mexico. Then, after a while, he noticed a few had flown up from Honduras.

Intrigued, Harden sent a few trucks of velvets to the state of Chiapas in southern Mexico and from Chiapas into Central America. They sold well. He then flew to Tegucigalpa, Honduras, with a few hundred velvet paintings. Setting them up in the lobby of one of the city's best hotels, he sold out of them in a day.

Harden concluded that a velvet goldmine lay in Central America, if only he could get product down there. Airlines were expensive. So to move his velvets down the isthmus, he founded a trucking company in Honduras. Leon Korol again fronted the money. By the late 1970s, Harden velvets were cascading through Mexico, Guatemala, into Honduras, and on down to Panama.

To tap these poorer markets, Harden's salesmen learned they had to sell velvets on the installment plan. They trekked through residential neighborhoods in Honduras, Salvador, and Costa Rica. Customers would put money down, then a weekly installment until the paintings were paid for.

Had the 1979 Sandinista Revolution not taken place, Harden's velvet operation might be there still. The year before the revolution, Harden had moved his trucking facility to Managua, Nicaragua. When the Sandinistas ousted dictator Anastasio Somoza, among the companies they took over was Harden's trucking firm, thus killing the enterprise. Harden's dream of high-volume velvet exports to Central America died with it.

As an outcast art, velvet naturally attracted outcasts as its purveyors wherever it was sold. Immigrants in the United States found that velvet sold well on the street corners, where permits weren't always required. With a little capital and rudimentary English, an immigrant could squeeze a living out of velvet. Painters along the border sold to visiting wholesalers whom they remember as "the Mexican guy from Arizona," or "Bart the Armenian" who lived in New Zealand, or the "Hindu fellow" who lived in Trinidad and Tobago.

In Canada, velvet arrived on the backs, literally, of another group of outcasts: Palestinians. Palestinian immigrants in Edmonton, in particular, fastened on selling velvet painting as a way to make money.

"They were street-corner peddlers," Harden said. "It goes back to the Bedouins, wandering the desert. They couldn't speak no English. But they would take three or four paintings and tie them to their backs and walk up and down the streets selling them to homes."

The first Palestinians to sell large quantities of velvet in Canada were two Harden clients: a Mr. Shawar and a Mr. Nabut. They formed the Jerusalem Trading Company in Edmonton in the early 1970s. But the brothers-in-law soon split and formed separate companies. From then on and for the next decade, Palestinian trading companies selling velvet paintings would form and then divide like amoebas across Canada.

Looking for virgin markets, Palestinians charged across the Great White North, from Edmonton to Calgary, to Hamilton and Toronto, to the Northwest Territories and Vancouver.

"We sold tons and tons and tons of that stuff," said Yaser Shawar, who is the son of A. M. Shawar and still lives in Edmonton.

And when Canada's urban markets were finally saturated, the Palestinians had nowhere to take their velvet but north to the Eskimos.

Edmonton's downtown airport had private planes for hire to traverse the Canadian outback. Palestinians began hiring these planes and filling their hulls with the smaller velvet paintings. Leaving no space unused, they'd tie equal numbers of large velvets to each wing of the plane. The velvet-clad planes would take off and fly north over the tundra looking for Eskimo villages. Harden went on a half dozen of these trips.

"You'd fly for hours into this flat country over what, from the air, looked like puddles of water. They were lakes," he remembered. "You'd get to a large lake. On the shores would be a village. The plane would circle. They'd land it on water. There'd be a post that you'd tie up to. In other places you'd taxi right up to the docks. When you land in the outback, the people come to you. The dogs come out barking, and the kids come out to see who you are. All the Eskimos would come out, and the Palestinians would sell the paintings for $300, $350, $400 each.

"You'd fly to one village, then you'd hear about another village a hundred miles off. That leads you to another one. Then the bush pilots—they called them bush pilots—would say, 'Oh, I know of another one two hours away, we'll try that one next time.' You'd try to make the trips fairly quick before you got caught in some of those updraft storms and had to spend a week up there."

As all this was going on, Juárez painters strained to churn out the velvets that not only the United States, but Central America and Canada now could not do without. They spent all week enclosed in rooms, breathing paint fumes. They were working-class kids. Now they were making dollars and could find anyone a job. They were the kings of Juárez. On the weekends, they hung out together and partied hard. Alcoholism broke like a rash among them. They dressed like pimps.

Chuy's workers spent their dollars on all-night carousing at Juárez's many cantinas. Chuy finally put a lawyer on retainer whose job it was to get his workers out of jail following their weekend benders.

"[Velvet painters] were like the *narcos* of today," said Juan Manuel Reyna. "When someone who's had no money all of a sudden gets a lot, he spends it all on vice—women, alcohol, all kinds of dumb things. Many painters died drunk."

It seemed that the trucks would never stop coming over from El Paso to load up with Juárez velvet paintings. "You don't see the big picture, because there is no big picture," said Daniel Ponce Márquez. "You only see the moment. There were no maquiladoras then. Velvet painting was the big industry."

Things got weird in Juárez. Harden, for one, bought a desert ranch on the outskirts of El Paso with the money he made from velvet. On it he built a zoo and kept foxes, bobcats, and ocelots. He bought a few wolves from Alaska and bred more than forty of them, selling them for twenty-five hundred dollars apiece.

He and the painters grew enamored with three-wheelers—the motorized bikes with thick wheels made for desert cruising. Harden bought sixteen vehicles for his painters to use; after a while, the Morán brothers and other painters bought their own.

They'd hold all-night barbecues in the desert. Many painters grew expert at chasing jackrabbits. On three-wheelers, wearing helmets with lanterns affixed, velvet painters would chase the rabbits at speeds of up to twenty-five miles an hour. When the animals tired, the drivers would sidle up to them and grab the creatures by the ears or hind feet. It became a game. The driver would paint each rabbit's ear with his own fluorescent paint and let the animal go; this made the rabbit off limits to the other drivers. Points were deducted for killing a rabbit. Each painter chipped in money, and the painter with the most points at the end of the night won the pot. The next morning, Doyle, the painters, and often velvet buyers from chain stores would emerge from the desert like gladiators, scraped, bruised, and bloody from the nocturnal pursuit of jackrabbits.

In no time, the velvet-painting business spread along the border.

By the mid-1970s, Tijuana, in particular, was shuddering in its own velvet orgasm. In Tijuana, velvet painting began slowly but with promise. By the mid-1960s there were only a handful of painters, but they were talented and committed. José Reveles painted beautiful bullfighters. The bandits that Nemesio Estrada painted were so lifelike that people said all they needed was blood for them to come alive; no one painted the facial crevices of old Mexican men like Nemesio's brother, Alejandro.

Tony Maya, one of Tijuana's finest oil painters today, learned his craft painting on velvet during these years. Maya had been a baker, a boxer, and a vagabond. He began painting by watching an artist he knew in Los Angeles. Moving to Tijuana, he honed his chops painting velvet by day to support himself and oils by night.

One man never mentioned as a great artist was José Velázquez. Velázquez had come from Mexico City, where he'd grown up in the tree-less neighborhood known as Tepito. There, he'd been in a gang whose trademark was robbing people and forcing them to disrobe before making its getaway. Velázquez had been a boxer. He won ten fights, lost his eleventh, and retired. He moved to the border. Somewhere along the way, he taught himself cartooning and to paint on velvet.

By the mid-1960s, this was how José Velázquez supported his family, and it was all he knew. When his twin sons, Juan and Abel, were fifteen years old, he sat them down and placed before them canvases of black velvet.

"Time for playing is over," he told them. "It's time to make money."

He took up a brush, dabbed it in pink paint, and, like an artisan in an Indian mountain village, proceeded to pass down to his sons the one craft he knew, starting with the simplest standard of Tijuana velvet: the Pink Panther. When his sons' attention or brush strokes strayed, he grabbed them by the hair and shook them.

"We just wanted to go out and play," said Abel.

For the next two years, the boys learned velvet's secrets. The Tijuana style of painting velvet is lighter than in Juárez. Tijuana painters cover much less of the canvas with paint, making defter use of the shadows black velvet can create. True to this style, José Velázquez taught his sons to keep their brushes nearly dry. Laden with too much paint, velvet would cake. Paint in one direction, he said; painting back and forth across velvet muddies the fabric's sheen. Above all, paint what sells, he said, and be literal. Tourists don't buy velvet impressionism.

Soon, the boys were learning the medium's Madonna con Bambino: the matador finishing off his bull. They mastered Snoopy, the *Playboy* Bunny, and prowling tigers. José Velázquez took his boys to visit the city's grand masters—men like Duarte, and the great Ramírez, who became one of Tijuana's finest velvet Elvis painters.

In time, their talents for reproduction were such that the Velázquez twins became known as "The Photographers." The family formed its own studio and through the 1970s painted round the clock, becoming the most important family in Tijuana velvet painting.

Velvet painting lifted the Velázquezes out of poverty. Dollars insulated them from Mexico's first economic crises. The twins built their parents a house. They married, had children, bought clothes and cars, and gave money to their sisters.

About the mid-1970s, they remember, Arabs from Canada came to town wanting everything painters could pump out. The Arabs spoke almost no Spanish. But every month, they'd come to a restaurant in Tijuana, and painters would line up with their wares. The Arabs would order fifty of this painting, a hundred of that one, a hundred of this other. The Velázquezes and other painters would frantically dash off the orders over the next two weeks. The Arabs would truck it all to Canada.

"They'd empty Tijuana every time they came," said Juan Velázquez.

Hurrying to fill an order for the Canadian Arabs, José Velázquez one day finished a canvas and tossed it aside. Later, he found it had landed face down against a blank velvet canvas. When he pulled the canvases apart, he noticed the painted canvas had left a print on the blank canvas. The Velázquez studio hushed. The boys looked at their father, then at each other. José swore them to secrecy. Such authority did their father possess that a decade after his death they still had to be prodded to reveal the trick.

Soon the family was painting one canvas heavy with paint then pressing it against blank canvases. Each blank canvas would retain an outline. The Velázquezes would fill in the detail and have a sellable painting in a fraction of the time it took to paint one from scratch. Their studio was the closest Tijuana got to the kind of velvet production line that Doyle Harden built in Juárez.

But techniques like this, along with U.S. demand, destroyed velvet's original promise. After a while, the city bustled with painters imitating whatever sold. Architects, policemen, truck drivers, even a few doctors, quit to become velvet painters. What did quality matter? Americans bought what was cheapest.

Tony Maya was one painter who finally could take it no longer. He quit in 1979, and, to escape, he spent a year walking the Baja California peninsula, drawing and painting watercolors. He never painted velvet again.

The Tijuana bandit showed how imitation gripped the art. Jesús Gutiérrez, a leading velvet painter at the time and today an owner of an art gallery in Tijuana, claims the man was his neighbor. He had rugged features and hard eyes. Gutiérrez said he photographed the man. Using the photograph as his model, he painted a bandit, with a sombrero and bandolier strung across his chest. It sold quickly. Gutiérrez painted more. Others copied him. Since then, in thousands of paintings, Tijuana artists have added whiskers, eye patches, scars, beards, mustaches, and cigarettes to the bandit, but the chiseled visage remains unmistakably the same man, though Gutiérrez says he moved from the city years ago and his name is forgotten.

As competition intensified, more artists began painting and selling in the street. Their presence caught city hall's attention. The artists tangled with inspectors who wanted taxes paid on the paintings they sold. With that, velvet painters crossed paths with the PRI—the party that ruled the country for decades by squeezing political loyalty from every part of Mexican life. And so began a brief, but curious chapter in the history of velvet painting, when a sector of the Tijuana PRI found a way to mine the ultimate kitsch art for political advantage.

The man who did this can be found on Mutualismo Street, in the heart of Tijuana's Skid Row. Mutualismo is lined with beaten houses, rundown hotels, and small markets. Thin dogs meander about. So do immigrants who, unable to break into the United States, have taken to drinking. Every so often, a police wagon pulls up and hauls a few of them away.

Overlooking Mutualismo are the offices of a group called the Confederation of Revolutionary Workers, but better known by its Spanish acronym, COR. The offices include several large meeting rooms, but to save on electricity they're dark most of the time. A secretary sits alone in a cubicle handling a phone that rarely rings. She takes documents from an occasional COR member who happens by, sliding open a glass window in her cubicle to receive them, as if dozens of people were in line and she needed the window to keep them at bay.

This is the fiefdom of Rafael García Vázquez, who has run the COR since the 1960s. Fliers laud his "constant struggle in favor of just causes." At the back of the hall is an adoring portrait of García Vázquez, painted years ago, during his prime and velvet painting's heyday.

The COR is an artifact of the days when Mexico was a one-party state. It is a federation of PRI-controlled unions of taxi drivers, musicians, flea-market vendors, and others who depend on the city government's beneficence. As the government, the PRI chose to whom the law applied—usually people who weren't party members. If, say, a vendor wasn't a party member, he discovered that selling on the street was strictly illegal. Only when he joined a PRI-sanctioned union could he pressure the PRI-run city government to allow him to sell on the street, whether or not it was illegal.

So federations like the COR exist across Mexico. Their leaders pushed the PRI government to let their members dodge some city ordinance. In exchange, union members supported the party and gave their loyalty and monthly dues to their leaders—men like Rafael García Vázquez.

As a young man, García Vázquez sold plaster bulls and sarapes to tourists. But conflicts over where these curios could be sold showed him politics was the more lucrative profession. He joined the PRI and began negotiating with the city government on behalf of merchants and taxi drivers, musicians and street vendors.

"I never detached myself from the people. I was always with them, organizing them, seeing what their problems were," he said, sitting in his office above Mutualismo Street, puffing a Cohiba cigar. "That's why I was able to help the Quetzalcoatl Painters Union."

The Quetzalcoatl Painters Union was formed by velvet painters as the art grew to employ hundreds of people and they fought tax collectors. Observing the painters' plight, García Vázquez offered to help. "Disorganized forces are forces in defeat," said García Vázquez. "We organized more than a hundred painters."

Others put the number closer to 350 painters. Whatever the truth, the painters, hounded by the city, took shelter under the wing of Rafael García Vázquez and the COR. He interceded with tax collectors. Finally, the city relented. But to paint and sell on the street, the artists had to join the PRI. The COR, meanwhile, converted the painters into a pillar of support for the political career within the party of García Vázquez, who was elected to Congress.

"He was always the boss," said Abel Velázquez. "He'd put in the president of the union. We'd vote for the candidate, but he'd say who could be candidate. He'd swear them in. We'd go to his meetings, rallies."

The union proved more than just politically profitable for García Vázquez. Painters' dues supported him. García Vázquez even tried to use the painters as bodyguards when a rebel faction within the COR wanted to kill him.

But to the painters, the union was serious stuff. It was their attempt to control the art's quantity and quality, which declined with every new doctor or truck driver who put brush to velvet.

"Tijuana seemed to live from velvet painting," said Jesús Gutiérrez. "We wanted to keep velvet as part of the tourism industry."

They failed. As more people painted, price and quality kept dropping. The Quetzalcoatl Painters Union lasted six years, long enough to see the art's demise. Jesús Gutiérrez was its first president and painted the portrait of García Vázquez that stands at the back of the COR offices.

Sometime in the mid-1980s, José Velázquez was elected the union's third and last president. His twins, Juan and Abel, tried to organize street displays of unionized painters. But by now the union was faltering. The best painters were leaving velvet. Eventually the bad ones did, too. It was understandable. Velvet paintings were piling up next to lava lamps and black lights in the thrift stores of America. The 1970s were over.

Before velvet painting collapsed entirely, though, one last group of out-casts discovered it.

In the mid-1980s, Scientologists, so widely scorned as cultists, took to selling velvet paintings on the street corners of America. Scientologists recruited people to join and take the religion's expensive courses. One way members made money to pay for the courses was by selling velvet paintings on the streets. It was profitable work and fit around a recruit's course schedule.

Hundreds of Scientologists paid for their courses this way. Perhaps the most important of them was a woman named Leona Logan in Clearwater, Florida, where Scientology has its headquarters.

Logan began selling velvets at the prompting of a friend in Texas. She deemed it a dubious way to make money at first, akin to streetwalk-ing. But one day in 1980, they set up a rack of paintings on a corner in a town in Texas.

"People got off of work, and all hell broke loose," Logan said. "I had people pulling these paintings out. They went crazy. I sold everything I had. It certainly changed my viewpoint."

Logan founded Making Magic, a company that sold velvet on street corners. Within a couple years, the company had vendors nationwide, many of whom were Scientology members. Logan would buy the vel-vets from Harden, then ship them to vendors around the country. Other Scientologists followed Logan's lead. For several years in the 1980s, the largest buyers of Doyle Harden's velvets were members of Scientology.

But Scientology was velvet's last hurrah. Towns began to outlaw street-corner vending, forcing merchandise to be sold within swap meets. Above all, American tastes were changing. The country had gorged on Aztec lov-ers and *Dogs Playing Poker*. Sales of velvet painting plummeted, and by the early 1990s the art had almost disappeared from Juárez and Tijuana.

Some of the painters from Harden's factory found jobs as ice sculp-tors in Las Vegas. A good number of them also hired on as design-ers at El Paso boot companies during the cowboy fad ignited by the

1980 John Travolta movie *Urban Cowboy*. Today, in what might be considered a cultural crisis, only a few men in Juárez or Tijuana know how to paint Elvis on velvet—and none of them is young. Daniel Ponce Márquez moved to Los Angeles in 1979 to start a rock band, but he kept at the art he'd learned through velvet painting. He now teaches art in California prisons.

Among the last of Tijuana's velvet painters are Juan and Abel Velázquez. Like bleary boxers after too many rounds, they lug their work around town trying to sell them to tourists, never with much luck. Their father, José Velázquez, stopped painting velvet after the painters' union dissolved, and spent his last years as a cartoonist in front of the Jai Alai hall. He died in 1992.

One day even the Canadian Arabs stopped coming. For them, velvet had been a way to accumulate capital without a bank. They used their velvet earnings to invest in hotels in Alberta. A. M. Shawar returned to Jordan and bought a dairy farm.

Yet today velvet's legacy is everywhere along the border. Velvet painting set the U.S.-Mexico border on the path to becoming an economic power and a refuge for poor people. By the 1980s, maquiladoras making televisions and car parts for the United States dominated the border economy. But their prototype had been the factories that Harden and others had set up to mass-produce velvet for the U.S. market.

Moreover, the border is where some of Mexico's most rambunctious art is created. The roots of that art scene are in velvet painting. Painting velvet for hours a day taught technique, discipline, and the art business to the region's first generation of artists—poor youths with no access to art school. Some of them went on to greater things.

"All those who started the fine-arts movement in Juárez were from velvet painting," said Mario Parra, who left velvet to study at the National Institute of Fine Arts in Mexico City and exhibit his paintings across Mexico and the United States. The Arts and Trades Workshops at the Autonomous University of Juárez that he helped found now teaches twenty-five hundred students a year and offers workshops in drawing, music, theater, photography, and dance—as well as painting. At workshops, students can learn to paint on canvas, glass, rock, and wood. Painting on velvet, however, isn't part of the curriculum.

Today, almost all the distributors of velvet painting are gone. Only Doyle Harden keeps on. He closed his Juárez factory following a tax dispute with Mexican authorities. But he still sells velvet paintings from his warehouse in El Paso. He buys them from the few Juárez studios that remain. Revenues in free fall forced him to invent new merchandise. He came up with the mandala—a round Indian shield of leather, on which are painted bald eagles, Native Americans, or the American flag—sometimes all three. The company has found fertile markets for velvet in Europe and Australia, but nothing like the boom of yesteryear is in the offing.

"We brought [velvet paintings] into the marketplace of the United States and many other countries," Harden said. Before that, "there were a few artists, but there was no wholesale, no warehouses. There was no place you could go and back up a truck and buy a hundred pieces. All this happened over many years and affected many lives.

"In Alaska, the aurora borealis will change shape as you stand there looking at it. Well, our lives were that way, too."

❋

Alcohol and money damaged the Morán brothers. Nacho committed suicide in an alcoholic depression. Miguel moved to Tijuana and continues to drink hard. José drank for years before turning to Jesus and is now a pastor in a town south of Juárez.

Chuy bought a topless club in El Paso. In 1980, with velvets earning less, he turned his studio over to his employees and devoted himself to his club. But his life was never as good as when he was the king of Juárez velvet painters.

Through that decade, a steady diet of alcohol and strippers ended his marriage. He owned a used-car lot in Juárez for a while, but lost it after the peso devaluation of 1994 forced customers to default on their payments. He moved to Rosarito Beach, near Tijuana, and opened a furniture factory with his son. Fire destroyed that, and the insurance company wouldn't pay. Broke, he returned to Juárez in the spring of 2003.

"Everybody does things they're sorry about, but I did more of them," he said. "It's very difficult to accept that I have to begin from the bottom again."

Velvet was all he'd ever done well. So after six months of looking for work, Chuy had gone to see Doyle Harden. Doyle had given him materials and promised to buy what he painted.

Wholesale velvet paintings were fetching no more than two dollars apiece. At that rate he'd have to produce two hundred paintings a week to survive. No matter.

"I don't need to earn as much as before," he said, sitting before his makeshift easel in his tiny house, his first completed velvet painting in twenty-three years standing to one side.

"I don't need to sell a thousand paintings a week. With three hundred, or even two hundred dollars a week, I can live well. Being careful in what I spend, I won't need to be the mass producer I was before."

And so, in that bare room on the southern edge of Juárez, the once-king of velvet painting propped another soft canvas against the wall and hunched forward, a fifty-four-year-old man beginning from nothing again.

"I know I can do two hundred paintings a week," he said, stabbing white paint at the black and again trying to bring light from the darkness. "Forty a day—I can do that."

Chapter Five

Delfino II

Diez in the Desert

The boy wasn't happy with his line of work, and in his short life he had never imagined that it was work he'd do. But by taking people illegally into the United States, he'd seen Ohio, Kentucky, and snakes in the desert, and he was proud of that. He was sure that he'd seen more of the world than men in his village who were twice his age. He had shepherded his first crew of people across the desert and into the United States before he could have legally driven in that country. Fear accompanied him always, but he'd seen that he could control it. One night, driving a group of illegals into Birmingham, Alabama, his car broke down; he calmly walked them all night along the highway into town. This kind of accomplishment was liberating and left him trusting his own abilities. Almost eighty people were in the United States because of him. He studied the awesome highways of America in a large book that contained maps of each state. He boasted that he knew some parts of the United States better than he knew Mexico City. He'd been to Georgia, California, and Colorado, and he was most impressed with the casinos that he thought were near Indianapolis.

His mother had named him Daniel, but everyone called him Diez—Ten—a nickname that was for his having been born on May 10, this in 1987. So he'd been sixteen for less than a month when, on June 7, 2003, he led a raggedy group of ten folks from Veracruz through the Arizona desert.

Diez was short and slight, but he had a confidence that protruded like a muscle beyond his thin physique and convinced many people who met him that he was bigger and more in control than he was. He had high cheekbones, with hair cut in a fade. His voice crackled. He punctuated it often with a dry laugh and spoke fast, slurring his speech, filling it with the slang of Mexican youth. He often ended sentences in, "you understand?" He hadn't known his father, who'd deserted the family for another woman when he was young. His mother, grandmother, and uncle had raised him. To them and to his siblings, whom he supported, he was an object of admiration.

Though he was a small-town boy, Diez had hip-hop tastes. He liked baggy shorts, baseball caps, and he had a barbed-wire tattoo engraved around his right bicep. Occupying the place of honor in the front room of his family's concrete-block house was a silver Panasonic stereo, which he obtained as partial payment from a client. On this he played CDs of Spanish rap, Eminem, and Mexican *ranchera* music. His dream was to have the nicest truck in his town. A few more trips north and he'd have enough money for a black 1994 Ram pickup that a friend was going to bring down from the United States.

Diez lived in Chocamán, which is a small town at the foot of mountains four hours west of Mexico City in the state of Veracruz. Rising from the center of these mountains was the Pico de Orizaba, a dormant volcano and the tallest mountain in Mexico. Diez was well known as a coyote in Chocamán, and people often came to his house asking when he could take them.

He had left school in junior high, ostensibly because his mother was ill. At times he regretted having dropped out, particularly when he saw kids his age wearing backpacks. But he had felt nothing for school and viewed it as drudgery. So he'd stopped going and, at fifteen, went to the United States with a coyote from a nearby town. With that coyote, he walked through the desert for the first time.

Eventually, he arrived in Phoenix, at the home of some friends. He stayed in Phoenix for eight months, but never could find work. However, the coyote who took him across had noticed something in him—a daring, a boldness, Diez figured, for this is what Diez saw in himself. The coyote offered to take him on as a partner, to help out in future trips. Every few weeks after that, Diez would head down from Phoenix to Sonoyta, a small Mexican border town. There he and his new partner would take north ten or twelve people at a time. This is how Diez, who first went to the United States looking for work, learned to smuggle illegal immigrants when he was not yet sixteen years old, and came to lead much older men through the Arizona desert.

Coyote was a term he disliked. He thought it sounded bad. In Mexico the word had sleazy, cowardly associations. Instead, he referred to smuggling humans as "the work." He didn't like the work any more than the job title, but he had nothing else. He wasn't afraid of the Border Patrol, for they hadn't caught him yet. Although he felt responsible for breaking up families, the people were desperate to go north. How else, he reasoned, could a junior high dropout like himself support his family and be in line to have the hippest truck in all of Chocamán? So, to cover his moral bases, he made frequent references to God. "God first," he said often. "God willing." It sounded hollow, but he knew that it pleased his mother to hear him talk like this. He spoke more believably of the necessity of faith, particularly when crossing the desert, and how it was essential to inspire his charges with the belief that they could make it through even as their bodies began to break down.

The city of Córdoba lies fifteen miles from Chocamán and serves as the hub of western Veracruz. The group Diez was to take on his second trip as leader met for the first time in Córdoba's bus station, on the afternoon of Wednesday, June 4.

There was Tavo, a boy he was training to help out on the trips. Diez brought two young men from a nearby village named Xocotla. Xocotla lay high up a tall mountain with no name; down at the foot of this mountain was Chocamán. One of these young men was Guadalupe Cocotle. He was eighteen and two of his brothers were already in a suburb of Los Angeles called Bell, where they had work installing carpeting and wood floors. Guadalupe was short and thin, the son of a retired teacher.

Shorter and thinner was the friend accompanying him. Delfino Juárez had worked construction in Mexico City since he was twelve. Since that age he'd been his family's lone source of support. His father had been a drunk for years, and his drinking drained the family of resources and most of its hope, which was kept alive only by Delfino's endless diligence. For eight years Delfino worked in Mexico City, coming home every so often on weekends. But he met a quiet, pretty girl named Edith Villanueva at a dance near the Alameda Park in downtown Mexico City. She was from the state of Puebla and worked as a maid in the capital. After a romance, they married, and she moved to Xocotla.

Eight months before Delfino left for the United States, Edith had given birth to a boy. They named him Axel. Now Delfino knew construction work in Mexico City wasn't going to be enough. He wanted to build a house for his new family. This was impossible on his Mexico City construction worker's salary of $130 a week. Plus, Guadalupe was going to the United States and was urging him to come along. So he went.

From a village named Tijan came two men and a teenage boy. There were also three women from the village of Cosaltepec—a friend and two sisters-in-law. Finally, there was a man from Guatemala, and he came to be known to all as simply Guatemala. Diez never knew the names of anyone on the trip. He preferred not to ask. It was business. He didn't want to know their personal lives. Each person would pay him fourteen thousand pesos—thirteen hundred dollars—to have him cross the border and get them to Los Angeles.

That afternoon, they took a bus from Córdoba to Mexico City. There, they boarded a bus for Sonoyta in the northern state of Sonora, abutting Arizona. For the next thirty-four hours, they cut west across Mexico to the Pacific coast and then north to the border. On the way, Diez imparted what wisdom his seventeen trips across the desert had taught him. He told them not to wear bright clothing that would stand out to a helicopter. They were to bring only one change of clothes.

Mexican buses show movies, which can make the trip pleasant or agonizing, depending on the film. Some bus drivers think it demonstrates the height of service to show harrowing high-tech shoot-'em-ups, or *Chuckie*, the rancid delinquent doll, or *Piranha*, a movie about dogs, kids, and oblivious blondes swimming in rivers and being chewed to death by mobs of carnivorous fish. This driver, mercifully, given the possibilities, showed *Spiderman* and *Scooby-Doo*.

In between the movies, as they settled in to the trip, the new acquaintances talked. The conversation naturally drifted to what each hoped from the United States and how long each would spend up north: a year, two years, three years, enough time to build a house back home. As many immigrants do, they spoke of the United States in terms of a fishing trip. How would they do and what stories would they have to tell when they returned? Visions of ten-dollars-an-hour wages danced before them.

One of the women was short and heavy. She was older than the two women—her sister-in-law and a friend—who accompanied her. She was determined, saying she was going to work really hard and hoped to earn a lot of money in Los Angeles, where her brother lived. Her husband had beat her and left her penniless with two children. She left the kids with her mother; one day she would send for them. Guadalupe noticed a couple times on the bus that she bled from her nose.

As they talked and their dreams animated the conversation, Diez watched and thought to himself, "God willing, it'll happen."

By the time the bus trip ended, these strangers were a cohesive group, and though they never knew each other's names, they were friendly and getting along. They arrived Friday in Sonoyta, directly across the border from the Tohono O'odham Indian reservation. Diez found them a motel where they slept that night. Before dawn the next morning, they took a taxi east several miles, to an isolated spot, got out, and began walking north and into the reservation.

A few miles outside Tucson, the Tohono O'odham Indian reservation is a silent land of two million acres splayed across southwest Arizona down to the Sonora border. The reservation is the country's second largest, the size of Connecticut. On it live no more than fifteen thousand people, scattered about the desert in settlements of low-slung houses and trailers.

Just across the border is Papago Farms, a farm run by the Tohono O'odham tribe. Running north from the farm is a paved two-lane highway, Federal Route 21. The road has few travelers apart from Border Patrol jeeps. The first population along this road is twelve miles north of the border—the Indian settlement of Santa Cruz, known for a large salt cedar tree with flowing branches giving lots of shade.

North of the farm, the desert is patches of low scrub brush and beige silt. This area is silent. It is so heavily trafficked by smugglers of drugs and people that the Tohono O'odham Indians say the animals and birds have been scared off.

A few miles later, large bushes and a stand of majestic saguaro cactus gradually emerge. Rising thirty and forty feet above the brush with their arms outstretched, the saguaros appear like mannequins caught forever in surprise, triumph, or joy. A saguaro cactus lives to two hundred years old, and must be fifty before it can grow arms. Saguaros are also 95 percent water—each one amounting to a living water-storage tank that is all but impossible for humans to get at.

After a few more miles, the saguaros disappear and give way to paloverde and mesquite—small trees of green and dark bark. Lower to the ground are ironwood, creosote, greasewood, and ocotillo, a bony, leafless plant whose many branches rise from the ground like electrified hair.

Most unnerving of all this desert's plant life is the cholla cactus. Its dark trunk is topped by a hydra-head of tubes covered with blond needles and spines. From a distance these spines appear soft and furry, which is why the species common to the area is called the Teddy Bear cholla. Up close, though, the spines look more like sharp clenched teeth ready to bite. Desert wanderers dying of thirst have been known to imagine the cholla is a container of water and stick their faces in it.

Like the cholla cactus, this desert, from a distance, appears almost lush and inviting. Rainfall averages about seven inches a year, which is enough to cover much of the land in vegetation. But the flora, on closer look, is menacing and turns the desert into an endless obstacle course for those walking through it. Each plant is a potential abrasion or a needle imbedded in the skin. Though the plant life is ample, it is so gaunt that it provides little shelter from the sun. Yet it grows tall enough to hide travelers who want to be hidden within it, which is why the region has become a smugglers' crossing point. To see over the shrubs, bushes, and cacti, the Border Patrol has devised elevated booths that rise twenty feet above the desert floor. From there, officers scan the desert floor with binoculars. The immigrant has no such tool and is often caught in the desert's trap, for the vegetation also grows tall enough to hide signs of help. Many people grow disoriented in the desert heat and wander until they die, with a house or road only a hundred yards away.

June is the desert's hottest month. In July, the summer rains begin. The saguaros produce their fruit, the ocotillo's bare branches grow a green fur and red berry, and the Tohono O'odham calendar begins. But the desert's denizens can only hunker down and endure June. Moisture vanishes from the air. The sun is at its highest point. In June, the National Weather Service often reports temperatures well over 100 degrees. But even when they are only 98 to 101 degrees, as they were on June 7, 2003, temperatures on the unprotected desert floor can rise to 130 degrees or more.

As it happened, Diez was aware of none of this. This was only the second group he'd led, though he had walked the desert with his partner many times and felt he knew the routine. Walking steadily, they would need ten to twelve hours to arrive at the Indian village of Santa Cruz, where Diez had a contact who would take them to Tucson. From there they would connect with the legion of private drivers that has emerged in Tucson and Phoenix. Diez could hire them to take each immigrant where he wanted to go in the United States.

Together, his group carried six limes, cans of corn and sardines, a sheet, a blanket, and twenty-two five-liter bottles of water. He'd told his charges to wear dark clothing—nothing white or red or yellow that might stand out. He wore tennis shoes, black jeans, a gray basketball jersey, and his lucky black baseball cap emblazoned with the letters SA. He had no idea what they referred to. He'd been given the cap about the time he took his first trip. It was tattered, and his friends had told him to get rid of it, but he always used it when he was taking people across. No one had sunglasses, and, other than Diez, no one had a hat. Diez, Delfino, Guadalupe, and the chubby woman wore tennis shoes. Others wore the cheap formal shoes that serve as all-purpose footwear for Mexico's poor. The group had eaten little on the bus trip, and nothing that morning, conserving their money for what lay ahead.

During the first few hours, the trek proceeded as planned. The group walked single file behind Diez. Guadalupe thought they were almost done when they crossed the border an hour after dawn. Delfino was filled with bravado. Walking a couple hours in the early morning, he felt nothing and didn't know what all the fuss was about, this desert and its heat. He figured he was just tough.

Within a few hours, though, the sun was high in the sky, and its intensity unnerved the tenderfoots. Diez kept walking and walking. Each walker quickly learned to concentrate on what was before him. The rocks could twist an ankle. Cactus spines pierced shoe soles and even slightly grazing a cholla could lacerate skin. Talking ceased. All their mental energy focused on avoiding the dangers the desert presented with every step.

Four hours into the walk, they passed Federal Route 21. And a half hour after that, things began to fall apart. The heavyset woman had been doing poorly. The group was walking fast, and she couldn't keep up. Guadalupe saw the blood again coming from her nose. She asked how far they had to go. They weren't even a quarter of the way, Diez told her. He tried to encourage her, but she had to stop.

They made her a shade hut by placing the sheet over some plants, while the rest of the group stood around her in the sun. She was scared and bleeding, and they joked with her to cheer her up. After a while, they asked if she could go on. She said she could. They began walking with her, pulling her along at times. But as she walked, she grew delirious. She hallucinated. She recognized no one, and finally she foamed at the mouth. She collapsed. The group stopped. Guadalupe saw she was going to die. He kept this to himself. The flow of blood from her nose increased and drenched her shirt. It terrified him.

Diez said they should turn back, put a quick end to the trip, and give up to the Border Patrol. The highway wasn't that far away. So they laid her on the blanket and began to carry her back the way they'd come. After a few dozen agonizing yards, they stopped to rest. The woman lurched her head to the side, threw up, and died.

"I don't think she's breathing anymore," said her sister-in-law.

Diez stood over her, stunned and panicked. The gravity of what had occurred set in. He began to cry. The others gathered around. Looking down at her, the sun above, their shadows fell over her corpse. They were terrified in the silent desert. She'd been talking, hoping. Now she lay dead. No matter what they'd seen on television about people dying in this desert, they were too flush with the dreams of dollars to believe they'd see it.

They looked at each other and stared down at her body. Quickly, what to do? Pulling himself together, Diez said they should reach the highway and give up. But now that the woman was dead, no one wanted to do that. Maybe we should bury her, suggested Delfino. Diez thought he should stay with the body, but realized that no one else knew the way to the Indian settlement ahead, and he didn't want to answer police questions about how they got where they were.

Finally, the woman's friends and Tavo, the coyote trainee, decided to stay with the body. Diez and the others would head on. Wait till we've been gone for three hours, he told the three who stayed with the corpse, then go back to the highway and wave down the Border Patrol.

Diez's group was now down to six men. They would have to make time. To lighten their load, he buried the cans of sardines and corn near where the woman died.

One of the first things Diez had learned about being a coyote was to remain positive and never show confusion or fear. His charges weren't used to the desert, and terror could easily infect them. Every group usually had at least one person who wasn't physically fit. As the sun rose, these people needed encouragement, a pat on the back. If they began to straggle or stop, it would slow the group and throw off the trek's timing. Some coyotes gave their crews stimulants to keep their heart rates up so they would walk faster. The Border Patrol had found immigrants, high on these stimulants, with heart rates above 160 beats a minute even while sitting. Diez didn't do this. Instead, he had developed a whole pep talk that he'd start giving about five hours into the trip. It had to do with how people in worse shape than they had made it. Think of the dollars you'll make. Keep on going. You can do it. Sometimes it included little lies, usually regarding how much farther they had to go.

This speech now deserted Diez as the diminished group he led continued beyond where the woman's body lay. Her death beat on him like the sun's rays. It drained him. He hadn't eaten since the day before. He salved his conscience thinking she must have had some physical condition he wasn't aware of. Still, he imagined the years he'd spend in prison. He tried not to let this show, fearing the others would lose heart. But he kept thinking, why me? Why does this happen to me? To Diez? He noted, in his misery, that he never asked this question when good things happened to him. So, he reasoned, it was all God's will. He trudged on through the brush and cactus. At times, compelled onward, rushing to get to the Indian settlement, he tried to run. He found he could only run a few yards in this heat. He was too weak.

Just twenty-four hours earlier they were watching *Scooby-Doo* and imagining their new lives in the United States. Now the trek had become a grim march. The woman's ordeal had slowed them irreparably. This terrified Diez. He calculated that they had spent two or three hours with her. Another seven or eight hours of walking remained. He didn't like walking at night. It was too easy to break a leg or walk face first into a cactus. They would have to spend the night in the desert.

All this coursed through his mind as he and his group walked on, each man alone with his thoughts. After three hours, shadows lengthened across the desert floor. They found a ravine and the six of them crumbled into its shade. Diez told them that the Indian's house was a couple hours away and they could do it easily in the morning. It was a lie, but he didn't want to upset them. It was ten miles to Santa Cruz. In their condition, that distance would take at least five hours of walking.

The others were quickly asleep. For Diez, though, the night seemed end-less. He tried to sleep but could not. He smoked cigarettes and tried to drink, but he threw up whatever went down. His mind churned over the day's events. The death of the woman whose name he didn't know weighed upon him. Out there alone, through the night, he thought of her dying on the desert floor. He'd go to jail. His mother would die of anguish. What would people say of him? Several times during the night, he closed his eyes. But the wind made a high cooing sound that Diez, in his panic, took for police radios. He'd start awake with a charge of adrenalin.

Through the night, he thought of what lay ahead. They had packed only enough water for a ten-hour trip. They were down to a few gulps of water apiece and the six limes. He didn't know if they'd make it.

None of this did he tell his charges as he woke them at first light. They trudged off into the desert again. They walked for one hour, then another, and another. They found nothing. The sun was high in the sky, and its rays drenched them in inescapable heat.

By 8:00 AM, they were out of water. They turned to the limes and sucked them ferociously. Diez's skin burned and was stuck with cactus spines. His face was lacerated from the brush. It was so hot, he felt, that if you had put a plate of beans on his head, it would have cooked. He wilted quickly, and now knew he wouldn't make it.

His charges, who had slept well, carried him on. They were terrified. He alone knew the trail to the Indian settlement. It was now they who gave him the pep talk. Come on, Diez, they told him, you can do it. How many times have you made this trip before? His arms slung around their shoulders, Diez slipped in and out of consciousness.

By midmorning, the limes were gone. They were oblivious to the tanks of water standing in the mighty saguaros around them. Only one source of liquid remained. To survive, Diez told them, they would now have to drink their own urine. They began to urinate in plastic baggies, but the liquid was too hot to drink. So they dug down beneath the topsoil and found cool earth and mixed this with the liquid. Diez was so dehy-drated that his body could produce no urine at all. He drank the urine of one of the men from Tijan.

This, however, was not enough to sustain him. He sagged as they carried him along, his arms draped across their shoulders. Finally, he told them, "I can't go on." Far off in the distance, he knew, was a white water tank and the Indians' houses. They couldn't see it, but he knew it was there.

"Go that way," he told them.

Some of the men wanted to stay and wait for the temperature to drop. Privately, Guadalupe said to Delfino, "Let's go. If we stay here, we're going to die." So the group left Diez lying there and walked on in the direction he had pointed them.

Diez's mother had always told him to think of happy moments when in a hard spot. He was now going to die. So he remembered his girlfriends. Rosanna, Silvia, Iris. He remembered diving in the river with Diana and drinking beer with his friends on the street corner back in Chocamán.

People who are dying in the desert often jettison money, gold, anything of great temporal value, as, without water, these become absurdly unimportant. One desert wanderer once told how he began to imagine an entire monetary system based on drops of water, so valuable does the liquid become to those lost in the desert.

From his pocket, Diez took a wad of three thousand dollars and threw it in the air. What good was money to him now? The bills fluttered and settled around him. Diez wanted the people who found his corpse to put the money to good use. He lay down and placed his cap over his face and passed out. He lay there for a long time.

The six men, meanwhile, stumbled on. They'd been on the desert floor now for a day and a half of sun. The woman was dead. Diez, with whom they trusted with their lives, was dying. They were out of water and had drunk their own urine. Their skin boiled, and they were near tears. Waves of chills swept over them and made them shudder. Their lips were torn and no one could talk. No one cared anymore about the dollars he was going to make.

Delfino fainted once, or maybe twice. There was no escape from the heat. He felt like screaming. In a frenzy, he ripped off his shirt and pants. The men began to separate. Delfino and Guadalupe walked on with the man from Guatemala. Guadalupe fell. He imagined that they would die and no one would know what had become of them. He wanted to be buried in his village. He wondered why he'd ever come.

Somehow, he pulled himself to his feet. As he did, he saw that Guatemala had kept walking and now veered away from the direction Diez had pointed them. Guadalupe stood and whistled at him.

"Come back, Guatemala," he called. "Come back."

"No," Guatemala said, "I'm heading on."

They never saw Guatemala again.

Their whistles, though, animated the three men from Tijan, who were now scattered about the desert floor. Believing someone had seen something, one of them scaled a paloverde and, finally, spotted a house in the distance.

"Casa," he yelled and pointed.

They made for it.

The house belonged to an Indian couple, who were startled to see five ragged Mexicans stumble out of the desert.

"Agua," they said. "Agua."

Then they collapsed in the shade under the enormous salt cedar tree in front of the couple's house. For one hundred dollars, the Indian couple filled their jugs with water and gave them bread and a few sodas. The kid who'd spotted the house broke down and sobbed.

As this was going on, Diez lay under the sun a couple hundred yards back. At one point he picked himself up and tried to walk but could not go far and collapsed again, facedown in the dirt. He passed out.

He woke to voices calling, "Diez, Diez." He raised his lucky *SA* hat and waved it listlessly, then his arm fell to the ground. The next thing he knew, they were over him, pouring water on him and plying him with soda. His skin was green, and his eyes were deep in their sockets. He had soiled himself and he was crying and couldn't talk.

The previous day, an hour after Diez and his group had left the woman's body, a Mexican woman waved down Border Patrol officers on Federal

Route 21. Angelina Contreras told agents that her sister-in-law had died in the desert.

A couple miles east of the highway, Border Patrol agents retrieved the corpse of twenty-nine-year-old Herminia Fuentes Sánchez. The next day, an autopsy by the Pima County medical examiner's office found that she died of heat stroke. Her body was flown home a few days after that, and she is buried in Cosaltepec. Contreras, her friend, and Tavo, the coyote trainee, were deported to Veracruz.

No one ever knew what became of Guatemala. Diez and the others figure the Border Patrol picked him up, as they were near the reservation houses when he split from the group. No one knew his name. The Border Patrol reports no deaths of men around that time, but the desert has many hiding places.

The following October, the Border Patrol reported that 346 migrants died crossing the border during the previous twelve months. Of these, 139 died in the Arizona desert.

Diez survived. The soda and water gave him cramps, but the cramps shot him full of life. Thus revived, he was able to walk under his own power to the Indian houses. He paid a Tohono O'odham Indian to take what remained of his group to Tucson in a pickup truck, stacked on top of each other. From there Diez had them driven to Phoenix, where a woman named María Elena ran a fleet of cars and an underground travel business for illegal immigrants. She brought them to a house, gave them food and toothbrushes. A few hours later, one of her drivers took the group to Los Angeles.

Diez stayed in Phoenix for a month working landscaping, fearing that police would be looking for him back home in Chocamán. One night, he saw on the news that 248 people had died crossing the border already that year. A month later, he bought a DVD player and went home to Chocamán.

For Guadalupe Cocotle and Delfino Juárez, the trip ended on a garage floor in Bell, a small working-class suburb of Los Angeles that is now almost all Mexican. They found work alongside Guadalupe's brothers installing carpets and wooden floors in suburban homes for weekly cash payments that amounted to something near minimum wage. The business owner, Porfirio Quiñónez, once an undocumented immigrant himself, gave them his garage floor on which to sleep. After a while he began charging them for the privilege. Without a car, or a license, illegally in the country and not speaking English, they were more or less captive workers of Mr. Quiñónez and his carpet business.

For Delfino Juárez, that garage floor in Bell was the end of a trip that had taken him from the freezing potato fields of Xocotla and his father's drunken binges, to the jobsites of Mexico City and through the Arizona desert in which he almost died.

"I told myself, 'I'll go work to see if I can make some cash,'" he said one night several months after the ordeal in the desert, as we drove down Sunset Boulevard in Los Angeles, having eaten hamburgers at In N' Out. "So many guys come here and quickly do well. How many years have I been in Mexico City, and I haven't done anything? I'm going to try it and see how I do. Hopefully I won't die."

❧

Two months later, on the Tohono O'odham reservation in the dead heat of August, a thin boy with a black baseball cap sat on a rock not far from where the woman died. He dug up the cans of corn and sardines he had buried and discovered they hadn't spoiled. Around him sat another group of seven would-be immigrants, heading to Los Angeles and counting the dollars they would make. This time none were women. As they ate, in his crackly voice and dry laugh, he told them the story of how the heavyset woman he'd known only as "Señora" had died, and how he'd had to drink another man's urine, thrown his money in the air, and almost expired himself.

"She died," he said, "right over there," pointing to the spot.

Chapter Six

The Beautiful Insanity of Enrique Fuentes

T here were several reasons why the opera *Pagliacci* was an appropriate first production for the Tijuana Opera Company, a year after going out on its own.

To María Teresa Riqué, the company's administrator, the reason was simple. The company didn't have much money, yet needed to build an audience.

"The music in *Pagliacci* is very beautiful, and the scenery and costumes aren't complicated to make," said Riqué, one chaotic morning a few days before the performance.

But like Tijuana, *Pagliacci* also had grit. Its plot revolved around a traveling troupe of clowns playing in a small village in southern Italy. Canio, the troupe's leader, is told by an evil hunchback in his troupe that his wife has fallen in love with a man from the village. Alone, Canio sings the aria that made the opera famous—"Vesti la giubba"—in which he laments that he must go on stage to make people laugh, while behind his mask of white paint he is in tears. In the next act, Canio and his wife perform for the village a light-hearted farce about marital infidelity. Art and life collide. During the performance, Canio can stand it no more. He pulls a knife and kills his wife. As her lover comes from the crowd to her defense, Canio kills him, too. The hunchback, who alone is pleased at the bodies all around him, closes the curtain with, "The comedy is finished."

An added advantage to *Pagliacci*, from the new opera company's point of view, was that few operas are so deeply imbedded in popular culture. Usually people who know nothing of opera at least know of the "clown opera." It was one of the operas Chicago gangster Al Capone most adored. Scads of pizzerias and Italian restaurants are named for *Pagliacci*. The phrase "the show must go on," and Smokey Robinson and the Miracles's "Tears of a Clown," are rooted in Canio's lament. Even the "Smile now, Cry later" clown faces common in Latino gang art are distant cousins to *Pagliacci*.

Pagliacci presented the melodrama of lower-class life as high art. Tijuana had been the quintessential border town, the seedy city of the working classes who'd come from all over Mexico; the city was, in fact, the setting for a good many tales of betrayal and murder. But Tijuana had also evolved beyond what the world knew of it. Amid its honking hodgepodge of shantytowns, its mansions, and its McDonald's, was a vibrant center for theater, painting, video, music, and, lately, for opera. So within *Pagliacci* could be glimpsed the old and the new faces of Tijuana.

Tijuana, with its constant flow of drugs and immigrants, was one of the great centers of Mexican corridos—bloody ballads about a real event or person. *Pagliacci*, as it happened, was the opera version of a corrido. The opera's composer, Ruggiero Leoncavallo, was the son of a judge in Calabria, Italy, in the mid-1800s. The judge told his son of a murder trial he'd overseen involving a troupe of actors. Like any corrido writer, Leoncavallo transformed fact into art, embellishing it with jealousy, sadness, and rage.

This, in turn, was what made *Pagliacci* one of the great examples of *verismo* opera, and verismo was yet another reason why *Pagliacci* was apt for Tijuana. Verismo was a short-lived school of opera in the late nineteenth century that focused on the lives of workers and the lower classes. It turned away from fables about Nordic gods and aimed to imbue opera with realism, with violence, raw passion, and the grime of life. Characters in verismo operas were not mountain kings or princesses; they were laborers, prostitutes, and peasants—the very people who had formed Tijuana.

For all these reasons, *Pagliacci* was an opera that seemed to belong to Tijuana. This was strange, because the city had never been meant for anything as delicate as opera. It was the Mexican city farthest from Mexico

City, and thus the country's elites deemed it least likely to forge any culture at all. Tijuana was where gringos went to indulge their basest desires. It brayed with rumpled shantytowns, traffic-jammed intersections, cripples selling gum, and shiny shopping malls. On the tourist drag of Avenida Revolución, *narcocorridos*, techno, and heavy-metal music blasted from strip bars as barkers attacked each passing tourist with promises of "no cover" and "lots of girls." Squat white maquiladoras—assembly plants—churned out televisions and more televisions. Tijuana has few tall old trees, but no end of yapping graffiti, and it all got hard to take after a while.

Yet in the midst of all this, opera had taken root and grown as an alternative, underground music, a refuge from the ruckus and jangle, and within its emergence was the story of how the city was changing. It happened because a few people set themselves, like rebel guerrillas, against the city's gale winds of commerce and tinseled pop culture. Amid the babble, they searched for harmony, exactitude, and discipline. They found it in opera. They nurtured it until it forged for Tijuana a soft soul where once had been only an economic combine. Achieving that required such passion and torrid pursuit that their stories came to resemble the very operas they adored. So in the end, the unexpected city of Tijuana could produce not only opera, but stories worthy of operas.

One of these people was Enrique Fuentes. Enrique is a soft-spoken man with a shy smile, a bit jowly in the cheeks, clean-shaven, with black hair graying at the edges. He lived over in the city's Colonia Libertad— a rough neighborhood where *Pagliacci* could have been set, in the hills wedged against the United States of America. Enrique thought the opera company's choice of *Pagliacci* important for one entirely different reason: the opera had a large chorus, with room enough, perhaps, for him.

Up to that point in his life, nothing about Enrique Fuentes had led anyone to think him a man capable of mad obsessions or magnificent dreams. On the contrary, most people would have described him as even tempered, stolid, and hardly given to outbursts of anger, passion, or hilarity. Now forty-six, Enrique had grown up in Tijuana, the youngest of eight brothers and sisters. His mother was a housewife, and his father had held a number of button-down professional jobs, one of which was as an accountant in a lumberyard. As a boy he'd been a loner and hadn't gone out much as a teenager. He'd finished a few years of college, meandered through a variety of courses, then dropped it all, not finding much that interested him. Through a sister, he'd found a job as a bilingual teacher's aide at an elementary school in San Diego. This is common on the border; thousands of Tijuanans cross every morning to work in the United States, then return home at night. The job he found didn't require a teacher's credential, so Enrique took it, and this became his life's path. For the next twenty years he commuted across the border into San Diego to work.

The Fuentes family had grown up in Colonia Libertad, next to the border. Most of Enrique's siblings were teachers, like Enrique himself. Not one played a musical instrument. Nor, before Enrique went off on his opera thing, had any of the Fuentes clan professed anything beyond a casual interest in classical music, much less opera. Enrique himself had never sung a note, and in his life he had purchased no more than three or four records.

But then he had attended a performance of *Rappacini's Daughter* at the San Diego Opera. A couple years later, in 1994, he took a forty-day trip through Europe with a backpack and a friend. It was the longest trip a Fuentes had taken—not counting Enrique's brother, Pepe's, service in the U.S. Army in Vietnam. "I wanted to get to know the Old World," Enrique said. He and his friend visited Paris, Italy, and Spain, but it was Vienna that awed Enrique most.

Tijuana is young, rootless, and anarchic. Vienna captivated Enrique because it was none of that. Operas were performed almost daily; he stumbled upon classical music concerts in parks, plazas, and museums. Enrique and his friend stayed in a small hotel overlooking an alley lined with old European homes. They saw a symphony perform Strauss in a palace and visited the house in Salzburg where Mozart was born. Enrique walked streets that were hundreds of years old, listening over and over to a tape of *The Blue Danube*.

It's not quite correct to say that he returned a changed man, but something was different. He had seen the world outside Tijuana, and it was so deliciously rich. So when, shortly after returning from Europe, he accidentally tuned in a weekly radio show called "Invitation to the Opera" hosted by a man named Manuel Laborín, Enrique didn't turn the dial. He counts it as the moment that started him down the path to what would happen later.

Heavyset, sixty-one-year-old Manuel Laborín is Tijuana's opera guru. An accountant by profession, Laborín lives for opera. The walls of his home in Tijuana's Playas neighborhood are tiled with photographs of the great Greek soprano Maria Callas. His closets are filled with opera videos. His pit bull is named Verdi.

For many years, Tijuana itself had nothing to offer the opera fan. So Laborín fashioned an operatic cocoon for himself, collecting records, then videos and compact discs of operas. From Tijuana, he could tune in U.S. public radio and television stations. For years he never missed the Saturday morning broadcasts of the Metropolitan Opera in New York over a classical radio station in San Diego.

"It was like going to mass," he said.

His accounting business grew, and this Laborín views as a happy event primarily because it allowed him to depart Tijuana to see live opera in San Diego and Los Angeles, occasionally in San Francisco and New York, and even Europe twice.

In 1993, at the behest of tiny public *Radio Tecnológico*, Laborín created the city's first opera radio program. "Invitation to the Opera" was where Tijuana's opera education began. Between arias, Laborín explained opera plots and terminology; he told anecdotes of how one singer had taken sick before this performance, and how Puccini had died before completing *Turandot*. He thrilled when calls came from taxi drivers and *piperos*—the truckers who take water to the shantytowns. The show was a little like wartime resistance radio in occupied territory. It let opera fans know that, appearances to the contrary, amid the broken sidewalks and concrete rivers, other hearts warmed to Verdi and Puccini.

Enrique Fuentes was one of those who, after hearing the show for the first time, never missed it. He would record Laborín's shows and sing along with them in his car as he waited to cross the U.S. border every morning. He purchased the laser disc of *Aida*, which enthralled him. Laser discs, precursors to DVDs, cost seventy dollars apiece, so Enrique could only buy one a month; only at Tower Records in San Diego could he find a decent selection. Nevertheless, he consumed opera laser discs as voraciously as his budget allowed. He began attending the San Diego Opera. The second opera he bought on laser disc was *Turandot*, and it became his favorite.

One day, Enrique tuned in to hear Laborín giving away a video to anyone who could name three Australian sopranos. He remembers being surprised that Australia, a land he associated only with being very far away, had produced any sopranos the world would know. But he'd just read the liner notes to a record that, by chance, named three Australian sopranos: Joan Sutherland, Nellie Melba, and . . . well, Enrique can't remember who that third Australian soprano was. But with liner notes in hand, he called the show and a few minutes later heard Laborín announce over the air that in the entire city of Tijuana the only person who knew the names of three Australian sopranos was Mr. Enrique Fuentes in Colonia Libertad.

By this time, opera was moving into Enrique's life like a lover. "I felt I was entering another world," he said.

Opera was such a lush, soulful place. It was far from Tijuana, a city he loved but whose jagged edges wearied him. And he felt it a shame, having discovered this beautiful thing, that he couldn't share it with anyone.

But we need to back up a bit first, to fully tell Tijuana's tale.

Several years before, on a balmy night in January of 1991, an Aeromexico airplane touched down at Tijuana International Airport. On board were four Russian musicians: Vladimir Fateev played flute; Sergei Maruschak, French horn; Piotr Turkin, bassoon; and Vladimir Goltzman, a clarinetist. They had been the wind section in a chamber orchestra in Moscow. Now the Soviet Union was collapsing, and the state-controlled economy was coming down with it. The musicians were getting out while they could.

Waiting for them at the Tijuana airport that night was a man named Juan Echevarría, who was trying to organize the first orchestra in Baja California. Echevarría was an astronomer by profession. He had moved to Ensenada, fifty miles south of Tijuana on the Baja California coast, in the mid-1980s to work at Mexico's premier observatory, which is on a mountain near the coast. Echevarría had also spent his life studying singing, and his wife, Encarnación Vázquez, is one of Mexico's great mezzo-sopranos.

When the couple moved to Ensenada, Baja California had no classical music. Finding this unacceptable, Echevarría formed a choir and called it Pro Música. Now he wanted an orchestra to go with it. An orchestra, Echevarría felt, would do more than accompany his choir. It would also bring talented musicians to the area; they could then teach young people. This, in turn, would help pollinate a musical culture in Baja California.

He found, however, that Mexican musicians didn't dare move from the center of the country where they had careers—from Mexico City and Guadalajara—to the musical wasteland of Baja California for an orchestra that didn't yet exist. No matter. Echevarría had really been looking east all along.

The socialist bloc had been in its death throes since the fall of the Berlin Wall in 1989. During the summer of 1991, a coup by Communist hardliners in Moscow attempted to knock Mikhael Gorbachev from power. An uprising of Muscovite citizenry foiled the coup, and with that the Soviet Union stumbled to its final days, leaving Russia in shambles and the world to ponder what the cataclysm meant for the future.

What it meant had long been clear to Juan Echevarría. The crumbling of the socialist bloc meant great musicians leaving the former communist countries for the West, and the United States in particular, desperate for work and stability.

"If the gringos are getting them, why shouldn't we?" Echevarría said. "I knew they were going to come cheap and extremely talented. The trick was to take advantage of this exodus and bring it to Mexico."

Echevarría found a young director named Eduardo García Barrios, who had just returned from ten years studying conducting in Moscow, where he'd directed a chamber orchestra. Echevarría offered García Barrios the directorship of an orchestra that didn't exist. García Barrios was an audacious fellow. It seemed to him an advantage that Baja California was the only state in Mexico without a professional orchestra, for it gave him a chance to show his mettle.

García Barrios left a secure job as director of chamber music at the National Autonomous University in Mexico City, the center of classical music in Mexico, and set out for the cultural wilderness of Baja California. He called his former musicians in Russia and offered them jobs: a small salary, plus lodging in the homes of the orchestra's patrons in Ensenada, with Gigante Supermarket providing coupons for food.

The Russians had to find Baja California on a map. When they saw it was near the sea, near California, that was good enough. "When we arrived, it seemed like paradise, after the cold of January in Moscow," said oboist Boris Glouzman, who arrived a week after the first four musicians.

Thus it was that the first professional orchestra in the history of Baja California came from Russia speaking no Spanish. Through that spring, more Russian musicians trickled in. By the time of the attempted coup in Moscow, a crew of fifteen Russians was in Baja California. The Orchestra of Baja California performed its inaugural concert that October.

For the next six years, the Orchestra of Baja California remained an entirely Russian ensemble, directed by a Mexican. Then it moved from Ensenada to Tijuana to have better access to the city's wealthy benefactors. This was how classical music came to Tijuana, and the city took from someplace else what it needed to jump-start a musical culture.

But this it had always done. Tijuana is a city from someplace else.

It was a coastal desert outpost surrounded by rolling hills until the 1920s. Then the United States prohibited alcohol. Hollywood types suddenly needed a place to drink, gamble, and screw. U.S. businessmen came down and built bars and casinos, which at first only employed Americans. As Mexicans were allowed to work in the racetrack and bars, the outpost began to grow.

Tijuana's dependence on California never fundamentally changed. Until a road from Mexicali was built in 1950, the only practical way to enter

Tijuana was via San Diego. Pesos were unheard of in Tijuana until the 1960s, and not in wide use until the 1970s. For many years San Diego provided the city with water and power. Before the early 1980s, many residents did their grocery shopping in San Diego because Tijuana had no supermarket.

In the 1970s, the American- and Japanese-owned maquiladoras began to replace strip bars and curio shops at the economic base of the city. By 2000, Tijuana produced more televisions than any city in the world: 20 million a year, according to one estimate. The plants employed tens of thousands of people, who came from Mexico's interior and turned Tijuana into a global-economy boomtown.

With Southern California so close, Tijuana channeled torrents of illegal drugs that came from Mexico and Colombia. The country's most notorious drug cartel emerged here, run by the Arellano Félix brothers, handsome and bloody middle-class boys who came up from Mazatlán. Meanwhile, the city was the passageway for the Mexican mass exodus into the United States. Legions of men would tramp through the city every day, lining its hills in the afternoon ready to run across the border when night fell.

In 1920, Tijuana had been a village of eleven hundred. Eighty years later city officials could only guess the population neared two million people. There were entire neighborhoods populated by people from different Mexican states—Oaxaca, Sinaloa, Sonora, Mexico City. Yet the federal government in Mexico City kept Tijuana's budget minuscule. So the city could neither control growth nor provide services for the newcomers. Shantytowns popped up on the ever-extending edge of town. "Cartonlandia"—Cardboardland, an awesome shantytown on the bed of the Tijuana River near the border—was almost a tourist attraction itself.

To the bureaucrats in Mexico City, and to most of Mexico, Tijuana was an ugly embarrassment, a virtually American city, and hardly Mexican at all. Government bureaucrats required extra salary to come staff federal agencies in Tijuana. In one sense, they were right. Tijuana resembled the global economy it depended on—an assault of random noises and images. "A modern-art painting" is how one Tijuanan described the city.

Yet Tijuana had a beauty that none of the country's exquisite colonial towns possessed. Young and far from Mexico City, Tijuana was free of history and tradition. It was close to California, the wealthiest U.S. state. This created better jobs and educational opportunities in Tijuana than elsewhere in Mexico. As a crossroads, its people were open to new ideas. To Tijuana came the hardworking poor escaping the limits and decaying economies of their hometowns. Many of these folks intended to sneak into the United States; but they found lives in Tijuana and stayed.

"A more egalitarian society formed here. It's part of what makes Baja California different," said David Pinera, who is a professor of Tijuana history. "It was a society in the process of forming, a society in which the culture of hard work predominates and less the culture of privilege. There aren't the closed social circles. The rich man here is someone who came from the bottom. His father didn't give him any leg up. He was a waiter or street vendor and made it according to his own efforts."

Thus a relatively large middle class could form. In the 1980s, banks, insurance companies, and auto dealers began to arrive to serve the middle classes. Tijuana then got its first supermarkets and shopping malls. Moreover, middle-class denizen naturally didn't want their children exposed to strippers, shantytowns, drunk gringos, and naked-lady playing cards. They wanted music lessons, ballet, and art classes for their children. So a constituency for a more evolved city was born.

It took years to get to this point, because if Tijuana had no history, neither did it have much arts heritage. People came here to enter the United States or make their cash and return home. No one was from Tijuana, so few people cared to make it a better place. Artists were considered talented only to the extent they could make a plaster piggy bank or paint a matador on black velvet.

But by the 1990s, that was changing. One element in this change was the theater known as the Tijuana Cultural Center. The CECUT, as it's known, is an enormous ball in the middle of the city and the finest performing-arts venue in northwest Mexico. Tourism Ministry planners off in Mexico City built it in 1982 to attract gringo tourists and put a dignified face on this grungy gateway to Mexico. Their minds danced with visions of buses packed with rich Americans crossing the border to watch Ballet Folklórico and orchestras from Guadalajara or London. At no time did those federal planners imagine any Tijuana arts groups performing in the Tijuana Cultural Center. What, after all, did Tijuana know about art?

But CECUT failed as a tourist attraction. Few gringos could navigate the city's maze of streets. Years after the theater opened, Americans still viewed Tijuana as more a place to catch syphilis than a Chekhov play.

Tijuana instead grew into its bulbous theater like a boy into his older brother's clothes. In the early 1990s, Pedro Ochoa, a local government lawyer, was named CECUT director. Ochoa expropriated CECUT from the clutches of Mexico City bureaucrats. CECUT invigorated Tijuana's arts groups with new funding and performance space. For most of the 1990s, CECUT presented little that wasn't homegrown.

This was all part of Mexico's larger liberation from its center during the 1990s. The PRI and its Mexico City bureaucracy had increasing trouble controlling the country the way they had for decades. In 1989, Baja California was the first Mexican state to elect a governor who wasn't from the PRI; Tijuana also elected its first non-PRI mayor.

The north's economy had always pulled Mexico along with it. In the 1990s, it emerged as a force in Mexican cultural life for the first time. The economy gave more northern kids the luxury of studying what they loved and not what was sure to make them money. Binational agreements allowed them to enroll at University of Texas, El Paso or San Diego State University. Young northerners not only studied music or literature more easily, they had a better chance at finding work in those fields. From the north, too, came the country's first regional literature. By the late 1990s, a crew of northern writers—Daniel Sada, Eduardo Antonio Parra, David Toscana, Luis Humberto Crosthwaite, Elmer Mendoza—drew their stories around immigration, drug smuggling, and the border's cross-cultural stew. They were the first Mexican authors to make their careers outside Mexico City, which they visited only on book tours.

As the 1990s ended, a leader in these changes was Tijuana, the Mexican city farthest from Mexico City. A city perennially under construction, it was used to drawing on ideas and influences from all over. CECUT became the city's arts school and offered classes in music, dance, and art history. Manuel Laborín's radio show was growing more popular. The all-Russian Orchestra of Baja California was headquartered at CECUT and playing regularly around the state.

As Juan Echevarría had hoped, the Russians began teaching young people at workshops. Their workshops were held mostly in sign language because the Russians still spoke little Spanish and no one in Tijuana spoke Russian. Nonetheless, these classes were the state's first organized classical-music instruction. In 1997, the Russians' workshops were formalized into the state's first music conservatory. At that point the Russians began to find other work. But by then, a musical seed had been planted from which everything else was to grow.

As it happened, Tijuana's evolution during these years resembled that of Enrique Fuentes. Opera had grown into more than just an interest for Enrique; it was becoming the one important thing in his life. Manuel Laborín held a series of talks on opera history. Sometimes two people would come to these talks, sometimes fifteen people attended; but one of them was always Enrique Fuentes. He read the books Laborín recommended. He learned the plots of operas and the difference between a soprano and a mezzo-soprano. Knowledge fanned his interest, and, when he had the money, Enrique would scurry off to Tower Records in San Diego in sweet anticipation of another laser disc. Soon Enrique was attending every performance of the San Diego Opera in the twenty-dollar standing-room section.

Nothing in the life of Enrique Fuentes had moved him the way opera did now. The sweeping music, the majestic scenery, the romance and melodrama—it all seeped far down inside him and awoke a giddiness, a bliss, a sense of wonder.

One Saturday night, on a whim, Enrique invited over some friends to watch the opera *Carmen* on laser disc. This went well. He decided to do it again and then again. In time, he turned Saturday nights into Opera

Saturdays, and before long, Enrique's Opera Saturdays were events that his friends didn't miss. If he was showing *Madame Butterfly*, they bought Japanese food. Enrique bought a thirty-six-inch television and shifted Opera Saturdays to the garage at his mother's house, which was bigger than his living room.

Opera Saturdays went on for more than a year. Meanwhile, a more grandiose idea germinated and took shape in Enrique's mind. It was only the vaguest notion at first, something that said, "a place for opera." But in those long hours in his car at the border crossing, the idea knocked around his brain. He added flesh to it as he watched his laser disc of *Turandot* again and again and as more friends attended each Opera Saturday. He imagined a quiet place, a refuge from Tijuana's chatter, an opera Shangri-La, with dim amber lights. He could present recitals by local singers and musicians. He could serve coffee and cake. And every Saturday night would be Opera Saturday.

He took the first irrevocable step a few months later. In a San Diego thrift store, he saw a hutch and credenza on sale for $375. They were elegant, dark brown pieces that fit snugly into Enrique's vision of his place for opera. Still, $375 seemed a lot to spend for an idea he wasn't sure he could pull off. Two weeks later, he returned and found the pieces selling now for $250. He hesitated. Then, as he stood there, a clerk walked up and cut the price to $150. That seemed omen enough. He bought them and trucked them to his mother's garage.

With two big pieces of furniture to his name, there was no going back. He began frequenting thrift stores. He bought a few tables and lamps with amber shades at secondhand shops in Tijuana. A friend gave him fifteen folding chairs. He bought a thrashed old piano. Before long, his mother's garage was packed as tightly as Enrique's imagination with the details of his opera café. One day, he said to himself, "It's time to do something with it."

Finding a home for his opera café turned out to be harder than he had imagined. He looked at several places around town. The owners thought the idea cockeyed; an opera venue might be noisy and disrupt their businesses nearby. They all said no. He was about to sign a lease for one place in an upscale shopping mall on the east side of town. But when he went to sign the deal, the landlady didn't show and never called to explain why.

Which is how, after weeks of searching, Enrique Fuentes found himself one day peering through the darkened windows of a concrete-block building on Fifth Street, around the corner from his boyhood home where his mother still lived.

The building belonged to Eugenio Romero, a construction worker, whose father had run a pharmacy out of it for many years. Romero knew nothing of opera, but he saw no problem with an opera café if Enrique could make the $450 monthly rent. And thus Enrique Fuentes's dream took root near where he'd grown up, two hundred yards from the steel wall dividing the United States and Mexico, in the pug-nosed neighborhood known as Colonia Libertad.

Colonial Liberdad formed in the 1930s as the city's first neighborhood. Today it drapes langorously across steep hills east of Tijuana's border crossing. The neighborhood is today a jangle of abandoned cars, shiny SUVs, two-story homes and taco stands, medical clinics and mechanics shops, Internet cafes and Pentecostal churches—all defaced with graffiti and shoved together in noisy conviviality.

Crammed up against the United States, the Libertad was where the poor from across Mexico landed when they came to Tijuana. Thus it embodied the city's essence. It produced the city's scariest street gangs, several great boxers, three mayors, and many of the city's successful entrepreneurs.

Many Libertad residents commuted to work in San Diego. They saw another political system every day they crossed into the United States. Years before Mexico's political change, working-class Libertad was a stronghold of the aristocratic National Action Party (PAN) because the party was the ruling PRI's only serious opponent in Tijuana.

Libertad's proximity to the United States also meant that its residents could use their smarts to jury-rig economic opportunity into new ways of making a living. The plaster figure industry started in Colonia Libertad and was the border's first handcraft, producing statues of Mickey Mouse and sleeping Mexicans to sell to tourists. Meanwhile, every afternoon,

Enrique Fuentes in his Café de la Ópera.

immigrants flowed through the neighborhood like a river of money. Entire Libertad clans learned to smuggle immigrants. Families discovered, too, that they could sell burritos, coffee, candy, maps, tampons, and other necessities to these weary travelers. That lasted until 1993, when the U.S. Border Patrol dammed the Libertad's river of money with a fourteen-mile brown steel wall from the Pacific Ocean east along the border and immigrants found other places to cross.

But the neighborhood's scrappy reputation didn't bother Enrique Fuentes as he rented that place on Fifth Street and busied himself with his opera café. He held a sing-along fundraiser to refinish his piano. He bought a secondhand stereo and, from a Tijuana bazaar, another television, a sixty-inch Magnavox. On a gilded frame he attached red velvet curtains and gold tassels. In this, he encased his sixty-inch Magnavox, giving it velvet curtains just like those across the stage at the Metropolitan in New York City, only smaller. At thrift stores, he found a plastic Viking helmet and a lyre. On the walls of his café he placed album covers—two dollars apiece at San Diego thrift stores—emblazoned with the faces of famous opera stars dressed as princesses and kings. His nephew knew computers, so Enrique added an Internet café to make money for the business. By then, he had invested five thousand dollars.

On July 10, 2001, in the middle of Colonia Libertad, Enrique Fuentes opened his funky, secondhand opera Shangri-La and called it El Café de la Ópera—just like the cafés in Vienna.

He figured opera fans had to be out there somewhere. He remembered Manuel Laborín telling him of the taxi drivers and piperos calling his program. Enrique had met other Tijuana opera fans at San Diego Opera performances. Colonia Libertad was so rough that in the minds of Tijuanans it resided somewhere near the Bronx, the New York borough synonymous in Mexico with urban barbarism. But Enrique felt at home and protected there. He knew the barber and the doctor down the street, and his mother lived around the corner.

"People who like opera will come," he told himself.

Nevertheless, he had to admit it was an adventure, perhaps the first in his life, that opera had led him to. *Aida, Turandot,* and the rest, the European trip, Manuel Laborín, the laser discs, the San Diego Opera, this restless search beyond Tijuana for what was precious in life. He often compared it to a virus that he didn't resist, but nurtured, and he luxuriated in it as it spread within him. He knew what he was doing was kooky and consuming, and for those reasons it thrilled him and compelled him onward.

Once he had finished, and the café stood around him, this mild-mannered man would look at his creation, at the plastic Viking helmet and the amber lamps, at the miniature curtains of red velvet over the sixty-inch Magnavox, at the old piano and the album covers with opera stars dressed as princes and peasant girls, and he would chuckle, shake his head at this shape of Tijuana music to come, run his hand through his hair, and quietly say, "What a beautiful . . . insanity."

As Enrique Fuentes was creating his opera experiment, not far away, atop an imposing hill, lived the ghost of Tijuana music's past.

The hill, towering out of Colonia Libertad, is the city's tallest. Scaling it amounts to a death march. By the end of the climb the knees wobble, and calves turn to rubber. You arrive light-headed, sweat pouring off your body.

At the top of this hill is a neighborhood of small concrete houses and corner stores. One house stands out. It is beaten and gray, with the exception of its front wall, which is painted bright yellow. On it is spray-painted the number 475, in enormous fire-engine red, as if the owner wished no one should miss it. Yet no one visits. The yard is bald, inhabited only by a large pirul tree with branches that dip to the ground.

Héctor Seemann lives here. For forty years, Héctor Seemann was Tijuana's only music teacher. At Lázaro Cárdenas Junior High School, he taught music to thousands of Tijuana children. He carried the torch of musical culture, dim as it was, through the city's Dark Ages. During these years, he composed two operas and several orchestral works. He gave private classes to young singers. He retired in 1991, just as the Russians and Juan Echevarría and García Barrios were beginning to nurture an appreciation of classical music in the state.

Seemann is sixty-nine and has diabetes. He never married and shares his property with several cats. He lives on a small government pension that doesn't allow for much in the way of food or medicine. He can barely walk. He hobbles about in a thin bathrobe, from which protrudes a plump tummy. He ties his long gray hair in a ponytail, and his white beard grows like an untended garden. Seemann's house is so torn up that he prefers to accept visitors in his front yard. He says he's bitter at ending this way.

"I've had no intellectual support, no material support. I'm not recognized," he says. "I have an opera fully written and orchestrated. It's a grandiose opera, like Verdi's. I've looked for people to produce my work, but it didn't happen. One maestro told me, 'We have to wait until there are musicians with souls capable of playing it.'"

Only two snippets of his compositions have ever been performed. He rails at government-paid artists and culture officials who stood in his way and at composers and musicians who've introduced dissonance into music. He no longer gives private classes, he says, and only one of his former students ever visits. Seemann yells at people walking on a vacant lot next to his house, which apparently is his property as well, threatening them with jail and ending his tirades with "goddamn Mexican jerks." Héctor Seemann feels his country betrayed him.

"I deny being Mexican," he says. "I'm going to die of hunger."

His opera, *Salvatierra*, is about a Roman Catholic priest sent to convert Baja California's Indians. Another opera, *The Count of Penaval*, is the tragic love story between a woman from the Yucatán and a Spanish count. He spent fifteen years composing these operas. If they are ever performed, each will last four and a half hours with no intermission. Another choral work he's arranged is for six hundred children; it's of arias written by other composers in eighteen languages, including Russian and a Mexican Indian language.

It's unclear whether Héctor Seemann was an important composer. A CD of a small San Diego college orchestra performing a waltz and an excerpt of *Salvatierra* shows he was competent, that what's on paper at least made sense, as sometimes his conversation does not. What is clear is that his great musical dreams never materialized. He recounts the story of a great pianist who told him his work should be played along side that of Liszt and Berlitz. Then he interrupts himself to yell at a young mother and child walking on the vacant lot adjacent to his home. "Hey, lady, this is private property! I've got twelve people already in jail for doing what you're doing. Don't teach your daughter to be a criminal!"

He treats his diabetes with water left in the sun for four hours, prescribed to him by a doctor who lost her medical license, but who, he insists, has cured twelve people of AIDS. He says he's converted to the African Yoruba religion and is rewriting the Mexican national anthem. "Mexicanos, bola de pendejos . . . Un cabrón en cada hijo te dio (Mexicans, bunch of idiots . . . Heaven gave you a jerk in every son)." "That's how it starts," he says.

A good many Tijuanans view Seemann's life today as the sad end to an ignored talent who dedicated himself to music at a time when Tijuana didn't want to hear it. His bad luck was to arrive before the city made a place for classical music. Now he is living out his last days in oblivion, worn out by relentless inattention, and alternating between esoterica and rage.

Yet his story may be a little more complicated. There's also a feeling around town that in the early years, Tijuana had so little classical music that townspeople, intimidated by "culture," which they didn't recognize but knew they didn't possess, applauded anything. The city's few classical musicians got used to it and held themselves to gradually lower standards. Artists began to feel they shouldn't dirty themselves with base self-promotion. The masses should know that four-and-a-half-hour operas with no intermission were the very definition of culture, and a composer shouldn't have to leave his piano to remind people of this fact.

Some in town believe that Seemann's music never found its place because he never went into the world to interest people in it. When it didn't come to him, according to this point of view, Héctor Seemann closed himself off in his hilltop house, and there he remains, hermit and artifact, railing at the world.

But as Tijuana was maturing, this attitude was changing. Musicians now courted their audiences, instead of regally expecting to be found and adored.

The new attitude's main proponent in town was María Teresa Riqué, a short, handsome woman of cheerful energy who had chanced to become Tijuana's main classical music promoter.

Her family was housing one of the Russians years ago when Juan Echevarría and Eduardo García Barrios asked her to become administrator of the new Orchestra of Baja California. A public-school English teacher,

Tere played guitar, piano, and cello, and dreamed of becoming a professional musician. Her daughter, Aiko, is the city's finest pianist and her husband, Manuel Yamada, is a nuclear physicist whose hobby is tuning and refurbishing pianos. Tere Riqué knew nothing about orchestra management. She took the job to be near the music.

As orchestra manager, she would sit enthralled as García Barrios rehearsed the Russians. She learned to negotiate contracts, where to rent harpsichords and piccolos, and which Tijuana venues had good acoustics. She studied what drew audiences. After a while, it became clear that her talent lay more in presenting music than in playing it. This was hard for her to face, but she filled her need for music by throwing herself into ever-more ambitious events.

It was slow going. Through the 1990s, the Orchestra of Baja California helped Tijuanans form the habit of seeing live classical music. But after a spurt of interest, the orchestra settled into drawing fifty or sixty people. Three years were needed to increase that to a hundred people—all feeling very lonely in the thousand-seat CECUT.

Somehow attendance like this did not emotionally crush Tere Riqué. She proved suited to promoting arts in a city like Tijuana, for she forged a religious zealot's imperviousness to reason and fact. To her, empty seats did not exist. She rejected traditional Mexican fatalism and developed instead an iron-willed optimism, particularly with regard to money.

"For me, to put on a concert or event," she said, "limits don't exist. A lot of it has to do with confidence, conviction. This is what makes people feel confident. Then they feel it's very natural that a concert gets done. At first I didn't realize this. When I understood that that's how it was, I never let myself think that a project wouldn't happen."

In 1999, she left the Orchestra of Baja California. She took a year off from teaching and, from a closet in her home, she formed Acorde Arts and Entertainment and became a freelance music promoter.

Given Tijuana's bleak support for any music that didn't fit in a strip bar, Acorde stands out for the craziness of its intentions. Riqué's idea was to promote under-heard music by unknown artists, throwing together music and ideas that hadn't been coupled before. One of the first shows was a tenor doing the songs of Mexican singer Agustín Lara, backed by a violin and piano, and alternating with a storyteller telling stories of love. Later, a clarinetist played Jewish music; a pianist and soprano sang songs from France, England, Spain, and Mexico. She arranged for a ballet dancer and pianist to perform the works of Chopin, Debussy, and Gershwin; she brought in a steel drum band from Trinidad and Renaissance music ensembles from the Canary Islands and San Francisco. Each event was like a canvas on which Riqué splashed her imagination, her love of music, and a promotional ability she'd forged during her orchestra years.

Acorde's 1999–2000 schedule of sixteen concerts was the first full arts season of any kind in Tijuana. It looked and sounded impressive: Acorde Arts and Entertainment with a full calendar of events. Behind the façade was Tere Riqué working out of a closet, frantically coming up with the ideas, booking groups, checking out venues, placing ads. Besides her brother, no one subsidized her ideas. She did shows anyway, dividing ticket proceeds with the artists, making money, losing it, making a bit more.

Not long after that first season, Tere was approached by José Medina. Medina is a barrel-chested tenor, the son of the bandleader at Tijuana's bullfight ring. He had grown up with music, taken what he could in music education from Tijuana, then left for years to study voice and perform in operas in New York City, Milan, and Mexico City. In the late 1990s, he saw Tijuana maturing artistically and returned to be part of it.

He asked Tere, What if Acorde were to include scenes from an opera as part of its season? Her company had a reputation for daring that Medina thought essential if the idea was to succeed.

"People were saying, 'You're crazy,'" Medina said. "'You can do a rock concert or Carlos Santana, but opera will never work.'"

Opera was expensive to produce. Luckily, Tere Riqué, who had learned not to see empty seats, also would not see that no money existed for the arts. This was a delusionary myopia, for it was clear to everyone that Mexico had no tradition of private support for the arts. The PRI government for years fostered a culture of paternalism and dependency, and found it a useful tool in controlling Mexico. Mexicans got used to expecting the PRI government to give them all sorts of things: housing and hospitals, basketball courts and soccer fields, clinics for the elderly and handicapped, eyeglasses for children. On this list was support for the arts.

The PRI also discouraged social involvement by the private sector; business's job was business, and the private sector avidly accepted its ghettoization. There were isolated cases of businessmen helping to build parks or low-income housing. For example, in December 1997, without government help, a coalition of businesses held Mexico's first nationwide telethon, to raise money for a handicapped children's clinic—now an annual event. But years of PRI paternalism created an addiction to government aid that many arts groups still haven't shaken. In Tijuana, even rebel rock bands scrub themselves up and go to the Institute of Culture for money to put on concerts.

This always seemed bizarre to Tere Riqué, because city government couldn't adequately fund the basics: sewers, streetlights, police, and health clinics. She saw how California arts companies found funding and directors among the private sector, so she went to Tijuana's business class.

Tijuana's wealthy had been contributing large amounts of money to the San Diego Opera for years. Contributing to the San Diego company swept a donor quickly to social prominence, while supporting Tijuana's nascent arts scene was to toil in threadbare anonymity. Tijuanans also trusted that their charitable donations would be used correctly in the United States. A donation to a Mexican charity, they had good reason to believe, was liable to end up in the charity director's pocket.

They were thus wary when, in 2000, Tere Riqué came asking for money for the city's first opera: a production of scenes from *La Bohème* and *Elixir de Amor*.

"But this woman worked twenty-four hours a day for six months," said Dr. Rodrigo Rodríguez, owner of IBC Hospital in Tijuana, who had given money to the San Diego Opera for many years. "You gave her money because you felt sorry to see her begging for money as if she were dying of hunger."

In August of 2000, scenes from *La Bohème* and *Elixir de Amor* played to a packed CECUT and surpassed Tijuanans' most intrepid hopes.

That night, Dr. Rodríguez sat transfixed by the scenery and the soaring singers he'd helped pay for. "That changed everyone's mind," he said. "You could see that every peso we gave had the effect of five pesos in her hands. Suddenly people realized that this kind of thing was possible without the government."

Businessmen were also encouraged when they saw Riqué tooling around town in the same Volkswagen Pointer she'd always had. Purse strings loosened. Over the next two years, other privately funded productions followed: in 2001 a full-length *Serafina and Arcangela* and then *Barber of Seville* played to standing-room-only crowds. Rodríguez and other businessmen began to shift their giving from San Diego to Riqué's productions.

In 2002, with a full-length production of *Madame Butterfly*, Riqué and Medina formed the city's first opera company—the Ópera de Tijuana. Other Mexican opera companies were supported by the government or a public university. The Ópera de Tijuana was the first designed to rely on private donations. On its board of directors were businessmen who had never promoted the arts but were enthusiastic about opera's first successes.

Meanwhile, a generation of musical youth was emerging. It was their luck to grow into adulthood in Tijuana just as Tere Riqué and José Medina were experimenting with opera. The operatic activity had made them see that music could be a profession and they headed full bore at it.

Mónica Ábrego, a twenty-six-year-old with a soaring soprano, had grown up in Colonia Libertad. Her father, Daniel, had migrated to Tijuana intending to cross into the United States. Instead, he stayed in Libertad and started a few small grocery stores and a beer distributorship. She grew enchanted with opera after seeing a performance of the San Diego Opera when she was fifteen. After high school, her parents sent her to study in Manhattan, and there she stayed to begin her career, in an Upper West Side apartment building that housed fifteen sopranos just like her.

Emmanuel Franco's father worked in the Tijuana city government. From singing at an aunt's wedding, Emmanuel discovered his talent. This quickly became a devotion. He began singing in choirs, school music festivals. He sought out teachers. On the day he turned seventeen, Emmanuel, a baritone, gave his first public concert. By nineteen, he had already appeared in two operas and soloed in several concerts.

The Paz siblings were especially impressive, as there were three of them. Manuel, Aurora, and Guadalupe had grown up singing in a church choir. Tere Riqué featured them in Acorde concerts as teenagers. After a while, the Paz siblings realized that a career in music was possible. Aurora and Guadalupe—soprano and mezzo-soprano, respectively—went to Siena, Italy, to study voice. Manuel was looking to spend time in Germany, which, as it happens, is a world center for tenors.

These kids were a radical thing for Mexico. Survival economics forced middle-class youths across Mexico to choose something remunerative as their life's work. Tijuana's economy, however, allowed these kids whose families lacked money or connections to nevertheless follow what they loved. Tijuana opera, like the city's economy, was not the domain of an elite but a fairer, democratic thing and open to whoever would work hard. By the time the production of *Pagliacci* rolled around, the city had thirty youths seriously planning a career in opera—a small number in a city of almost two million people, perhaps, but far more than ever before.

Tere Riqué found that parents—friends of hers—would call now for advice, terrified that their son or daughter wanted only to study music. How would their children live? Wouldn't it be better if they studied something serious—like accounting or dental hygiene—and music on the side? And though Tere understood these parents' fears, it upset her that Tijuana still treated music as frivolity, something to turn to when the real work was done.

"These parents say, 'My child has to study a profession,'" she said. "But I tell them, 'Their profession is *singing*. They'll always have work. Their work is music. Sometimes it's not that well paid, but they can live from it.' We have to stop thinking of music as something extra. We have to integrate it into our lives. Music is essential in our lives and we can't do without it."

❦

This is what Mercedes Quiñónez had always believed.

Mecha, as friends call her, is a stout woman, with a rosy, warm smile and a self-effacing way about her. As a girl, she didn't play house; she played at being a singer. She had once studied music seriously but felt compelled to stop and had to return to Tijuana.

By the late 1990s, she had spent a desiccated decade hunched over bills in the windowless office of her hardware warehouse out in a dusty neighborhood of Tijuana called Guadalupe Victoria. She had stacked and sold miles of garden hoses and gray duct tape. It was a good living, feeding hammers and nails, water tanks and measuring tape into Tijuana's manically growing maw. Yet she knew she had no heart for hardware, and all she'd ever wanted was to sing. Now all that remained of her once-luxurious musical dreams was a small church choir that she directed. With no other music around her, she clung to it for years like a mountain climber to a crevice on a sheer rock face.

Her parents, José Quiñónez and Mercedes Ruiz, had been fruit vendors in Manzanillo, a city in the state of Colima, well down the Pacific coast. Nine of their sixteen children lived. Mercedes was the next to last and the couple's final daughter. When Mercedes was two, her parents took a boat up the coast to Tijuana, where life was better.

Mercedes's mother was a tough woman. José Quiñónez gambled on horses, dogs, and roosters. He rarely gave his wife enough to provide for the family. This caused rows throughout the couple's married life. So Mercedes Ruiz set up a tortilla stand downtown, and it was from this that she gave her children the essentials.

Mercedes Ruiz sang often. When she was happy, when she was sad, she expressed herself through song. Yet she had a horror of singers. She forbade her daughters to be either nuns or singers, believing the former to be hypocrites and the latter to be loose women. Nor did she believe music was work. Life had taught Mercedes Ruiz to respect jobs that made money; that did not include singing. So she offered no support to her one daughter who wanted more than anything to be a singer. She told Mecha that after she was gone she expected her to care for her older brother, Pancho, whose brain had been damaged by fever.

Early in life, Mecha had wanted to be an elementary-school teacher. But her mother couldn't pay for her education through high school. So after Mercedes finished elementary school, her mother pushed her toward secretarial school, and at age fourteen, Mercedes became a secretary, a profession that inspired her not at all. She went to night school to finish the courses she needed to be a teacher. But long hours at her secretarial jobs didn't allow her to continue.

At seventeen, Mercedes joined a youth choir. The choir opened her to organized music for the first time. Slowly the desire to teach was replaced by the need to sing. As Mercedes would spend more time at choir practice, her mother would roll her eyes and say, "Let her have her fun." Mercedes Ruiz saw her daughter sing only once—in a mass that her daughter had to drag her to.

After a while, Mercedes joined a choir at Lord of Mercy Catholic Church because the church had a piano and she wanted to learn. The director gave her piano lessons.

Mercedes needed time free for her music and no longer wanted a full-time job stealing options from her the way her secretarial jobs had kept her from night school. She began to sell things door-to-door: books, clothes, jewelry—it didn't matter. When she was twenty-three, the priest at Lord of Mercy gave her the church's old upright piano. She put it in her room at home. Long into the night she would practice hand exercises and play the "Moonlight Sonata" to the studied indifference of her parents.

For several months, she even stopped working and lived on her savings while studying piano with the church director. A former boyfriend called. He was about to graduate from medical school in Guadalajara and invited her to the ceremony. It would cost a lot, and she didn't have much money saved. Yet within the offer was the hint of marriage, or at least reignited romance.

Her teacher at the church urged her to make up her mind.

"I'll give you classes and charge you very little," he told her. "But I need to know if you're going to go to Guadalajara to the graduation of this boyfriend. The money you spend on the trip you can use to take music classes."

She called Guadalajara and declined her young man's invitation. It was the closest she ever came to marrying.

"I went to live in music," she said.

The life of Mercedes Quiñónez now became one long trek through Tijuana's cultural desert in search of oases of musical instruction, detoured constantly by departing teachers, family duties, and the need to make a living. When the church director left town, Mercedes was again without a teacher. She was young and isolated out in her working-class neighborhood. She didn't know how to look for such things and had no one to guide her. Still, by now she had enough piano training that the priest at Lord of Mercy Catholic Church asked her to start a choir. Church choirs would connect her to music for the rest of her life.

A few years later, she found a voice teacher in Ensenada. Professor Bañuelos was a piano teacher and wasn't vocally trained. Still, these were the first lessons that approached being serious. Professor Bañuelos had a passing interest in opera and had her learn her first aria, sung by Mimi, the main character in Puccini's opera *La Bohème*. Mercedes boarded a bus to Ensenada every morning to attend classes with Professor Bañuelos. After class, she returned home and went door-to-door selling tomb space in a Tijuana graveyard called Colinas de Descanso—Resting Hills.

Seeing her daughter going to such lengths, her mother said, "You're crazy. Why are you studying that?"

"Because I like it," Mercedes would reply, and it would hang between them, her mother's disdain for what she loved.

Then her money ran out, and Professor Bañuelos died. Undaunted, she read in the newspaper of a choir forming at a local university and joined that. They performed on television one night, and Mercedes pleaded with her mother to watch.

"Did you see us?" she asked when she got home.

"Oh, no, *hija*," her mother said. "I forgot all about it."

Through singers in the university choir, Mercedes learned of summer courses offered to adults at the Las Rosas Music Conservatory in Morelia, in the state of Michoacán, two thousand miles to the south. That summer, she took her savings and went to Michoacán to study piano, voice, and harmony.

Las Rosas was formed from a religious school for girls built in 1743. It remains one of Mexico's best music schools, focusing especially on voice, and is home to the Morelia Boys Choir. With its baroque brick arches and interior garden, the school exuded achievement. Mercedes remembered this as her life's pinnacle. The conservatory's teachers were strict and serious, and she drank deeply from their high standards. They told her that her voice was the best of all the adult students. For years, she had felt anxiety as she searching in vain for musical instruction. Now, at the conservatory, she felt harmony, peace, the kind of resolution that ends a piece of music. She thrilled to the chance to develop not just sight-reading and vocal technique, but to nurture her musical heart that had gone untended in Tijuana. Her voice was becoming a full lyric soprano.

She was chosen to solo in the recital that ended her summer course. She'd never sung alone before a crowd. It was a dream, something she waited for all her life. That night, in the venerable Morelos Theater in downtown Morelia, Mercedes stood before the audience as the pianist began to play "Virgin Tutto Amore" by Francisco Durante. As she began to sing, she forgot the words. Terror gripped her. She tried again and nerves overwhelmed her. Finally, a teacher gave her the music. Mercedes was so rattled that the music seemed gibberish before her. Somehow she got through it. When she ended, the audience, watching her agony, burst into wild applause. Mercedes burst into tears.

She kept on despite this mortifying debut. She stayed at the school for the fall term. She was thirty, a good age for this kind of discipline. She had started at seventeen and behind her were years of practicing and scratching for a chance like this.

Yet the moment ended abruptly. Her mother took sick and called Mercedes home. Other siblings lived in Tijuana, but Mecha did not have it in her to refuse. She left the conservatory for what she intended to be a brief absence; she even left her clothes at the school in Morelia, so sure was she that she would return soon.

Finances and her mother's health kept her in Tijuana for the next two years. Mercedes would remember this like the death of a child. Her voice needed tending right then. Something in her never got the chance to grow when conditions were perfect for it to flourish. God knows why He does things, she told herself.

Two years later, her mother seemed to be doing better. Hoping it was not too late, Mercedes returned to the conservatory. She was thirty-two and meant this departure from home to be her last. At the airport in Tijuana, she told her father she would not be returning. She asked for his blessing. He gave it, and she boarded the plane. It was the first time she saw her father cry.

In Morelia, however, her studies consumed her time. She couldn't work. Her savings ran out, and again she had to leave the conservatory. Desperate, she went to an aunt's in Mexico City. She found an Italian voice teacher. She studied and sold selling rubber stamps door-to-door.

Then her mother took sick again. So in the summer of 1985, less than eighteen months after leaving home for good, Mecha was back in Tijuana caring for her ailing mother. Mercedes Ruiz died a year later. By the time she died, her youngest daughter had become both the nun and the singer Mercedes Ruíz abhorred: in the steadfast way a nun is married to the idea of Christ, Mercedes was wedded to music.

It was the union Mercedes preferred. She saw few examples of happy couples around her. Mexican women married, she felt, out of economic vulnerability. She had supported herself since adolescence and didn't need a man to take the job. She saw women across the border in the United States who didn't marry. She took heart from that. Anyway, the men she knew were interested in television and soccer, and too willing, she felt, to accept as immutable what life had plopped in front of them.

When her mother died, it fell to Mercedes to support her brain-damaged older brother, and her aging father as well. She yearned to return to Mexico

City and study again with the Italian teacher. But she could not bring herself to shirk the responsibility her mother had always said would be hers.

For succor, Mercedes formed a twenty-three-voice choir at San Martín de Porres Catholic Church and became the church organist. She began selling hardware to support herself, her brother, and father. Hardware sold for decent markups. It withstood peso devaluations. Mercedes cared less than ever what she sold. She opened a small warehouse and worked there twelve and fifteen hours a day. One last time, she rummaged about Tijuana for a music teacher, but found no one.

It was here that Mercedes finally gave up and relinquished the search for music instruction to which she had dedicated half her life.

This was the 1980s. Mexico's economy was imploding. Caravans of people streamed north, carpeting Tijuana's distant hills and ravines. They all needed hardware. Her company expanded to employ eighteen people. Her singing dreams wilted as her business grew. She corseted her mind into accepting this and hunkered down to wholesaling hardware and tending her brother and father, while prying what satisfaction she could from the church choir.

For eleven years, Mercedes trudged on like this. Maybe this was how God wanted her, singing for Him alone.

"My singing has always been for the church," she said. "My singing wasn't for the world."

Her choir's commitment didn't approach her own. The singers wouldn't practice. They were often late for rehearsal and sometimes didn't show up at all. She would explode at them and stalk off. She would call them a couple weeks later, though, telling them there was rehearsal and they would all come together again and the choir would continue on as if nothing had happened. She pretended they needed her.

She once gave music lessons to a convent. She was supposed to stay for two weeks; instead, she remained for two months, resting peacefully away from the world. She might not have left had her father and brother and hardware warehouse not needed her.

Then in 1997, as abruptly as the first day of spring, life began to change for Mercedes Quiñónez.

A friend told her of the conservatory that had formed a year before with Russian music teachers, of all things. Cocooned in her hardware business, Mercedes had heard nothing. She rushed to it. The conservatory was full. But through the school she met Elena Vostrakova, a Russian choirmaster, whose husband played in the Orchestra of Baja California. Vostrakova took Mercedes as a private student.

Suddenly at forty-five, when she least expected it, Mercedes Quiñónez was studying music again. It made her giddy. She cried and thanked God. Her search for music had been so arduous. Her life had been one of yearning postponed. The needs of others had always come before her own. She was unmarried and childless; she lived at home to care for others; to support them she ran a business that deadened her. Now Tijuana, the city from which she'd never expected more than a living, was offering her music.

To her choir at San Martín de Porres she spoke bluntly. "I'm going to take classes, and you should, too. I gave you a lot. I don't have time now." Anyhow, she felt her musical skills were too limited to teach them much.

She immersed herself in her voice classes. At first, the number of lessons it took to learn a piece of music agonized her. She'd spent so many years running a business that she saw only the cost. After a while, though, she realized that with time her music could reach beyond technique to a higher plane of musical expression. With the hardware business doing well, she made peace with the money. She delved into each new piece of music and soon came to see her potential differently. With every aria she studied, she sought not just to sing the notes. She wanted to attain the point where technique was instinctive and forgotten, and her voice became a vehicle that revealed her heart's essence.

After a few years of study, she found she could achieve this. When it happened, she was no longer Mercedes Quiñónez, hardware wholesaler; she was the music, the character whose part she sang. She hadn't the theatrical flair of many sopranos when she performed. There were no expressive hand movements, no plaintive shaking of the head as she sang. Instead, Mercedes barely moved. She would stand erect, wrap her arms together at her waist, and close her eyes. Then her body seemed to reduce to lungs, throat, mouth, and voice as a powerful ribbon of sound slowly rose from her and floated over her audience.

She sounded like a religious mystic when talking about the many layers of ineffable beauty that lay within the music she could create, occasionally stopping distractedly in midsentence at the wonder of it all.

"Each piece of music," she would say, "I try to understand why it exists, where it came from, where it goes, why it's there."

Out in her hardware warehouse for so many years, Mercedes had forgotten any of this was possible. Now she barely considered her hours at the warehouse as time lived.

Within a year of taking classes again, she began giving solo recitals at restaurants, at the conservatory where the Russians taught, then at Tijuana's Casa de la Cultura. After several years, she developed a contingent of fans that went wherever she performed. It's not stretching the truth to say that by the time *Pagliacci* was presented in the summer of 2003, Mercedes Quiñonez, now fifty-one, was Tijuana's premier soprano.

When Enrique Fuentes had opened his opera café a couple years before and presented a series of Friday-night recitals, Mercedes Quiñónez was the second singer to appear, but she was the first to pack the place.

By the time *Pagliacci* was in rehearsal, ever-more ambitious plans for the Café de la Ópera were gripping Enrique Fuentes.

Within a year of the café's opening, people passing in the afternoon heard the loopy, semihysterical sounds of voice exercises and piano scales. Manuel Acosta, a baritone, had begun offering voice lessons at the café. Enrique was one of his students. Enrique found teachers to offer piano and classical guitar classes. There weren't always students, but there were teachers.

In addition to Opera Saturday, Enrique began offering Friday recitals by local singers, who were young and often green. Before a small, encouraging audience at Café de la Ópera, they could make mistakes and hone their talents like jazz musicians in some after-hours dive.

Mercedes Quiñónez, Tijuana's premier soprano.

He named the computers at his Internet café for operas. One computer he called *Aida*; he named others *Carmen, Madame Butterfly*, and *La
Traviata*. The title character in his favorite opera, Puccini's *Turandot*, was
a controlling, ice-cold Chinese princess, so he christened his computer
server for her. He named an iced-coffee drink *Turandot* as well. His high
caffeine espresso he named "Nessun Dorma"—"No One Sleeps"—for the
most powerful aria in *Turandot*.

Enrique's neighbors on Fifth Street watched bewildered and talked among themselves. Eduardo Gómez, a construction worker who lived across the street, didn't know what to make of it. Two years after the café opened, he hadn't yet been inside it. "I don't know anything about opera," Gómez said. A few women up the street looked askance at the café. Several neighbors were concerned that their parking spots not be taken on the nights when Enrique held events. The barber a few doors down thought that anything that brought more culture to Colonia Libertad merited applause.

Eugenio Romero, who owned the café's building, knew nothing of opera either but developed a proprietary interest in the place. He even helped Enrique knock down a wall to expand the café and remodel a music room.

Meanwhile, El Café de la Ópera became a petri dish both for new artists and for Enrique's own business ideas where opera was concerned. Hunches would form there, separate, modify, then morph into more developed plans. He planned to drop the Internet café and turn the café into a music school, a cultural arts center. Propositions that were for the moment financially impossible, Enrique noted for later. When he passed the broken-down Cine Libertad across the street, a movie theater from his childhood converted now into a dusty warehouse, he imagined what a fine performing-arts venue it would make.

After a while, you could imagine Enrique the hero of his own opera, beset by a vision that would not let him rest, struggling to make an opera café work in Colonia Libertad as a chorus of neighbors around him commented at what his beautiful insanity was creating on their street of broken sidewalks.

As *Pagliacci* approached in mid-August, Enrique was making plans to hold a daylong opera festival in the street the following summer to celebrate the café's third anniversary. He wanted to involve the neighbors in it. Fifth Street would see what had been going on behind his doors all this time.

At 8:15 PM on a Friday in August, with a raise of the conductor's baton, the orchestra fell silent, and after months—decades really—of preparation for this moment, the curtain finally went up on Tijuana's production of the luscious street brawl of an opera called *Pagliacci*.

Pagliacci was the first opera production for which Tere Riqué and José Medina had auditioned a chorus. In the past, with few options, they'd given parts to anyone who wanted to sing. This time, though, they wanted higher standards. Several people who sang in choruses of earlier productions were cut.

The *Pagliacci* chorus was where Tijuana's musical evolution could be measured. Emmanuel Franco and Manuel Paz, as well as a dozen younger boys, were in the chorus. Mercedes Quiñónez played the town widow. The rest of the thirty-odd members of the chorus were folks in whose lives music was finding a place. They played common citizens, which they were. José Ángel Álvarez, sixty-nine, had owned a pest-control business and had only begun to study voice in retirement. Humberto Ramos sold construction materials and had sung all his life. Indalecio Rivas, a thirty-six-year-old engineer, was a supply executive at a maquiladora that made headphones.

Somehow passing the audition, too, was Enrique Fuentes, only a few months into his voice classes. He'd been practicing his loopy voice exercises in his car as he waited to cross the border each morning.

"At times I stand there and can't believe I'm here," he said, the afternoon of the performance. "But I feel sure of myself and as if I've been doing this all my life."

He was given the role of the baker, and thus in rehearsals he'd walked about with a tray of bread, which, to his relief, gave him something to do with his hands.

Pagliacci played to a sold-out house. That night, Tijuana, known far and wide for the cheap and the desperate, gathered to celebrate exactitude and harmony. The show was attended mostly by the city's middle classes, so intent on finding an alternative to the ragged notion of their city. Enrique had bought a ticket for Héctor Seemann, who allowed himself to be persuaded to descend from his hill. Amber lighting and peasant costumes gave the show a warm, welcoming feel. Even chorus members cried when tenor José Ordóñez, brought in from Monterrey to play Canio, sang "Vesti la Giubba" and showed that, in art, unrestrained passion is best expressed through firm control.

Backstage after the show, thin chorus boys ran about singing the aria's most powerful line—"ridi pagliaccio" ("laugh clown")—in the deepest voices they could muster, throwing their arms out like 250-pound Italian tenors. Audience members flocked around Ordóñez, who was still splashed with clown whiteface.

La Ópera de Tijuana was still searching for sponsors on opening night, needing ten thousand pesos to cover the show's expenses. Yet its *Pagliacci* had been relatively free of government assistance. The federal government gave free use of the CECUT; the city put up money for the scenery. Six more businessmen had signed on to sponsor the production, and the volunteer staff had grown to twenty. Three months before, La Ópera de Tijuana had started its own fundraising group, Amigos de la Ópera, each of whose members was to put up five hundred pesos a month to give the organization a year-round income. By the night of *Pagliacci*, it had its first two members.

To Emmanuel Franco or Manuel Paz, *Pagliacci* was another step toward a career in music. Franco would be heading to Spain within a few weeks to study with a baritone in Madrid. Manuel Paz would be looking for a way to get to Germany to study with tenors there. His sister, Guadalupe, was waiting to hear from teachers in Siena, Italy, to see whether she would return or head to a conservatory in Mexico City. They were all children of midlevel government bureaucrats—not a profession in Mexico that typically earns enough to support children in great things. But the opera was a sign that in Tijuana now music did not have to be what you did when you weren't studying accounting or dental hygiene. It could be, as Tere Riqué had said, indispensable to life itself.

Backstage, Enrique Fuentes waited a long time to take off his makeup. He beamed incessantly, had his photo taken with José Ordóñez, and was generally at a loss for words.

"I did it," he said. "My first time."

❋

Three weeks after the presentation of *Pagliacci*, in his house atop Colonia Libertad, Héctor Seemann collapsed and died.

It was four days before anyone knew he'd passed. The owner of the shop across the street smelled an odor and called paramedics. He'd died of a heart attack. He was cremated. Students remembered that he used to say a dead body needed to lie in state for three days before being cremated or buried or the soul wouldn't be ready to move on. Héctor got four.

He'd refused his siblings' entreaties to come live with them. Several students tell of offering to take him shopping or bring him things from San Diego. One student even took him to the new music conservatory and pushed the school's director to hire him as a composition teacher. Seeman let that idea die without following up on it.

"He liked to say how much he hated the idea of dying alone," said one of his former students, "but he sought it out."

It wasn't hard to see the passing of Héctor Seeman as the end of one musical era in Tijuana as another began. Tijuana now treated its musicians better and expected more of them, as well. No longer were opera choruses formed with whoever was available without auditions. Students no longer had to leave town for musical educations. On the contrary, children from Mexicali and Ensenada were coming to Tijuana to study. For the musician or singer who would go and get it, Tijuana offered possibilities, and one of them was that the possibilities would only get better. Artists and musicians, Tere Riqué had once said, had to be part businessmen and learn to promote themselves. No longer could they sit back and wait for the world to recognize their genius.

❋

At 8:30 PM, a few nights after the presentation of *Pagliacci*, Fifth Street in the Colonia Libertad was settling in for the evening. A streetlamp threw the shadows of two boys twenty feet up the concrete sidewalk. The boys called to each other as they crossed the street, making plans for the next day, then headed home. Another kid rode his bike along the sidewalk. Down on the corner, the lights of the neighborhood ice-cream shop were still on, though customers had departed.

The only other lights on the street came from the Café de la Ópera—a string of Christmas lights that Enrique had fashioned into a low-budget imitation marquee on the face of the building.

Outside the cafe was a poster announcing the first event of the city's 2003–4 opera season. The café would present short scenes from operas by Bizet, Verdi, and Rossini, performed by five local singers and commented on by Manuel Laborín.

Enrique's opera ideas would continue to grow more majestic. In July 2004, he and La Ópera de Tijuana would hold the city's first free outdoor opera festival on tiny Fifth Street to celebrate the café's third anniversary. More than five thousand people crammed the street to hear singers do scenes from *The Barber of Seville* and arias from Puccini. Enrique walked about dressed as a Renaissance courtesan. His neighbors sold fruit drinks and tacos from their doorways. Almost seven thousand people attended the festival in 2005. By then, tourism officials were seeing gold in opera. They began promoting the festival as part of Tijuana's cultural life. Two decades after Mexico City officials built CECUT Theater to attract tourists, Enrique Fuentes and the city's opera devotees did it in Colonia Libertad with far less. In this city of many vices, opera had become another.

But tonight, inside the Café de la Ópera shortly after *Pagliacci*, Enrique, Mercedes Quiñónez, and others from the chorus sat in a semicircle with sheet music before them. Down the street came a growling car, and this set a dog to barking from a yard nearby. His yelps echoed across Fifth Street as the chorus's first strains of "Va Pensiero" floated from the café.

"Va Pensiero"—"Go, Thought"—is a mournful choral piece. It is from an opera called *Nabucco*, written by the great Italian composer, Giuseppe Verdi. The opera is about the fall of Jerusalem and the Hebrews' exile. "Va Pensiero" is Hebrew slaves' lament at their imprisonment in Babylon. Italians at the time seized on lost Israel as a reference to their own country, then ruled by Austria. "Va Pensiero" was Verdi's first "hit." On opening night in Milan in 1842 patriotic Italians erupted in a near-riot that Austrian police struggled to put down. The opera marked Verdi's emergence as a figure of Italian culture and nationalism. When he died in 1901, Milan halted, and the thousands of mourners who lined the streets spontaneously broke into "Va Pensiero" as his casket went by in horse-drawn carriage.

Now, in Colonia Libertad, the Hebrew lament was at first barely audible as it ushered from the Café de la Ópera. But as the chorus inside swelled in power, the long lines of song funneled out onto Fifth Street. There, briefly, "Va Pensiero" commingled and wove a counterpoint to the car's metallic ruminations and the barking of the penned-in dog, before finally evaporating into Tijuana's night.

Chapter Seven

Atolinga

On the evening of March 6, 2001, Raúl Briseño and an employee were preparing food at his new restaurant in McHenry, a small town northwest of Chicago.

Briseño had opened Raúl's Burrito Express only six months before. It was a lunch place for tacos and burritos and soft drinks, the first Mexican restaurant in McHenry. This was Briseño's second establishment in what he felt one day might become a chain—the original Raúl's Burrito Express was in the nearby town of Wauconda. And, as the McHenry place was a new business, it was taking up a lot of his time.

So at a little past 7:00 PM, long after the lunch rush, Briseño and his employee were still at work when two young men in black ski masks burst into the restaurant demanding money, one of them waving a gun. Outraged to the point of fearlessness, Briseño, the immigrant entrepreneur, ran the punks out of his restaurant with a butcher knife. During the chase, he collared one of them and began to drag him inside, yelling to his employee to call police. The second robber, seeing this, stopped and shot Briseño, hitting him in the chest. Briseño fell and died outside his restaurant.

In the days that followed, shrines were erected at Briseño's place in Wauconda, where he had been a well-liked member of the business community. His family offered a five-thousand-dollar reward for the killers' arrest.

The murder of Raúl Briseño, a thirty-five-year-old father of two, happened to be the first in McHenry in five years. Television stations and newspapers ran stories about his death and its effect on his family and the town. They noted, too, that the Mexican community in the tiny suburbs north of Chicago had grown large through the 1990s.

But what the news coverage didn't quite catch was that Raúl Briseño was part of a much larger, more nuanced story of Mexican immigration.

Briseño was from Atolinga, a village of about three thousand people in the state of Zacatecas in north-central Mexico. Beginning in the 1970s, Atolingans began arriving in large numbers in Chicago to work as dishwashers. They came timid and fearful, wanting only to make some money and go home. In Mexico, and especially in the state of Zacatecas, the world of business is reserved for the monied classes. As one immigrant put it, "He who has power can do things, and he who doesn't can only suck his thumb." So, few of these new immigrants imagined ever starting a business.

Yet over the next thirty years, Atolingans would become pioneers in Chicago's Mexican restaurant business. They spread taquerías across Chicago. By the time of Briseño's death, immigrants from tiny Atolinga, Zacatecas, owned forty-five restaurants, mostly taquerías, in and around Chicago. After a while, it was hard to find anyone from the village in Chicago who didn't have some connection to a taco and burrito place. Briseño himself had three restaurants—his two taquerias and a family sit-down restaurant that he owned with his brother Sergio in Wauconda. Four of his brothers and sisters also owned restaurants.

Atolingans' voyage out of their cloistered pueblo and into the world invigorated them as it tested their abilities. Using a chain of restaurants called Golden Nugget Pancake Houses, the example of one of their peers, and the only capital they had available—each other—Atolingans jump-started themselves into the restaurant business. In time, an informal Atolingan self-help network emerged in Chicago that could put up a restaurant like the Amish raise a barn. As they moved farther into the world, Atolingans found that they discarded not only poverty but a way of thinking.

❖

The village of Atolinga sits out on a highland mesa in the southern finger of Zacatecas. The state is suffering from a prolonged drought, so the short grasses on the plain leading into town have the color of straw.

Prickly-pear cactus and hearty huisache trees, looking like bonzais that grew out of control, provide the occasional burst of green against a canvas burned brown and yellow. Glancing away from the highway that leads into town are walls of stacked brown stones that wind into the distance. Far off to the left is the small adobe home the Briseño family grew up in and then abandoned.

Many Atolingans grew up in adobe houses. Since moving to the United States, they have returned to replace the adobe shacks with beautiful homes of two and three stories, with tile floors, plumbing, and sliding-glass doors. These houses now pack the town. Reflecting their years in the north, some immigrants have even built houses in suburban American style—with houses set back from the street, with driveways and lawns. Yet, apart from a few weeks every August and December, these immigrants have not returned to Atolinga. So the houses in which they've invested so much are empty.

Like a becalmed ship sitting at sea, Atolinga sits mired in scary peace and quiet. A pickup truck will occasionally trundle through town, a twelve-year-old boy in a baseball cap at the wheel. Otherwise, visitors can walk down the streets at midmorning, through silent canyons of houses, and never have to move aside. The skies above the village are clean, and rooster calls echo across the village. Yet all this, while quaint, is further sign that the conditions that caused the desertion of Atolinga have not changed.

Some thirty-two hundred people live in the municipio of Atolinga, which includes the town and fifteen hamlets nearby. Almost ten thousand Atolingans live in the United States, with enclaves in Chicago, Indianapolis, Atlanta, and Pasadena, California.

"Our economy runs entirely on dollars," said Alejandro Castañeda, a veterinarian and the mayor of Atolinga, sitting one afternoon in his office in city hall. "When a boy is fifteen, sixteen years old, the father or brother or uncle says 'Send the kid up, there's work for him up here.' The kids get to junior high, maybe high school, and they're gone. Very few keep studying. People leave out of economic necessity, but leaving has also become a culture."

Prices for land, cows, cars, and homes are quoted in dollars. Those who aren't connected to the United States find the dollar-boosted cost of living too much for their peso salaries, so they, too, start to think of leaving.

In its isolation, Atolinga could probably attract businesses only through the promise of low salaries—about fifteen dollars a day is the norm.

"(But) you ask people to work, and they say not for that little," said Castañeda, who also owns livestock and has looked in vain for people to help him on his farm. "They get dollars from their family. So they have what they need to live."

Job-creating industries have thus avoided Atolinga. Dependent on U.S. dollars, Castañeda said, the folks who remain behind retain the debilitating feeling that nothing is possible without outside help.

Scholars of Mexican immigration contend that the working-class people who leave Mexico for the United States are those who are most eager for a future, those unhappy with the status quo back home, those willing to risk a lot for something different.

This described Raúl Briseño. He had only a second-grade education, but an active mind. He was always making plans; "muy vivo"—quick thinking—is how his family describes him. In his first years in America, he often held two jobs and for a while worked four jobs.

Though he was the seventh-born Briseño child, Raúl was the first in his family to start his own restaurant.

"My brother set the example. He was the one who showed us the path we all took," said Raúl's older brother, Alonso.

In the early 1970s, an entire generation of young people left Atolinga for Chicago. The older Briseño siblings were part of that. For a while, Atolingan youths filled an entire apartment complex at Broadway and Irving Park Boulevard in north Chicago.

"We were young and thinking of the future, and there was no future (in Atolinga), unless your parents were rich and could give you a college education," said Luis Briseño, another of Raúl's older brothers, who left Atolinga in 1972.

Raúl Briseño joined the exodus in 1980 at the age of fourteen. By then, his brothers had settled in the resort town of Wauconda, in lake country northwest of Chicago. Wauconda and its neighboring resorts were evolving into bedroom communities, as Chicago sprawled north. Rising land prices and insurance rates for private beaches finally put an end to most of the tourism in Wauconda. A few factories arrived and brought more bustle to the town.

This, in turn, attracted more immigrants. As its economic base changed, the township became part of a Mexican-immigrant expansion from Chicago to the suburbs. Today, the village has a population of ninety-four hundred people, of which more than eleven hundred are Latino, mostly Mexican immigrants.

Raúl spent the 1980s working in Wauconda restaurants. He married and had two sons. He spoke often of starting his own restaurant.

By the end of the 1980s, this had become a real possibility. Years before that, the lives of most Atolingan young men in Chicago had intersected with a chain of pancake restaurants, and that changed everything.

Golden Nugget Pancake Houses are a chain of all-day breakfast restaurants decorated in ersatz Gold Rush style, heavy on the vinyl seating and plastic-coated menus. A restaurateur named Howard Quam founded the chain in 1966 and in the 1970s began to expand. There are seven Golden Nuggets in Chicago today.

Golden Nuggets expanded in Chicago based on Mexican labor, and much of that from Atolinga. No one remembers which Atolingan immigrant first found work in a Golden Nugget. But by the mid-1970s, a first job at a Golden Nugget was almost as much a part of Atolingan culture as crossing the Rio Grande.

To the new young immigrants, Golden Nuggets held several advantages. The menu consisted of easy-to-learn dishes like omelets and pancakes. It took an energetic kid about two years to go from dishwasher to kitchen manager. Plus, turnover was high. And once a few Atolingans were in a position to hire people, they hired their friends from the village. Dozens, perhaps hundreds, of Atolingan boys started their Chicago working days at a Golden Nugget Pancake House. Some thirty Atolingans eventually managed Golden Nuggets in Chicago. By the mid-1980s, a few of them had moved on to manage major Chicago restaurants.

One of these was Carlos Ascención Salinas, a short, stocky, garrulous, and fast-talking fellow, the son of an Atolinga stonecutter, and known to all as Chon.

Chon Salinas almost single-handedly established Atolingans in restaurants and pushed them to explore the possibilities of America, even as he himself spent decades torn between whether to put down roots in the United States or return to the village.

Salinas had only an elementary-school education when he came to Chicago in 1973 at the age of fifteen. Like those before him, he found work dishwashing in a Golden Nugget Pancake House. By seventeen he was the night-shift kitchen manager.

Chon Salinas was not the first Atolingan to manage a Golden Nugget. But, in about 1976, he became the first to leave a Golden Nugget to manage a major sit-down restaurant when he was hired to run Ratso's, a local jazz dinner club. The owner enrolled him in food-service management classes. Salinas studied English and business administration at a local college.

"I was always wanting to return to Atolinga after getting together five hundred dollars or something," he said. "A friend told me, 'Don't be an idiot. Learn English.'"

In 1981, Salinas found a job at John Barleycorn's, a classic eatery in Chicago's Lincoln Park neighborhood. The owner lived in Hong Kong. The restaurant manager, a fellow by the name of Jimmy Lee, encouraged Salinas to take on more responsibility. Soon, Salinas was managing the multimillion-dollar business as if it were his own.

"There I learned what we later put into practice: that you can do things well, in a team, without envy and backbiting," Salinas said. "I began to believe that the most important support you can get was not economic, but moral—the encouragement, that there's someone who tells you, 'You can do it and you won't fall.' This is something we all need."

Chon believed that having left Atolinga poor and done well in the United States gave him license to show people back home a few things. He owned a slim parcel of land in Atolinga. On it, he built what's believed to be the first house in Atolinga designed by an architect. The house efficiently uses space. It placed storage compartments under the stairway, which was backed, in turn, by a bathroom. Below its large planters are storage closets.

"I wanted to give the village a message regarding the quality of a product and not look only to produce what's cheapest," he said. "Plus, we have to leave something behind, a trace, evidence that we existed. There's no point to living if you don't leave something behind."

The house took more than two years to finish. It resembled a typical Chicago three-flat—narrow and three stories tall—but stood as testament to Chon Salinas's belief that he would one day return to Atolinga to live.

In 1986, meanwhile, John Barleycorn's was put up for sale. Salinas, the son of a stonecutter, put together a group of investors and a $1.25-million offer to buy the restaurant. He was outbid, and he left the restaurant.

Casting about now for something to do, he bought a faltering taquería from a friend. The taquería, in a storefront in north Chicago, had once housed a hamburger joint run for many years by a couple of Greek brothers. Salinas named it Taco and Burrito House. After the hectic pace of John Barleycorn's, he found this taquería remarkably easy to make work.

His Taco and Burrito House was a simple concept. It served American versions of Mexican food, geared to gringo tastes. Salinas tinkered with a menu to come up with food that was easy to make, tasty, and eaten quickly. He added a bacon burrito, a Junior Burrito and a Super Burrito, a small chimichanga. His tacos were large and topped with lettuce, sour cream, tomatoes—nothing like the small tacos typical of Mexico. It was Mexican fast food for Americans, and for Chicago it was new.

People from the village predicted he'd be bankrupt in six months. But when six months passed and Salinas's low-overhead, fast-food concept did well, a rumor ran through the Atolingan community that he was smuggling drugs. Successful Mexican-immigrant businessmen in the United

States often face this rumor—Chon insists it's untrue—and it usually comes from people from their villages they've known all their lives.

"Mexicans believe that any Hispanic who comes to America and makes money is making it from drugs," he said.

After a while, though, friends would approach him to ask how they could do what he was doing. Chon wanted to dispel the drug-smuggling rumor and saw the virtue of lending money to people he was sure would repay the loan. So he encouraged them and loaned some of them money for a down payment on houses. They, in turn, used their home equity to borrow money and opened taquerías similar to Chon's Taco and Burrito House.

Atolingans, years after finding their first restaurant jobs in Golden Nuggets, were ready for this. They needed only to see someone else do it first.

"We're like goats. Where one jumps, the rest jump as well," said one Atolingan immigrant.

Thus the late 1980s and early 1990s saw an explosion of Atolingan taquerías in the Chicago area copying the Salinas concept. Cousins would pool their money. One owner would lend money and advice to a brother or uncle. Sometimes owners would sell to, or help finance the restaurant of, a trusted worker. Salinas started six taquerías among family members in Chicago and two more in Madison, Nebraska, where a sister lived.

Like Golden Nuggets, Salinas's taquería concept had the virtue of simplicity. It was geared to what an immigrant could run with only on-the-job business training. A taquería could open in a storefront with a friend's loan of only a few thousand dollars.

Few Atolingans varied Chon's business model. Their places had names like Taco and Burrito Place; Taco and Burrito Palace, Famous Taco and Burrito King; Fast Burrito; Burrito Loco; Sergio's Tacos; Taco Mex; and so on. The menus mostly copied what Salinas came up with at Taco and Burrito House.

They became part of a Chicago ecosystem of immigrant nonfranchised fast-food restaurants that included Chinese food, Greek gyros, Italian hot-dog stands, and sandwich and donut shops owned by Indians.

Several Atolingan taquerías replaced Polish and Italian hot-dog stands that went out of business.

Atolingans pooled knowledge, shared experiences, aided those in need. For a while, they formed an informal cooperative to buy vegetables and supplies. When one of Salinas's taquerías burned down in 1998, he reopened two weeks later using equipment from other Atolingan restaurateurs.

This kind of cooperation was a radical concept for men from an isolated Mexican village. Back home, anyone who wedged his way into a small business wasn't about to help or cooperate with the competition. *Envidia* was rife and pernicious. Envidia means "envy," but it also implies backbiting and in commerce, even sabotage. Envidia is behind the common Mexican proverb "Pueblo chico, infierno grande" (Small town, big hell). When discussing envidia, particularly as it relates to business, many Mexicans tell the story of crabs in a pot of boiling water. When one crab tries to get out of the pot, the others pull him back down; if they can't get out, why should he?

Chon Salinas came to view envidia as a devastating force. He felt it was behind the drug-smuggling rumors with which he'd had to contend. A significant cause of Mexican poverty in small villages, he believed, was the way people not only wouldn't cooperate in business, but at times actively tore each other apart. He told the story of Urbano García, a great carpenter in Atolinga years ago, who so feared competition that he refused to teach the trade to his own sons. As Salinas went out on his own and then helped others do the same, he railed often against envidia.

"The loans we eventually gave each other weren't that important," he said. "What was important was to recognize the strength of unity, this support, backing each other up, this confidence that we all need. It's what I learned at John Barleycorn's and what other people taught me there. I'd tell those who were starting restaurants that we have to break the pattern of those famous crabs."

Chicago was a huge market that offered opportunity for everyone. The new immigrants found themselves together in the same strange land, facing the same challenges: the English language, U.S.-born children, business permits, leases, taxes, snow. The envidia impulse withered, and unity came easier.

One of Salinas's most fervent disciples was Raúl Briseño. In 1990, at twenty-four, Briseño opened Wauconda's first Mexican restaurant—Raúl's Burrito Express, "home of the six-foot-long burrito"—with advice, encouragement, and a loan from Chon Salinas.

In Briseño, Salinas saw a youth lacking confidence but willing to work hard. He also saw a chance to expand his taquería concept to the suburbs. Wauconda residents already knew Briseño from his days as an employee at a local Irish tavern, where he organized regular Taco Nights. Raúl's Burrito Express had customers from its first day.

What Atolingans had created among themselves in Chicago— a kind of mutual-aid society—Raúl Briseño now created within his family. He brought a born-again fervor to restaurants. Everyone should have one.

In 1994, Raúl lured his brother, Alonso, out from California, with the promise of helping him start a restaurant in the nearby town of Mundelein. "When you see others doing it, and you know they haven't even been to school, you say, why not me?" said Alonso.

Raúl financed Rosa's Mexican Restaurant for his sister, Rosalina, in the nearby town of Rochelle. His brother, Luis, left factory work to start his own restaurant in the town of Island Lake. Raúl partnered with his younger brother, Sergio, to open Dos Hermanos, a sit-down restaurant in the ailing Wauconda Shopping Center, a move that town officials credited with helping revive the mall.

Again, the rumor spread among Atolingans that Raúl's money had come from drugs. His siblings insist that Raúl made his money honestly. Indeed, their brother's enthusiasm was infectious. With his encouragement, the Briseño family had created a little restaurant empire in the suburbs north of Chicago by the time he died.

In 1987, just as Chon Salinas was starting Taco and Burrito House, which would give birth to a generation of new immigrant entrepreneurs, he was gripped by the idea that it was now time to return to Atolinga to live. It was a startling and ironic notion. He was bootstrapping himself into the American tradition of small businessmen, yet wanted more than ever to be back in Mexico for good.

His wife, Ana, balked. Women's lives in the village were brutish. She liked Chicago's services—the dishwashers and refrigerators and supermarkets. The kids were growing up. She didn't want to go back to Atolinga to live.

Chon insisted. What would it take to get her to return? he asked. A house, big and luxurious, she said finally, built in the American style, with a driveway, and a lawn, and set back from the property line. She found a photograph of a house in a magazine and gave it to her husband. He gave it to an architect.

"Build me something like that," he said.

If the first house Chon had built in Atolinga looked like a Chicago three-flat, this one was a California ranch-style house, and, the way Chon saw it, it embodied the ideal of how to live. The house was made of brick on an enormous piece of land. It had two stories, four bedrooms, two living rooms and a dining room, a balcony, a large garden, a basketball half-court, and a barbecue.

For three years, as his taquería concept took hold in Chicago and then boomed, what quietly consumed Chon Salinas was building that house back in Atolinga. He thought of almost nothing else. He made lists of the special fixtures, the carpeting, and the curtains it would need. He sketched where the basketball half-court would go, where the barbecue pit would be. Not wanting to drain his savings, he took on extra work to pay for the house. He sold sour cream from Wisconsin to Mexican restaurants and took on other odd jobs.

By 1990, the house was pretty much done and could be occupied. Then, almost as soon as Chon finished the lavish house, he began finding reasons not to return to it. His kids were growing up, he told himself, and in private schools. They'd be in college soon. Maybe then, he'd go back. His taquerías were doing nicely. It'd be a shame to leave them now.

He thought this curious—that, while continuing to invest money and energy in the new home's upkeep, he didn't move his family back to Atolinga. Instead every year for the next decade he found reasons to say, "Next year."

❖

By the 1990s, Atolingan immigrants' restaurants were doing well. This was felt back in Atolinga. A home-building boom transformed the village into what it never had been: a town with services and paved streets.

The village's annual fiesta on August 7—in honor of San Cayetano—had once been confined to one day, with a mass, a parade, and a dance in the evening. But as Atolingans' life improved in the United States, the fiesta stretched into nine full days of revelry. One sign of economic success was when an immigrant could hire a ten-piece banda—blasting trumpets, clarinets, bass drums, and tubas—to follow him and his friends around the plaza. After a while, bandas from across the state descended on the village in early August. Atolinga's small plaza would seem to levitate on the roar of two dozen brass bands, gridlocked like Mexico City traffic, each playing different songs at the same time.

The young people who came down from the United States seemed to speak less Spanish as time went on. The fiesta became, in the words of one old lady, "Puros chiquillos hablando inglés" (Nothing but kids speaking English).

With the Chicago restaurant success, Atolingans formed one of the first Zacatecan clubs in Chicago—Club Atolinga. Chon Salinas was its president.

Over the next decade, Chicago grew into a major center of Zacatecan immigrant clubs with thirty-two, headquartered in a building on the south side that had once housed the Polish-American Polka Museum. The Zacatecan clubs practiced a version of the Atolingan mutual-aid philosophy. They raised money for public-works projects in each village—money that's now matched by Mexico's federal, state, and local governments, in a program called "3-for-1."

Club Atolinga remodeled the village elementary school, paved streets, renovated a plaza, and built a park. The projects helped the immigrants as much as the village. They'd left home urchins. Now, wealthy and magnanimous, they returned to improve it. The club and village improvements brought them together and reminded them how they had changed. They had lost the old timidity with which as villagers they had viewed power, business, and the great El Norte. They were now very American, but couldn't bring themselves to abandon Atolinga.

Even so, Atolingan immigrants had to admit that their village had become less a hometown than a place to spend a couple quiet weeks a year. Atolinga's residents, they knew, generally viewed them as wealthy and arrogant. When asked to vote for the town's next public-works project, most year-round residents preferred a chapel for wakes and funerals; immigrants in Chicago wanted a rodeo arena for use during the August fiesta. A party that Chon Salinas and a friend attended in Atolinga emptied when they arrived. On village streets, poor men with whom Chon had gone to elementary school who'd never left town hit him up for money and scolded him if he didn't recognize them immediately.

"The things I used to feel returning to Atolinga I don't feel here anymore," Chon said at the fiesta in Atolinga a few months after Raúl's death. "Atolinga is no longer for Atolingans. Now it's a village for people from someplace else."

Huichol Indians from the neighboring state of Jalisco had found a home in Atolinga. They didn't speak much Spanish, and they looked and dressed very differently from the light-skinned native Atolingans. These new residents tended immigrants' empty houses or were construction workers on the odd immigrant home not yet built. Immigrants in town for the August fiesta hired Huichol Indian string bands, who played Spanish versions of "Deep in the Heart of Texas" and songs by the slain narcocorrido singer, Chalino Sánchez.

The beautiful houses lining village streets were built on the premise that immigrants would return for good. But as their restaurants in Chicago succeeded, this seemed less feasible. The focus of their investment switched to their American-born children in Chicago private schools. So just as Atolinga acquired all the services, and perhaps some of the opportunities, that immigrants left to find in the United States, immigrants were no longer around to enjoy them.

"I always say I'll return but I know I won't," said Jesús Carlos, one of the few nonrestaurateur Atolingans living in Chicago. "I'm lying to myself. But if I say otherwise, I'd be like the patient who's sick who admits he's going to die."

Indeed, in Chicago, Atolingans were busy pushing out into other business frontiers. Wives of several restaurant owners started their own beauty parlors. Several Atolingans in Indianapolis had their own taquerías. In 1993, Rodolfo Carlos opened the first family dining, sit-down restaurant owned by an Atolingan in the suburbs of Chicago, then opened four more, prompting others to look to the suburbs as the next entrepreneurial horizon.

Atolingan taquerías in Chicago, meanwhile, became to recent Mexican immigrants what Golden Nuggets had been: schools to learn the restaurant business. Another Atolingan, Rudy De la Rosa, employs twenty-four people in his taquería, most of them from the village of Taranda in the state of Guanajuato, who are learning the restaurant business. De la Rosa has helped a couple of them go off on their own.

All this is merely to say that Atolinga existed more in the United States than it did in Zacatecas. A website, www.atolinga.com, got twenty-five hundred visitors a month, many more than the village itself. U.S. Atolinga had businesses, a news bulletin, an annual beauty queen, periodic dances, and, holding it all together, clubs in Chicago and Los Angeles where those who shared a background and position in America could be comfortable and together.

More than four hundred people attended the memorial service for Raúl Briseño a few days after his death.

He had served on Club Atolinga's board of directors and returned to the village every year. Yet he was fully involved in a new life in Wauconda. Townspeople remember him buzzing around Wauconda on rollerblades or his motorcycle. He helped with fund-raisers for the high school and fire department. He donated food to Waucondafest—the town's annual fair. He and his brother, Sergio, brought the first mariachi band to the fair.

A good part of Wauconda attended his funeral, as did Atolingans from as far away as Indianapolis. News of his murder spread through www.atolinga.com. The line of cars to the cemetery stretched for two miles.

Two months later, McHenry police announced the arrest of three men and a woman in Briseño's killing. Two of them, police believed, were the robbers, while the other two waited in a car. They were charged with murder and robbery, which police alleged was committed to get money for drugs.

"It is obviously a great relief," said Raúl's sister, María, shortly after their arrests. "On the other hand we reopen the wounds in our hearts thinking what really went on that night and what Raúl's last thoughts might have been."

Raúl Briseño's legacy is the entrepreneurial energy nurtured in Chicago that made restaurateurs out of a family of poor ranchers from a thirsty highland mesa in Zacatecas.

The youngest Briseño, Palemón, took over Raúl's Burrito Express in McHenry. Sergio opened The Foot-Long Burrito in Round Lake Beach. Dos Hermanos in Wauconda and Rosa's Mexican Restaurant in Rochelle continued to pull in customers. Alonso hoped to open a large suburban restaurant soon; his son was studying to be a chef.

"I sometimes tell my wife: We don't have much, but everything in due time," Alonso said. "We bought our house. We bought a new truck. It was really satisfying to be able to give my son a new truck for school. I have credit. You can see the advance in the Briseño family."

❀

In August of 2003, thirteen years after completing construction on that California-style house in to Atolinga, Chon Salinas put the finishing touches on it. He'd put them off for years. Knowing it wasn't quite finished gave him another excuse not to decide whether to return to it. But now he painted it. In front of the house, he installed a fountain of a little boy peeing into a pool. Then he killed a pig, hired a mariachi band, and held a party for seventy people.

It was a going-away party for himself. Little remained for him in Atolinga. His wife's parents had died, as had his father. His mother was a U.S. citizen and lived in Nebraska. Childhood friends had moved to Chicago, and his brother was once kidnapped in Atolinga.

"After thirty years in Chicago is when I found myself," he said, as he drove his SUV through the city's north side one winter afternoon several months later. "All that time I thought I was going back [to Atolinga]. Imagine all the energy it uses up—all that time you're thinking that you're going back. It keeps you from growing and involving yourself in life here. It takes over part of your brain. It's not so much what you spend in money. It's that it uses up all your energy; you don't do other things because you're so involved in this one thing, all so you can go back, which is something, finally, that you never do. A lot of immigrants spend most of their lives doing that."

And to this day, Chon Salinas hasn't spent a night in that California ranch-style house in Atolinga that took so much to build.

He now thinks he might sell it.

Chapter Eight

A Soccer Season in Southwest Kansas

Because Garden City High School had trouble finding white students who could kick the ball, Juan Torres was the field-goal kicker for the school's football team for one sweet year and knew the rarified world of privilege and glory that comes with playing America's sport in western Kansas.

In the year 2001, Juan Torres and Miguel Benítez, both sophomores, had the strongest legs on the school's soccer team. So they were made the kickers for the football team, as well. Miguel had the stronger leg and was used for kickoffs. Juan was reserved for field goals. Even so, the coach showed little confidence in Juan's leg. Toward the end of one game, down by two points, the team was close enough for a field goal but the coach opted to try for a touchdown. The attempt failed, and Garden City lost. "We could have won that game if they'd put me in," Juan said.

Despite their essential roles, Juan and Miguel were strangers on the team. No one called either of them anything but Kicker. This was how Garden City had evolved since the beef plants had brought Mexican and Salvadoran immigrants to town. Native Garden City—which is to say, the city's white and assimilated Mexican-American residents—depended economically on the immigrants and were mostly polite. But neither group knew much about the other with whom it had come to share streets, schools, and, occasionally, neighborhoods. An awkward coexistence was expressed in a million little ways, and one of these was the way the football players grew to call each of their two young kickers simply, Kicker.

But when Rockhurst High School came to town, Juan Torres earned a place in history. Rockhurst is a Jesuit school in Kansas City, a school reputed to recruit its players as early as middle school, put them on weight plans, and field kids of enormous size every year. By the time Rockhurst came to Garden City that season, no one had scored against them. There was no question who would win the game. But as no one had scored against Rockhurst so far, Garden City's coaches decided they would try a field goal if the team got close enough. Sure enough, in the first quarter, the team found itself at Rockhurst's twenty-yard line. They called on their sixteen-year-old Kicker.

"I was so nervous," said Juan. "I actually thought I was going to get hit by one of those kids. They snapped the ball, and I just ran up there and closed my eyes and kicked it and hoped it went in. I didn't even see it go in. I just heard the crowd cheering."

Garden City lost the game 40–3.

A tall fellow with confidence beyond his years, Juan Torres possesses the handsome jock cache that, as a senior two years after his field-goal glory, made him a presence on campus in a way that some of the smaller, thinner Mexican kids were not. Still, he spoke of his year on the football team the way a kid remembers a favorite summer vacation. On the road, you ate your fill at restaurants, and sometimes you even went to steakhouses. The school held pep rallies for you. The cheerleaders and the trainer were always at your games. Everyone on campus wanted to know you. It was intoxicating. Most of the Mexican population in town slaughtered cattle for a living and spent mostly unnoticed lives, unless they committed a crime, which was then duly reported in the *Garden City Telegram*. By joining the football team, it was as if Juan had been allowed into a special club, the benefits of which he'd been only partially aware of until then.

Most of all, he remembered wistfully, "it was great to play on Friday night, under the lights, and have your name announced over the speakers."

Two years later, in 2003, in the sky over western Kansas one afternoon in September, the sun had beaten away any errant wisp of cloud and was now

The 2003 Garden City High School soccer team, varsity and junior varsity.

beginning its decline in the west. Had a breeze not trickled in from somewhere, the soccer field might have been deadeningly hot, as September afternoons often are on the High Plains of Kansas.

Coach Joaquín Padilla shielded his eyes, looked into the sun, and yelled at his players to send the ball forward. On the field before him ran the Buffaloes, the varsity soccer team for Garden City High School, in white uniforms with black numbers. A slower opponent was outhustling his boys. Padilla groaned, turned away, and stomped the grass, as his players gave up on another loose ball.

Joaquín Padilla is a short, affable man now in his fifties, with gray hair and a mustache. Twenty years ago, as Mexican immigrants were arriving to Garden City, he'd come to town, hired as a high-school guidance counselor. Over the years, he had pestered the administrators and school board for an activity in which the immigrant students would want to participate. The school created a soccer team in 1996.

Soccer at Garden City High had gone largely unnoticed since then, however. Padilla's players insisted some students on campus didn't even know the school had a soccer team. In Wichita, Kansas City, and Topeka, soccer was a middle-class, white sport. But out here on the High Plains it was as foreign to the native white residents as the immigrants who played it. Southwest Kansas was farming and cattle country, which made it football country. Soccer was the sport Mexicans brought with them, and Mexicans went out for it. A few white school administrators attended soccer games, but players suspected they did so out of obligation.

As the 2003 season got under way, the team suffered the kind of indignity soccer players at Garden City High School were used to by now. A girl from the school's yearbook staff showed up at practice with a digital camera she didn't know how to use. She told the players that everyone on the staff who knew how to operate the camera wanted to take pictures of the football team, so they'd sent her to shoot the soccer team. She asked if any of them knew how to work the camera.

The varsity team she would photograph was made up of eleven children of Mexican immigrants, five of Salvadoran immigrants, one Vietnamese, and an Anglo. Padilla hoped this team would be different. Every year, he usually lost eight or nine players, who'd be academically ineligible or whose families would leave for work in other states. Each fall Padilla would start anew, patching together a team from whoever was left and whoever had moved into the area over the summer. But this year he'd lost only three guys, and eight of his returning players were seniors.

Juan Torres had dropped football to concentrate on soccer and had been the team's leading scorer the previous year. Rey Ramírez was a quick forward and played a lot of midfield as well. Hugo Blanco was small but fast. Armando González and Elbin Palencia alternated at the other forward spot. Luis Posada was a midfielder whose speed allowed him to cover enormous territory. Carlos Reyes, a thick, tough junior, and Pablo López, a thin sophomore, were at midfield. Defense was a solid wall made up of Rudy Hernández, Hernán Macías, and Servando Hernández. Backing them all up was Miguel Benítez, the goalie, who had remained as the football team's now all-purpose kicker.

These kids, or their parents, had come from different parts of Mexico and El Salvador. They were out on the desolate High Plains prairie of Kansas for one reason: IBP, the world's largest beef slaughtering plant. It was a few miles out of town and employed some four thousand people, virtually all of them Latino immigrants.

Seniors Tri Dang and Chuck Dodge were the team's only non-Latinos. Tri came to Garden City when he was nine. His father was a former officer in the South Vietnamese Army who had spent years in a communist reeducation camp after the war and who also worked at IBP. Chuck was born and raised in Garden City, and, alone on this team, his family had never worked in the beef plant.

Years before, when they were ten and eleven years old, seven of Padilla's players had played on a team that traveled around southwest Kansas playing other youth squads. That had been the start of organized youth soccer in Garden City. So by now, they knew each other's game. They were talented and fast. For all these reasons, Padilla allowed himself to hope. None of his teams had ever won even a first-round playoff game, but Padilla thought this team could advance beyond regional playoffs. He wanted the school to notice the team and by extension the Latino student body. This would only happen if the team did well.

Yet early in the season he watched as his boys played timidly. They showed up out of shape for practice in August. On this sunny September afternoon, they wilted when opponents pushed them out of plays. When his team won anyway, 1–0, on superior skill not effort, and the sun went down and his players walked off the field, Joaquín Padilla was not pleased.

His mood did not improve two nights later, when Garden City played Great Bend, another High-Plains town. Padilla's guys seemed to collapse when they couldn't score easily and discovered instead that Great Bend battled them all game long and won 3–0.

By the end of the first week of the 2003 season, the Buffaloes were 2–1. But Padilla believed they could easily have been 1–2. It was not the way he liked to start a season, and this year especially.

What bothered Padilla most was that there seemed to be a lot of Mexico in the way his kids had played soccer up to now. As the season progressed, this became one of his favorite subjects, and he would go on eloquently about it for quite a while.

Padilla had grown up in the town of Pátzcuaro, in Michoacán, several hours west of Mexico City. Pátzcuaro is the center of a region where people make handcrafts—guitars, furniture, and copperware. As a boy, Padilla learned to guide tourists around the area. As the artisans would pay him 20 percent of whatever they sold to his tourists, it was a lucrative business.

One day, he met a busload of tourists from Kansas. Among them was Henry Watkins, a railroad foreman, rancher, and state legislator. Watkins took a liking to this boy and asked Padilla if he'd like to come back to Kansas to live and go to school.

Padilla talked it over with his parents. Learning English would make him a better tour guide. So in 1962, at fourteen, alone and speaking no English, little Joaquín Padilla moved to the town of Erie, in eastern Kansas. Every morning he'd milk cows on the Watkins farm, then hop a bus for school. He sat in the back of his classroom, lost and bewildered, the only Mexican in the school. But he was a plucky kid. He memorized words and what they meant. He could understand the math and science. He would read to his English teacher during lunch break, and she would listen and correct him. Within six months, Padilla was pulling Cs. At year's end he was speaking English.

That summer Padilla returned to Pátzcuaro. He now knew enough English to be a great tour guide. But Kansas had changed him. "I went back to the same house, and I didn't find myself," he said. "The lake was there, the mountains were there, the trees were there, the house was there. Everything was the same, but I was not. When August came, I said, 'I can't stay here.'"

He returned to Kansas, leaving his family, who remain in Pátzcuaro to this day. Over the next seven years, he lived with two other families. The father of one of these families was the high-school basketball coach. So Padilla played on the basketball team and ran track at his high school.

Upon graduating, he received a track scholarship at Pittsburg State University in eastern Kansas, where he studied psychology. That led to a master's degree, and when he'd finished that, the school had an opening teaching Introduction to Psychology. At twenty-four, ten years after coming to the United States speaking no English, Joaquín Padilla stood before a college class of a hundred Kansas freshmen and taught them the basic concepts of psychology.

Padilla therefore had distinct ideas about what was possible in life. The cardinal sin, he felt, was to let life happen to you. That was how it was in Mexico.

"Mexicans are taught to be submissive. In Mexico, we're taught not to compete," he said. "A lot of those ideas come over here with families."

Mexican immigrants showed remarkable daring in coming to the United States. But once here, Padilla believed, many immigrants settled too easily into the enormous and oft-replenished Mexican enclave. The enclave helped immigrants find work and housing, then insulated them and did not force them to change.

As bilingual guidance counselor, Padilla would watch as, paralyzed, his students stared at the list of elective classes from which they had to choose three per semester. They'd ask Padilla what he recommended. He would tell them the choice was theirs.

"But the classes are all in English. There's a lot of Americans in there," they'd say.

"Of course," Padilla would answer. "If we were in Japan, there'd be a lot of Japanese."

He noted ruefully how they dropped the classes when they got difficult.

His players would buy their shoes through Padilla because he had a coach's discount through a catalogue. This was also often a tortured, drawn-out process, as some of his players anguished over what shoes to buy. On the field, too, his players seemed afraid to assert themselves—particularly when the other team was tall and white. They gave up on loose balls and took an elbow in the chest without giving one back.

Padilla felt this was part of a fear of standing out that was widespread among Latino students at Garden City High School. It was why the school, with a thousand Latino students amounting to a huge vein of soccer potential, had only about thirty boys go out for the varsity and junior varsity soccer teams each year. No Latina had ever gone out for the cheerleading or dance squad. The school newspaper, which published an article a week in Spanish, had no immigrant kids on its staff. The school formed special activities to get Latino students to participate; Latin Lingo began as a dance squad for Latinas.

Some students' poor English held them back; others were academically ineligible. Just as often, though, Latino students suffered from feelings of inferiority. "You know in Mexico how most people look down on poor people," said Artemio Rodríguez, a junior, whose parents came from Jalisco. "They think it's that way here, that white people look down on them. I think it's self-imposed. They always stay to themselves."

On campus, being Mexican had come to mean showing less interest in school and participating less. A Latino student who got good grades or did after-school activities was a "coconut": brown on the outside, white on the inside. Many soccer players, therefore, preferred the more comfortable Sunday adult leagues in town, playing against other immigrants—though competition was uneven, injuries were common, and college coaches never scouted these leagues.

With few boys to choose from, Padilla felt he couldn't ask of his players what a football coach would have demanded. His players whined about running sprints. Padilla would relent. Players were late or sometimes didn't show up at all. Football players would have been cut for any of these infractions, but Padilla said little.

"If we ran them hard . . . we wouldn't have a kid out here," he said, one day watching an unfocused practice. "It's a fear of excelling, of achieving."

Like any coach, Padilla compared his sport to life. Neither soccer nor life was determined by "Lo que Dios diga—Whatever God wishes." "It's you who makes things happen or not happen," he said. "This is hard for them to buy into."

Still, Padilla had faith in soccer in the United States. Until they joined the team, certain of his players had never showered in a locker room, competed face-to-face with white people, or stayed in a motel far from family. In the United States, soccer fulfilled the mission of student athletics in a way that football and basketball often didn't anymore. Those sports, in fact, tended to teach Old World lessons: that your behavior has fewer consequences if you belong to a privileged elite. In the United States, soccer was assiduously ignored and was therefore more egalitarian. Soccer players didn't often get the breaks on grades afforded a star running back, but that was a good thing. They had to work hard for recognition. Because of this, Padilla felt, soccer scholarships could offer real educations and open more important doors in life. But, again, the team needed to do well for the scholarships to come.

It was for all these reasons that his team's hesitant play distressed him in the first weeks of the 2003 season. This year was the culmination of a lot that Joaquín Padilla had been waiting for since he started the soccer program.

"This is the year," he said. "This is it."

This would indeed be a different kind of year for soccer in Garden City, Kansas. A high-school soccer season in the High Plains heartland where football was king would afford glimpses of America, of the Mexico within it, and of what had become of the country's melting pot.

Somewhere west of Wichita, the eastern United States ends and the West begins. Rolling hills bow to semiarid, flat land; the tall grass of eastern Kansas becomes short and scruffy out in the western part of the state. These are the High Plains. They stretch out before the Rocky Mountains from South Dakota down to Texas. At their center is western Kansas.

On the prairie, the trees that grow are thin and weather-nagged and mean nothing to the wind. A fall wind can rally across the plains and blow unobstructed for hundreds of miles. As remarkable as the flatness of western Kansas is its weather. It changes insanely. This part of Kansas has seen rain, snow, and hard sunshine, all in the same day.

Two hundred miles west of Wichita—equidistant from San Francisco, California, and Norfolk, Virginia—in the very middle of what Americans consider their heartland, lies the town of Garden City, Kansas.

The town, twenty-nine thousand people, is flat, too. Surrounding it are the cattle feed yards and the farms and the natural gas wells that make up the region's three principal industries. The largest edifices in Garden City are the water towers—each broadcasting the town's name across the prairie—and the white grain storage elevator. Only two-lane state routes bisect Garden City; no interstate comes anywhere near the town. Garden City's restaurants are mostly of the Burger King, Subway, and Lonestar Steakhouse chain variety that have crept across the country, homogenizing city and small town alike.

Garden City has always been a regional shopping center and is today the home to the only Target and Home Depot stores for 180 miles. Downtown Garden City is usually empty, and people are rarely seen out walking. Nor is there much to do at night, which people say is one reason the region has among Kansas's highest teen pregnancy rates. Seven miles away is the town of Holcomb, famous as the setting of *In Cold Blood*, Truman Capote's chronicle of the murder of a farm family.

This part of Kansas has always scared people away. The 2000 census showed that the state had 2.68 million people. Of these, only about 350,000 souls were brave enough to live west of Wichita.

The first European to see the region was a Spanish explorer named Francisco Vásquez de Coronado, in 1541. An Indian guide told Coronado that he would discover an Indian land of unimaginable wealth, of fish the size of horses and rivers six miles wide. Instead he found a few hundred Indians in huts and oceans of buffalo. Coronado recognized that the land had rich black soil that could, with effort, be farmed and where trade routes could be developed. But the Spaniards wanted gold and weren't inclined to settle for less. Coronado and his crew strangled the guide who'd led them there, turned around, and went home.

Three centuries later, in the late 1800s, the pioneers in western Kansas would understand how Coronado felt. Promoters of the region had to invent ploys and get-rich-quick schemes to attract settlers, because people tended not to stay, and without people the region had no future. Those who responded to these come-ons hoped for a place to escape limitations, to reinvent themselves. They were black "Exo-dusters" leaving the collapse of Reconstruction in the South; Mennonites from Austria escaping persecution; Czech, German, and Bohemian peasants; city folk from the east looking for fresh air to breathe.

Out on the plains, their lives became an epic grapple with nature. Blizzards froze them and their livestock. Their crops withered under hailstorms in July, then droughts. Con men fleeced the settlers. Rattlesnakes dropped from the roofs of their sod houses onto their dinner tables. Children died from the flu, from pneumonia, and scarlet fever. Walls of prairie fire could race across the flatlands, swallowing pioneer homes. As the pioneers slept, centipedes entered their ears, and fleas nipped their legs. Poor farming techniques withered the land, and by the 1930s terrifying dust storms moved across the High Plains, turning day to night and filling homes with silt. Only the most willful people, or those with no choice, stayed and survived.

One of the best tellers of their stories is a man named Craig Miner. Miner is a tall, thin historian with wispy white hair who teaches at Wichita State University. His great-grandfather, William Miner, came from Connecticut in the mid-1880s, looking to be a land speculator. He invested in extending street rail lines between the towns of Ness City and Sidney, a scheme that failed when Sidney blew away in a tornado. He founded the town of Harold, which disappeared when a railroad planned for the area failed to materialize. Two generations later, Miner's father was a lawyer and moved the family to Wichita.

Miner's father would take him to the family farm in Ness City. Miner remembers the lights of the harvesters at night crawling like huge insects across the fields. The farmers he met were leathery men conversant in the exotic themes of truck engines and bull castration.

"I was a city kid. I had that imagery about western Kansas—which may be partly a myth and maybe always was—as where double-distilled U.S. of A. is," Miner said. "Of course, I didn't have to live there, which everyone was always reminding me."

Studying history, his romantic notions of western Kansas faded as he discovered stories of immigrants' spirits crushed by land fraud and mean weather. Through Miner's books pass marauding Indians gang-raping pioneer women, towns that choke to death on the dust of failed crops, and locusts—which one year formed a cloud 250 miles wide and 20 miles deep, devouring even children's clothes, and driving people insane.

Yet much of what Americans think of themselves and the origins of their country is bound up in the lnd Miner described. The hard land promoted the values of self-reliance, directness, frugality, and calloused hands. It sculpted a classless society where weather and economics humbled all, regardless of station. Thus, no region outside New England contributed more of this country's historical icons: pioneers, sod houses, family farms, fields of corn and wheat, small towns and Main Street, Sioux and Cheyenne Indians, buffaloes, Dodge City, cattle drives, cowboys, the Santa Fe Trail—all of it the subject of ballads, novels, and a hundred western movies.

Southwest Kansas was America in another way, too. No one who stayed here remained the same. As recently as the 1950s, a woman suffering through a drought could be found in Miner's book, *West of Wichita*, writing: "Those who can stand it [here] have had to learn that man does not modify this country; it transforms him, deeply."

In 2003, tourism to Kansas was rising. A principal reason for this, state officials discovered from tourist surveys, was that Americans longed for something rooted and authentic to nourish their lives amid soulless chain stores, nonstop shopping, and twenty-four hour news cycles. Naturally, they looked for it in Kansas.

"People have that yearning for that Grant Woods sort of family—homesteader, pioneer stock that's independent and honest and sort of free of all this load of junk," said Miner one October day, sitting in his university office. "We imagine (these families) are not on the Internet getting spam. They're out there on their tractor, close to nature, close to God and heaven and livestock. We think about them earning their own way, independent of the taxpayer. We'd all like that to be true."

But western Kansas had been changing in ways relevant to this story for at least fifty years.

In the 1950s, the invention of the turbine water pump allowed them finally to suck water from the massive Oglalla Acquifer, a sea of underground freshwater that stretches under the High Plains from South Dakota to Texas and New Mexico. New irrigation systems let them spread that water across wide swaths of land and decreased the threat of drought. Farmers could grow huge amounts of grain—corn, milo, and alfalfa—which could be fed to cattle. With that came the cattle feed yard.

In 1951, a Garden City farmer named Earl Brookover built the first cattle feed yard in Kansas, with large pens in which cattle ate locally grown grain from a trough. Cattle fattened faster and more efficiently—on high-protein milo, corn, and alfalfa—than when they grazed aimlessly on the range. Dozens of ranchers opened feedlots across the High Plains. The Irsik family, another feedlot operator near Garden City, built the first processor that turned corn into cattle feed. Today, there is feed yard space for a million head of cattle within a sixty-mile radius of Garden City.

Poets would find potent symbols of America's vanished frontier in these yards, with their acres of penned and tagged cattle that once roamed the range. The cowboy was now as penned in as the cattle. He rode from yard to yard, culling the sick head.

Still, the feed yard changed the American diet. The price of beef dropped. On rangeland, cattle exercised as they grazed, making their meat lean and tough, so not much of the animal was usable for anything other than hamburger or pot roasts. America's hamburger tradition was due to the fact much of the range-fed cattle was appetizing only when it was ground up with some of the animal's fat. But in feed yards, cattle didn't move much, so their meat was fattier and thus more tender and better tasting. Demand for beef rose. This added protein to the U.S. diet. Cattle producers could now harvest more profitable specialty cuts—brisket, chuck, inside skirt, flatiron, and flank steaks—from all over the animal.

Brookover's idea was to keep in Kansas what was raised in Kansas. Up to that point, Kansas and a lot of rural America resembled the Third World: its commodities—cattle and corn, in this case—were shipped away to be transformed into more profitable products elsewhere. The feed yard transformed Kansas corn into a more profitable product—cattle. Thus a bit more of the wealth that these rural communities produced remained in the area.

By the 1970s, southwest Kansas was a cattle center unlike anything early settlers could have dreamed. Yet it was only a hint of what was coming.

The man who completed the transformation of southwest Kansas—and changed America in the process—was a tall, jowly fellow with a slow Iowa drawl named Andy Anderson.

Anderson cofounded a company known as Iowa Beef Packers—later IBP. Anderson had intense energy and creativity where building things was concerned. He'd been a butcher, then a meat wholesaler in Los Angeles. Anderson had no schooling in engineering but would become an expert, and endless tinkerer, in the science of meat-packing and refrigeration. He built the meat-packing plant of the future.

Meat-packing began in the big cities, near large populations of workers, many of whom were Eastern European immigrants. Legions of well-paid union butchers in Chicago, Omaha, and Kansas City slaughtered the cattle that came in on trains from the High Plains. Anderson and IBP moved the meat industry to the small town in the American heartland where the cattle were raised. Anderson retired from IBP in 1970 and died in 1990 at the age of seventy-one. But by then, he and IBP had reinvented the way meat was slaughtered and sold. They'd also ended butcher unions and brought millions of Mexican immigrants to the heartland.

In 1960, Anderson and his partner, Currier Holman, used a U.S. Small Business Administration loan to form IBP in the town of Denison, Iowa. Anderson applied assembly-line principles to the disassembly of cattle. In this factory, the jobs of slaughtering, cutting, vacuum wrapping, and boxing the meat for shipping were mechanized and consolidated under one roof. His factories broke down these tasks until anyone could do them. A production line would send a cow carcass on a hook through the plant. A worker would make one cut, then the carcass moved to the next worker, who made another cut, and so on, until the skeleton remained. The cuts were then sealed in plastic and boxed for shipment.

Boxed beef was easier and more sanitary to ship than the swinging carcasses that were touched by dozens of hands before they were eaten. Packaged in plastic, the meat kept fresh, and it didn't lose weight, as happened when carcasses were handled excessively. Also, only the edible parts of the animal were shipped to market. In the old days, retail butchers might throw away the small quantities of unsalable fat and bones that came with the large slabs of beef. An IBP factory could accumulate great quantities of this detritus and sell it in bulk for use in other products. More than forty products—from perfume to shoes—are today made from one cow.

After Brookover's success, feed yards spread across the High Plains. They supplied the huge numbers of cattle Anderson's factories required to run efficiently. IBP built or acquired boxed-beef factories in small towns in Nebraska, Iowa, Kansas, and Minnesota. In 1980, the company built the ultimate expression of Anderson's innovations: the plant near Garden City, which can slaughter eight cattle a minute.

To IBP, rural towns had an advantage in addition to their oceans of livestock: they had a nonunion culture and were mostly in states that had outlawed the union shop. Unions correctly viewed IBP's plants as a threat to the skilled tradesmen they represented. The two sides waged fierce, occasionally bloody battles for two decades.

The tale of IBP's rise to dominance in the meat industry is too long to fully recount here. It is studded with antitrust investigations, lawsuits alleging price fixing, armies of injured workers, and fines from the Occupational Health and Safety Administration. In 1974, company cofounder Currier Holman was convicted of conspiring with a Mafioso to bribe the company's way into the New York meat market. Consumer groups decried IBP's cozy relationship with federal regulators, whom they said watered down investigations of the company's pricing and labor tactics. Meanwhile, IBP's competitors needed similar plants, and their battles with meat unions further wracked the industry.

By the end of the 1980s, IBP and Anderson's boxed-beef factories had closed urban meat-packing plants and busted the unions. The skilled union butcher in the city was replaced with low-skilled assembly-line worker earning less than a third the wages in the heartland.

IBP applied its model to pork as well. Tyson, the chicken titan, was mechanizing poultry slaughtering and locating chicken plants in small, nonunion towns in Tennessee, Arkansas, and North Carolina. Meat plants would come to Joslin, Illinois; to Lexington, Nebraska, and Jamestown, Tennessee; to Storm Lake, Iowa, Guymon, Oklahoma, and Fort Morgan, Colorado.

Mechanized meat plants allowed rural America to retain even more of the wealth from the product it generated. But slaughtering cattle at a ferocious pace without union protection made meat-packing the most dangerous job in the America. Workers were prone to repetitive-motion injuries, knife cuts, and stress. They came home with their hands frozen in a grip. Turnover was high.

While these towns had the poultry and livestock the factories needed, they lacked people willing to do hard, fast, nonunion work. The only people who would work these jobs in the required numbers—the people the heartland needed to extract the wealth from what it produced—were from Mexico and Central America. It again attracted immigrants—this time not from villages in Czechoslovakia or Austria, but from Mexico, El Salvador, and Guatemala.

Once in the heartland, many of these immigrants later moved on to its cities, forming the core of the working class in Denver, Nashville, Memphis, Des Moines, Wichita, Oklahoma City, and Kansas City. By the beginning of the twenty-first century, the mass movement of Latino immigrants to the heartland, which the meat plants had ignited, was one of the country's most important demographic trends. The Midwest hadn't seen this kind of influx of foreign-born workers in a century. The South hadn't seen it since slavery.

"It was the IBP revolution," said Don Stull, professor of anthropology at the University of Kansas, who studied meat-packing and the effect of immigration on Garden City. "You could credit or blame IBP—depending on your point of view—with bringing immigrants to these areas. They certainly were the industry leader with all these innovations that lowered wages, busted unions, and sent packing plants out to the country. We have IBP to thank for the modern beef-packing industry."

Perhaps the first rural town in the American heartland that Mexicans sought out in large numbers was Garden City, Kansas. IBP's plant opened with twenty-three hundred jobs, and that number soon jumped to above three thousand jobs. Garden City's population almost doubled. A town that in 1980 was 82 percent white was by the year 2000 almost half Hispanic. New languages befuddled schoolteachers. Hundreds of workers slept in their cars at first. Then trailer parks were built.

Garden City, and the towns of Dodge City and Liberal, formed meat-packing's golden triangle, with five plants in all, employing twelve thousand people and slaughtering about five million head of cattle a year. The companies were desperate for workers; one company briefly advertised in the Garden City High School newspaper. They first recruited workers from Texas and New Mexico. They arranged for newly arrived Vietnamese refugees to settle nearby, giving jobs to anyone. In time, though, many of the Vietnamese took their savings and left southwest Kansas.

By the late 1990s, workers in these plants were mostly from Mexico and Central America. Kansas ranchers and farmers of bygone eras had relied on their own labor to extract wealth from the region. That was now Latino immigrants' job, which was an alarming development for a state that had prided itself on its classless society.

But a lot of what Americans imagined as quintessentially American about the heartland had, in western Kansas at least, been fading for some time.

Two-thirds of Kansas farms were on the government dole. Farmers in Finney County, where Garden City was the county seat, received $151 million in government subsidies between 1995 and 2003—more than any county in the state. Most Main Streets were empty, thumped by farm crises and then finally sucked out of western Kansas towns and regurgitated onto the floors of numerous Wal-Marts. The local bar and grill had bowed to Applebee's, the faux hometown diner with fifteen hundred branches nationwide and plans for a thousand more. Boot Hill in Dodge City and the Dalton gang's hideout a few miles away in Meade—symbols of the untamed American spirit—had been made into fun parks for tourists.

Much of what these prairie towns had been was now found only in their historical museums. These museums were always worth a visit, as much for the conversation with the old ladies who ran them as for the wondrous displays of church organs, tractors, Victrolas, and old stoves. Museums reminded visitors of how small-scale and locally owned America had been. The photographs in these museums were especially telling. They were reminders that a generation ago the people here had been as thin as rails.

By 2003, an obesity epidemic was in full bloom across southwest Kansas, as it was across the country. Doctors in the area reported hundreds of patients who were seventy-five to one hundred pounds overweight. Women five feet nine weighing 250 pounds were almost common. Garden City High School served pizza, French fries, and Pepsi and called it lunch. Unpleasant parallels could be drawn between the feed yards where thousands of cattle fattened at the trough all day and the "All-You-Can-Eat" buffet at the Golden Corral restaurant in Garden City.

Obesity was especially unsettling to see in western Kansas, which had been so associated with wizened pioneers and gratification postponed. Viewed from western Kansas, it did not seem coincidental that Mexicans came to the heartland just as Americans were attaining unprecedented sizes. It wasn't that the immigrants weren't fat—many of them were. It was that, in the words of one doctor, "physical activity is left to the immigrants, for the most part."

As the twenty-first century began, the sparse prairie of southwest Kansas again offered a clear view of an America under construction. It was different from that which earlier pioneers had created. Its values included not gratification postponed, but excess consumption; not self-reliance, but dependence on others' labor; a class, not classless, society.

What seemed closest to the American spirit that southwest Kansas had forged was the attitude of the Latino immigrants who'd come to work as hard as it took to get ahead. Even behind the great symbols of authentic Americana, there was often a Mexican doing the heavy lifting and ensuring that Kansas looked as the country expected.

Pheasant hunting, for example, was a time-honored western Kansas tradition. With wild pheasants long dead, however, pheasant farms had popped up—worked by Mexican immigrants. These farms raised pheasants but sold fantasy. Farmers bought the birds, then rented their land to groups of lawyers and businessmen from Chicago, Denver, and Kansas

City. These lawyers and businessmen came to southwest Kansas with shot-guns they didn't always know how to use, looking for pheasants and the illusion that they were roughing it on the High Plains. Meanwhile, the immigrant workers said nothing to upset the effect the lawyers sought.

Perhaps the best example of this dependence, however, was in the town of Liberal.

Liberal is the hometown of Dorothy in *The Wizard of Oz*. The book's author, L. Frank Baum, never lived in Kansas, but he set his story there to emphasize his heroine's innocence. During the 1980s' farm crisis, Liberal was persuaded to build a Land of Oz to draw tourists. The town stages its OzFest there in October.

OzFest 2003 featured Robert Baum, great-grandson of L. Frank Baum, and five tiny actors, now in their 80s, who had played Munchkins in the film. Organizers held look-alike contests for kids dressed as Dorothy, the Cowardly Lion, and the Tin Man.

Moving invisibly through the crowd was the handyman at the Land of Oz, a man named Eduardo Barrios. Barrios grew up in the state of Durango, in northwest Mexico. A taciturn fellow of fifty-four, Barrios lived and worked for many years in Southern California. In 1999, he came to Liberal, where two sisters live. He found work at the National Beef plant, but then cut his hand. The company patched him up, gave him some money, and sent him on his way. The Land of Oz hired him.

Today not much happens at the Land of Oz without him. Barrios paints the Yellow Brick Road yellow and the Emerald City green. He mows the lawns, cleans the bathrooms, and replaces the toilet paper. Were it not for Barrios changing the light bulbs on one display, a vision of Glinda the Good Witch would never appear. And if you look behind the curtain at the Land of Oz in Liberal, Kansas, you will find not a frumpy white professor, but Eduardo Barrios, a Mexican immigrant, tending the dials on the tape deck that pipes in the Wizard's booming voice, creating the icon Americans most associate with what is theirs.

On a sunny, breezy afternoon in October, the calls of soccer players echoed like wind chimes on a field near the western Kansas town of Great Bend.

The Garden City High School soccer team was again playing the team that a month before had made them look weak. This time, though, Garden City seemed to have found itself. There was a new urgency to the way they played. It was startling to see Rey Ramírez and Rudy Hernández push opponents out of the way, to watch Luis Posada buzz back and forth, covering the entire field in seconds.

The intervening month had been a good one, the kind that Joaquín Padilla had expected of his squad as the season started. Since that early loss to Great Bend, the team had won all its games. Now at midseason, its record stood at 8–1.

Winning, it seemed, had jolted them awake and helped them shed the losing attitude. The hesitancy of a month before was gone. They confidently elbowed opponents or streaked together down the field with the ball, like a pack of gazelles in perfect choreography, then turned together to backpedal.

Most players would say the tougher attitude emerged during two close wins a month apart in which the team had ample opportunity to give up but did not.

The first was a home game against Dodge High School. Trailing Dodge 2–1 with six minutes to go, Juan Torres tied the game with a magnificent bicycle kick—flipping in the air with his back to the goal and kicking the ball in for a score. Hugo Blanco scored with two minutes left to win it. The team went on to win its next five games.

Then, in early October, Garden went south to play Liberal High School. The team took an early 2–0 lead. Liberal surged back to lead 3–2. With three minutes to go, Juan beat defenders to a loose ball in front of the Liberal goal and scored, tying the game. In overtime, Servando Hernández rocketed a penalty kick from thirty-five yards out that the Liberal goalie couldn't corral. The ball caromed off the goalie, and Juan was there to kick it in for the 4–3 win.

"The attitude began to grow that we can beat anybody," Padilla said. Luis Posada believed the team was no longer intimidated by higher expectations. "People expect us to win, and we expect to win," he said.

This was new for Garden City High School soccer. Since the team's inception, soccer had long been a metaphor for Mexican immigrants' standing in town. The team's annual mediocre showings were due, as Padilla said, to losing a lot of players each year. But also, on campus, soccer was considered low class. No one at school cared much about the team. Few Latino students, nor even many players' parents, attended the home games. So as each season went on, players would grow demoralized, stop caring, and lose. All this would, in turn, support the idea that soccer was as unworthy of attention as the immigrant population in town.

Even the team's one decent year—in 2000, when it went 12–4—wasn't much recognized. Attendance didn't rise; few people came to the team's one playoff game, which it lost. Soccer, after all, wasn't football, and it was simply too soon after the school's football team had won it all.

The story of Garden City High School's rise to football greatness was well known to all the soccer players. Most of them were not so young as to have missed the football team's one truly great year in 1999. Four years later, the soccer team felt it still competed with the wistful memories of that championship year that the town fervently clung to. When it came to football's glory days, Garden City was like a jilted lover who refused other suitors hoping the one great romance would return.

Garden City had spent the 1970s and 1980s developing a losing tradition in football that seemed unshakable. As the 1990s approached, administrators vowed to change that. They hired a coach named Dave Meadows from a winning high school in Oklahoma. Meadows's job, he was told, was to win, period. Wanting to retain nothing from Garden City's losing years, Meadows brought his entire coaching staff with him from Oklahoma. Meadows was made the school's athletic director. He was an old-style southern football coach and had a dictatorial way about him. This miffed a lot of folks, but they stifled their criticism as the new coach crafted the school into a statewide football force.

Under Dave Meadows, Garden City's team made the state playoffs eight of the next ten years. It played for the state championship in 1998, losing to Olathe North, from Wichita. The next year Garden City won it all, beating Olathe South High School 14–7. The team's trophy stands next to Sodbuster—the stuffed, full-size buffalo that is the school mascot—that is enclosed in glass in the school's main hallway.

High school football never reached the level of religion in Garden City. After all, as one parent said, "this isn't Oklahoma." Still, the great 1990s enshrined the football team as the town's central social preoccupation and unequaled source of civic pride. There was resistance to starting a soccer program for fear that it might detract from the football team. At public events, mayors mentioned the football team's record and its Friday night opponent. Hundreds of parents joined the booster club each year. They would travel the many hours it took to go to games in Wichita, Manhattan, and Salina.

At school, football players formed a privileged caste. They were expected to remain silent on the bus to away games, concentrating on the task ahead. But they were winked at when they did poorly in class, and they roamed the halls during class uninterrogated. The booster club ponied up money for them to eat at steakhouses while on the road. Football players got the pep rallies. Cheerleaders pined to date the star players. Students ached to say hello to them in the halls; teachers clapped them on the backs.

As much as anything, the sign of the football team's status was that it played at the school's stadium, under the lights, with bleachers and a scoreboard. Soccer, meanwhile, played on a nondescript field attached to Kenneth Henderson Middle School a mile away. The field had no scoreboard, no snack bar, no dressing rooms. Nor did it have lights. Games, therefore, had to begin at 3:30 PM. The field had only one bleacher, though this had been more than ample seating for the dismal attendance at soccer games.

To the town's credit, winning football games at any cost did not interest Garden City. In 1999, the very year the team won the state championship, Dave Meadows was pressured to resign. Meadows was feared, but not loved. When he was found to have supplied two players with a salve usually applied to injured horses—an ointment known as DMSO—outraged parents and teachers mobilized and forced him out.

But the school's football team had never been better than mediocre since then. Meadows's successor had been fired after only two losing seasons. By 2003, the school's football dominance was a memory. What hadn't changed, however, were the traditional privileges that the 1990s had conferred on the football team. Both the local and student newspapers, for example, spent far more prominent space on the football team than on soccer, though in 2003 the soccer team was having a stellar season.

This unequal treatment of football and soccer is true of most U.S. high schools. Football is more popular, has a longer tradition, and is a bigger money earner. Thus, it gets more attention and larger budgets. At many schools, the inequality stops there. Most high school soccer teams are made up of middle- or upper-class white kids, who feel socially equal to their football peers. But at Garden City, the inequality in the two sports simply magnified the town's class and racial differences. The recognition of football reflected the class of the kids who played it. Likewise, when soccer went begging, it seemed to emphasize to the players their status on campus. Just as meat-plant workers never made the papers, no student at Garden City High School had ever been recognized or popular because he played soccer.

It was easy for Padilla's players to dwell on this inequality. As Rey Ramírez put it, "Their parents own farms and cattle feed yards. Our parents work for their parents."

But as the fall of 2003 progressed, a few things began to happen in Garden City. First, the football team once again began to lose. At homecoming, the team's record was 1–4. Attendance dwindled. Who wanted to watch a losing team? Students now came late to the games and left once they had an answer to the evening's central question: where are the parties?

Observant folks discerned that the town's demographics meant football's glory days probably would not return. The city was growing, but the Anglo population was declining. Replacing them were families from Mexico and Central America. By 2003, their children made up more than half the two-thousand-student body at Garden City High School. Immigrant kids quietly acquiesced before school traditions, of which the football team was the most important, but the sport they prized was not football, but *fútbol.*

"When the school was defending state champion, there were easily seventy kids—sophomores, juniors, and seniors—who went out for the football team," said Brad Hallier, the high-school sports reporter for the *Garden City Telegram.* "Now you're looking at forty or fifty kids. Liberal, same thing, and they're a football town, too. Maybe five families move out, and ten Hispanic families move in. How many of them have played football in their lives? Pretty much all they know is soccer."

It was in 2003, as Garden City football declined, that soccer ascended. The early loss to Great Bend jolted players awake. They stopped focusing on what they weren't getting and began to ask more of themselves. By the second Great Bend game, players were charging for loose balls. In fearless and elegant slides, they would launch themselves feet first at the ball, stealing it while leaving opponents sprawled on the ground. That October afternoon, they easily beat Great Bend, and their record stood at 9–1.

Now, for the first time, the soccer team became the talk of Garden City High School. Suddenly people noticed the sport, and thus the immigrant kids who played it. Soccer players were startled when teachers stopped them in the hall to ask how they'd done the day before. They could hear other kids talk about the team in the halls. Students put up posters with newspaper articles and photos of players in action, urging the team on.

As excitement built around the team, the city commission took up an issue related to soccer. The commission decided to name the soccer field at Kenneth Henderson Middle School for a member of the community. Several Latinos were mentioned as possible candidates, including a former street-department worker and a radio DJ. Hearing of this, the family of Martín Esquivel thought the field ought to be named for him.

Esquivel was born in Somberete, Zacatecas, and grew up in Ciudad Juárez. In 1976, at the age of nineteen, he came to Garden City and found work in a small meat plant. Later, he helped build the IBP plant and was hired at the plant when it opened.

In 1977, Esquivel organized the town's first soccer team, made up of Mexican immigrants. The team traveled to play in Texas and elsewhere in Kansas. It was a rag-tag crew. Still, soccer in Garden City began with that team Martín Esquivel founded. Ten years later, Esquivel was shot and killed by a young man he confronted who had been bothering his sister, Manuela.

In the fall of 2003, his sister, Manuela Esquivel, drew up a petition asking the city to name the field for her brother. Taking the petition to IBP, McDonald's, the local schools, and the Sunday adult soccer leagues, the Esquivel family came up with fifteen hundred signatures and presented it to the city. As the Buffaloes' season went on, in the background was the debate over how to name the field where the team played.

Meanwhile, the team won game after game. Attendance climbed beyond the demoralizing fifteen or twenty spectators. The school moved bleachers from the football stadium to the soccer field to handle the overflow. Toward the end of the season, even the cheerleaders, white and Asian girls, started coming to the home games, urging the Buffaloes to "F-I-R-E, Fire Up!" After each win, the students in the crowd, now numbering in the dozens, lined the field, and the players ran by high-fiving them all. This became a tradition, and the line of students grew longer with each win.

All this had an almost physical effect on the players. They walked taller on campus. "Around here it's always been football, football, football," said Rey Ramírez, midway through the season. "But the other day, the athletic director asked me how we'd done the night before, and I said we'd won and he said, 'All right! High five!' It caught me off guard. I've never seen anybody show excitement for soccer other than us."

The team was something for immigrant kids to be proud of, and some of its glory reflected on them. "It seems like it shouldn't matter, but it did," said one student. ESL students met the team at their bus before it headed to an away game. Kids who'd never attended soccer games before began showing up at home games. After a while there were enough spectators that for the first time cheers were chanted in unison, in Spanish. One frigid afternoon in late September, dozens of students huddled together wrapped in blankets to watch an entire home game despite a lacerating wind and temperatures in the 30s.

By midseason, the school newspaper, *The Sugar Beet*, for the first time wrote long stories about the team and ran them with photographs. The posters in the school hallways got bigger with each victory.

One result of that was some Latino students gradually began to lose their fear of participating. One of these was a girl named Vanessa Ramírez. Vanessa, pretty and bright, was a lively sophomore. Her mother was eight-months pregnant with her when she swam across the Rio Grande to enter the United States. Her parents came to Garden City and found work at the IBP plant. On Valentine's Day of 1988, Vanessa was born.

By the early 1990s, the Mexican community in Garden City had grown so large that Vanessa didn't learn English until the third grade. This enclave had been most of what she'd known up to then. But her bubbly personality allowed her to move beyond the limitations of the Mexican enclave at school. In eighth grade, she had tried out for choir—the first Mexican-immigrant student to do so.

In ninth grade, her grades fell, and Vanessa lost some of her ambition and spirit. Much of this had to do with her parents, who saw no future for her in school and told her so. "I'm not smart," she said. "I get told that every day at home: 'You're dumb.' They call me *burra*, *pendeja* (dope, idiot). 'Why are you in school? Just drop out and get a job.' My dad just told me yesterday, he said, 'Soon you'll be sixteen, and you can drop out.'"

But as the soccer team's season electrified the Latino students at Garden City High School, one of those it transformed was Vanessa Ramírez, now a sophomore. By midseason, she was the team's most faithful fan. She began to regain some of that fearlessness that her parents' low expectations had discouraged. She never missed a soccer game. She painted her face in school colors and made T-shirts supporting the team. She carried a large school flag to home games and ran up and down the sidelines with it when the team scored.

Vanessa recognized this as radically new behavior for the child of Mexican immigrants at Garden City High School, but she didn't care.

"Hispanic students isolate themselves," she said one afternoon at a home game late in the season. "They say, 'I'm going to look stupid if I participate.' They feel like they don't want to be involved in school. They just want to be involved in their own little world. They're scared."

As the team kept winning, more immigrant students began to consider after-school activities. More boys spoke of trying out for soccer the following year. Several Latinas were actually planning on going out for the girls' soccer team in the spring. Five girls promised to become the first children of Mexican immigrants to try out for the school's cheerleading squad next fall. Whether they'd make it was an open question. The parents of Asian and white girls had money to send them to cheerleading camps that most Mexican girls' parents couldn't afford. Still, the chutzpah it took to even plan on it was impressive. It was as if a Mexican boy were talking about trying out for quarterback.

The ringleader in this was Vanessa Ramírez. Inspired by the team, Vanessa vowed to play soccer in the spring and try out for cheerleader next fall. Though her grades were sagging, she showed no signs of listening to her parents' opinion of her scholastic abilities, but instead met with a University of Kansas counselor and now spoke of attending college to study nursing.

"I know we can do something for this school," she said. "It's not only them (the white students) at this school. It's us, too. We're part of it. It's just that we feel neglected. We feel they don't pay attention to us. Whatever we do isn't going to count. That's why we never try for anything. We're just as capable of doing something as they are, we just haven't realized it."

Through that fall, the Garden City Buffaloes won game after game. The school took notice. So did the *Garden City Telegram*. The paper's reporter, Brad Hallier, understood the sport and explained the fine points to the school's other coaches, who were caught up in the excitement. Finally, more or less all of Garden City—immigrants and whites—awoke to what was happening. The Spanish-language radio stations mentioned their success. The mayor stopped asking about the football team and now inquired how the soccer team had done each week.

Among the townspeople, though, one white couple needed no prodding to follow this team. They were Andy and Sidni Musick, and they watched the team's success that fall with a mixture of bitterness and satisfaction.

Sidni Musick has a grandmotherly look about her, with long gray hair often kept in a bun or ponytail. She teaches English as a Second Language (ESL) at Garden City High School. All her students are immigrants, and in 2003 these even included one or two of Padilla's players. She is also the advisor to the school's Asian Club. Andy Musick is bald, with a mustache and goatee, and works as a church musician and substitute teacher.

The Musicks are among the few white people in Garden City who live in an entirely Mexican neighborhood. There are people in town who would describe the Musicks' attitudes on politics and society, including the issue of immigration from Mexico, as "bleeding-heart liberal."

The Musicks had been a driving force behind the youth soccer team in 1996 that included many of the players who were now on the high-school team. That youth team marked the first time in Garden City that immigrants and the native white population—children and parents—were thrown together socially, outside a school or workplace. Then, abruptly, the team dissolved when Latino families took their children to form another team. The white kids dropped soccer for other sports.

The experience had challenged some of the Musicks' ideas regarding Mexicans and the American melting pot. Now, seven years later, watching the 2003 Garden City High School soccer team made up of kids from that team, the couple still wanted answers for the break-up of the experiment into which they'd put so much work.

The Musicks' involvement with soccer began when their son, Theo, was six and playing in a parks-and-recreation league. Andy Musick had never played soccer, but he learned to coach it. Eventually he became a certified soccer referee. The rec league was informal, and the teams rarely practiced. So as Theo grew, Andy Musick looked about for more competitive soccer for his son.

The way Andy Musick tells it, when he'd referee rec-league games, one of the coaches, Juan Rucker, was particularly critical of his calls. Rucker is a Mexican immigrant, a proud, intelligent man who had played high-level amateur soccer in Mexico. He had no children in the soccer leagues but volunteered to coach a team anyway.

One day after a game, Musick said he approached Rucker and proposed they work with, instead of against, one another. Rucker agreed. They set about forming a team of the more talented kids in the rec league. Their idea was to practice regularly and travel to play better teams far from Garden City. They chose the best players for the team.

What they formed was meant to be a traveling soccer team, not a social experiment, but it became both. About half the players chosen were white, the other half were Mexican and Salvadoran. On the team was the nucleus of players that would make up the 2003 team for Garden City High School: Juan Torres, Rey Ramírez, Carlos Reyes, Miguel Benítez, Hernán Macías, Rudy Hernández, and Chuck Dodge.

Those involved in the team remember it, by and large, as a pleasant and beneficial experience. The team practiced twice a week and played teams in Lawrence, Emporia, Dodge City, and Liberal. Once, though, at a tournament in Topeka, the players, tiny nine- and ten-year-olds, were greeted with calls of "beaners" and "taco vendors" from white parents. The Dodge City coach was equally nasty. At the Dodge City game, the opposing team's parents' insults got so vicious that a referee finally ordered them off the field.

The Musicks said they dove into the team's organizational details. They arranged lodging for the boys on their trips. They recruited parents to drive the team to games. They helped put together fund-raisers. During the summer of 1996, the couple was busy arranging nonprofit status for the team.

That summer, Andy Musick invited a soccer coach from Wichita to hold a three-day camp for the kids. Rucker had been away for several weeks. Musick arranged the camp, then called Rucker to tell him that the camp was scheduled. Rucker showed up, but left without saying a word. The Musicks never heard from him again.

Suddenly, the Latino players stopped coming to practice. Just like that, the biracial traveling soccer team ended. The immigrant parents took their kids and formed a team with Rucker—a team that itself fell apart a short while later.

The Musicks never understood what happened. They ran into a wall of what in Mexico is called *hermetismo*—which translates into a social silence, an unwillingness to give direct explanations, combined with a desire to avoid confrontation. Immigrant parents looked away when they saw the Musicks in stores or at school.

"Even when we had their kids' personal items, like socks or something, we called them, and parents never returned our phone calls," said Sidni Musick.

Sidni Musick says she heard later through her students' grapevine that parents were telling their relatives not to let their children take her ESL class because she was prejudiced. Meanwhile, the immigrant players stopped saying hello to Theo Musick at school.

Rucker said he broke with Andy Musick over the soccer camp because money the kids had raised for uniforms was used to pay for it. "We'd done three car washes for uniforms, and I didn't think that money should be used for the summer camp," Rucker said.

If true, the Musicks say no one told them. Andy Musick's family had been migrant farm workers in Oklahoma. He remembered his folks as direct and straightforward. "I thought Mexicans would be the same as my family," he said. But years later, Andy Musick still had no explanation for the split, except for from one boy, who'd told Theo Musick that they were going to form a team just for Mexicans. When Theo reminded the boy that he was not Mexican, but Salvadoran, the boy replied, "Well, we Hispanics got to stick together."

Undeterred, Andy Musick continued to referee adult-league games on Sunday. Then players began calling him racist for the calls he made against them—though all the players in the games he refereed were Latino. After a while, the league stopped calling him to referee.

To the Musicks, wrapped up in the episode were Mexicans' complicated feelings toward America and toward white people whom they perceived as wealthy by definition. Perhaps, too, there were attitudes, accepted implicitly from years of PRI government education, that gringos will always want to usurp what's Mexican. Also part of the mix may have been Mexican envidia—or envy, usually involving someone feeling that he doesn't get enough credit or attention, or that someone else gets too much. "Maybe this is why IBP has been so successful in keeping unions away," said Sidni Musick.

Americans talk often about racial diversity, but it isn't an idea that seems to appeal to many Mexican immigrants. On occasion during the 2003 season, when Tri Dang dribbled the ball downfield, some of the Mexican fathers of his own teammates made fun of him by babbling in imitation Chinese.

"I think there was prejudice against us because we were white," said Sidni Musick, talking about the team seven years after its demise. "Prejudice because they perceived the fact that we had more money, when in reality we probably didn't. There was a perception that we thought we were better than they were. I think they thought they were inferior. When I see people kind of duck and turn away now when I come by, I can see that they're embarrassed."

Sidni Musick also thought the experience a result of Mexican immigrants' unwillingness to let go of Mexico and be absorbed into America. She saw this in the vehemence with which her ESL students—with better futures and better educations in Kansas than ever possible in Mexico— spoke of the United States taking Mexican territory 160 years earlier.

"The people who are treated the worst [by Mexico] are the ones who turn around and are the most loyal to Mexico," she said. "It's an interesting human puzzle."

One mother remembered the traveling team well. Sylvia Trevino is Juan Torres's aunt. She is a frank, strong woman. Both Juan and her youngest son, Sergio, played on the traveling team. She often sold candy and made enchiladas to raise money for the team. Race was part of what split the traveling team, Sylvia said. The bitter welcome the Mexican kids received in places like Topeka and Dodge City hardened these views.

"I think that's what made it so racial among the kids. They grew up with it," she said. "They want something that they don't have to share with anybody. 'This is just for us.' The white kids truly knew they weren't wanted. It kept going into the high school. I listen to the guys talk. They see it as a Hispanic game, a Hispanic sport—'We're the best and nobody can do what we can do.'"

Youth sports often get tangled up in the egos of parents who covet athletic success for their children. Andy Musick may well have wanted more success and playing time for Theo, who played goalie, than the Latino parents thought right. He may have considered himself a coach of the team, while Rucker may have believed his experience meant that he alone was the coach. Some of the Latino parents may have felt the white kids were not as skilled as their children.

All of which is to say that there are probably many reasons why the town's first biracial soccer team dissolved. Yet the result was undeniable: it chased a generation of white kids out of soccer in Garden City. Left without a team, they went on to other sports, and from that moment, soccer in Garden City has been an almost exclusively Latino sport. The city recreation department still holds weekly games at which every child in town is welcome, but these games aren't competitive, and children don't develop many skills. There are more competitive leagues for older kids, but no one who plays in them is white. Thus the high-school team will also likely be uniracial for years in a way that would be unacceptable for any other team sport.

Also watching the Garden City High School team's season unfold was Adam Hunter, who was beginning his third year as soccer coach at Dodge City Community College, seventy miles away.

Hunter was twenty-eight, an outgoing fellow with a gruff baritone, and short-cropped reddish-blond hair. He was from a small town near Wichita, and he'd gone to college on a soccer scholarship. Upon graduation, he found a job coaching the boys' and girls' soccer teams at Dodge

City High School. In 2001, the community college hired him to start a soccer program, wanting to attract Latino immigrant kids and generate some scholarships for them at four-year colleges.

Hunter's job was to recruit kids from the meat-packing towns of Dodge City, Liberal, and Garden City. He didn't speak Spanish. Nor had he much contact with Mexican kids besides the few with whom he'd played. But he didn't figure his new job would be too complicated.

"Go pick the players you want and coach them," he told himself.

That proved to be only half the job. The other half, Hunter came to find out, was administering pep talks and seat-of-the-pants psychology to Latino players from meat-packing towns to get them to accept the scholarships that four-year colleges were begging them to take. So far, these talks had failed, and Hunter was at his wits' end.

"There's definitely a pattern developing," he said one October morning in his office at the school's physical education department.

He had coached three great players in his first two years. Plaques honoring them were affixed to a wall of his office.

"All three of these plaques are for Garden City guys," he said. "All three are our only All-Conference players to ever play here. All three had, or could have had, scholarships to a four-year college. But all three aren't playing anywhere now. All three live with their moms. In fact, every single Garden City kid who's come here to play is back with his mom."

One of these plaques belonged to Guillermo Tamayo, a good-hearted fellow, tall and thin, from La Piedad, Michoacán, with whom Hunter was particularly close. Guillermo's parents had brought him to the United States when he was sixteen. He had been a kicker for the Garden City High School football team in 1999, the year it won state. He was also a tenacious, driven soccer player.

When high school ended, Guillermo figured he'd follow his parents into the meat plants. They wanted him to work there. Hunter, though, had seen him play, offered him a scholarship, and urged him to come to Dodge City Community College. So Guillermo went, without giving much thought to what he was going to study.

Junior college transformed Guillermo. It removed him from the immigrant enclave and his home. Selecting auto technology as his major, he found the classes and the auto lab intimidating at first. But in time, his confidence grew. After two years, he virtually managed the school's auto lab that he'd once been terrified to enter. He had never thought of going beyond high school, yet here he was doing well in college. For the first time, he had to cook for himself, wash his clothes, and pay bills. At first, he went home every weekend, but as he grew accustomed to school, his visits home became monthly.

Guillermo figured his schooling would end after two years at Dodge and he'd go to work in the meat plants. "But when Hunter heard of us stopping school and going to work, he didn't really like that," Guillermo remembered one day, as he sat in a Denny's in Wichita. "He told us that we'd be doing a job because we had to, not because we enjoyed it. He was saying, 'Get an education, and you do the things you like to do.'

"My parents were saying, 'Quit school and start working.' That was their attitude. They had bills to pay. They think that even if you don't have education, as long as you work, you can go through life."

Being away from his family had given Guillermo other ideas. Several schools offered him soccer scholarships. Pittsburg State University, in southeast Kansas, had a top automotive engineering program, which interested Guillermo, but the school had no soccer team. With prodding from Padilla and Hunter, Guillermo tried out for the university's football team as a field-goal kicker. The school's coach liked his kicking, but Pittsburg State didn't give scholarships to junior transfers. The coach told Guillermo he could only fund his senior year. Guillermo decided to attend the school anyway.

He worked that summer in a meat plant in Dodge City and lived with Hunter to save money. The coach persuaded him to take out the first bank account anyone in Guillermo's family had ever had.

That summer, though, Guillermo didn't save as much as he hoped. As fall approached, he had second thoughts about college. Hunter urged him to take out a student loan. Guillermo was terrified of debt— even at the lowest interest rates. His parents moved to Hot Springs, Arkansas, and were telling him to come down and find a job. Two weeks before the 2003 term started, Guillermo pulled out of Pittsburg State and moved to Hot Springs. He told himself he'd attend the school in the winter.

But by midfall, Guillermo pushed off his entry date a whole year. He was battling mightily to decide what to do. Hunter would give him more pep talks over the phone, urging him to leave his parents and go to school. Meanwhile, Guillermo was working at McDonald's.

It drove Hunter crazy. Hunter had begged, cajoled, and browbeaten many of these players to get them to go on to a four-year school. By now, he was getting very practiced at this, though no more successful for the trying.

It wasn't just the star players from Garden City like Guillermo whom he had trouble persuading to stay in school. In his office, Hunter had a roster from his first two years. He ticked off the names of Mexican-im- migrant kids from Dodge and Liberal, as well. Every one who finished the two years of college, and several who didn't, had turned right around and gone back home. Just three weeks before, Hunter's star player in the 2003 season, a premed student from Liberal, had left the team to go home and work in a meat plant. Kids who were passing calculus and engineering classes would suddenly leave school and go home. Most of them returned to work in the beef plants in Dodge, Liberal, or Garden City. At twenty or twenty-one, they had wives, children, or both. Their futures were becom- ing as narrow and hardened as the chutes down which the cattle went to slaughter in the meat plants.

At first, this so confounded Hunter that he was on the phone con- stantly with Joaquín Padilla, out in Garden City. But Padilla had had no better luck with his kids. In six years, only one of his Latino players had gone on to a four-year college. Several of his players were at the plants. It drove Padilla crazy to see this, too, but leaving the enclave and making the jump into the unknown of a four-year college, competing with white people, was too much for a lot of these kids. Padilla commiserated with Hunter but couldn't help much.

"There's a leap that they have to take themselves, but a lot of them don't," Padilla said.

Still, Hunter kept on. The four-year colleges had offered to his players only partial scholarships, and each kid would have had to put up money, sometimes many thousands of dollars. That's what student loans are for, Hunter told his players. But like Guillermo, a lot of them brought from Mexico a terror of debt that years in the United States had not diminished. On top of that, many of these kids feared leaving family. At home, their mothers and sisters cooked and cleaned for them and did their laundry. In Mexico, this syndrome—the way mothers spoil their sons—was called *mamitis*. Several of his kids were afraid to cut that cord and go far away to a school where few people spoke Spanish and they'd have to compete scholastically with white people. So they returned to mom and to the packing plant. This gave them what they wanted now, regardless of what it sacrificed over the long term.

"What I try to explain to them," Hunter said, "is this: your parents came here so you wouldn't have to do what you're trying to do right now. Your parents didn't move up here so that you can go to work in the pack-ing plant, too."

Even there, Hunter found he was only half-right. Certainly, many parents didn't want their kids in the plants, and many wanted their kids to get an education. But a lot of parents, he discovered, also didn't want their children far from home. Southwest Kansas has no four-year colleges, so these parents' attitude sentenced a lot of kids to a junior-college educa-tion, at most. Hunter rarely got a chance to convince the parents other-wise. In Mexico, poor, uneducated parents felt intimidated around schools and rarely participated in school activities. This attitude survived in the Mexican enclave in the United States. Few parents of Hunter's players at-tended their games.

So while soccer in the United States opened a door to a better future, Hunter's Latino players couldn't bring themselves to leave the comfort of the Mexican enclave to walk through it. Three years after starting a soccer team to get Mexican-immigrant kids into college, Dodge City Community College was instead turning out second-generation meat-plant workers, some with AA degrees.

One of these, it turned out, was Padilla's assistant coach for the 2003 season, a young man named Anselmo Enríquez. Anselmo had been the best soccer player ever at Dodge City Community College and the best to come out of southwest Kansas. He is a high-cheekboned, handsome fellow, with a powerful left leg and delicate touch with the ball that, though he was never the fastest guy on the field, allowed him nevertheless to dribble through slaloms of defenders. The second of those plaques on Hunter's wall was his.

As a freshman in 1996, Anselmo had been a member of Garden City High School's first official soccer team. That team was made up mostly of Mexicans, many of whom were timid and tiny kids. They spoke little English and were thoroughly cowed by their taller, older white opponents. Over the next three years, though, they improved and began beating some of the white schools that once had crushed them. His senior year, Anselmo was second in the state in scoring with twenty-three goals.

"Sometimes you feel like you're less when you come to the United States," he said one afternoon, watching the Garden City team practice. "But once you win, you begin to inflate with pride. You feel you can play on the same level. You feel that you've got two legs, just like them."

After high school, Anselmo took a scholarship at Cloud County Community College, four hours north of Garden City. For the first time, he was away from Mexicans and among middle-class white kids. Anselmo's mother had cut beef at a meat plant; his white teammates' parents were doctors and lawyers who drove BMWs. What struck Anselmo was that these kids who had everything only wanted to drink. Every night, it seemed, they were out getting drunk. The next morning, after wind sprints, they'd be bent over throwing up. Anselmo never threw up after wind sprints. He tried to get along with his teammates, but he didn't have money for endless parties. He didn't drink, smoke, or use drugs. He took soccer seriously.

Moreover, Anselmo had come to Garden City from the state of Durango, where his father had been a state-police officer. One day, when Anselmo was about eleven, his father and an uncle went to town to buy fertilizer. They were stopped by a group of men claiming to be state-police officers as well. They arrested Anselmo's father and drove off with him.

The next day he was found shot to death, presumably on the orders of a local drug smuggler. With that memory in tow, Anselmo, his brothers and mother moved to Garden City, where relatives lived.

Anselmo's background distanced him ever further from his privileged Cloud County teammates. Their behavior seemed to him frivolous and wasteful. What Anselmo also noted was how his teammates couldn't wait to leave home for college, in part so they could drink and carouse away from their parents. "Mexicans, we're very close as a family. White people, you leave home, and you don't care," he said. "There in Cloud County, I don't even think the white guys remembered their parents. When they had free time, they wouldn't even go visit their parents. They'd just drink. Me, as soon as I had a chance, I'd come visit my mom in Garden City, then go back to school."

That semester, his mother lost a job and was on unemployment. Anselmo didn't feel right in Cloud County. So after the season, he dropped out and went home. He took a job in the IBP meat plant. The next year he accepted a scholarship at Hunter's soccer program at Dodge City Community College.

That year, Anselmo again displayed his left leg and his spectacular dribbling. He led the team in scoring. Four-year colleges from South Dakota, Oklahoma, and several in Kansas rushed to offer him scholarships. But, again, none offered a full scholarship. Student loans were out, as Anselmo, too, feared debt. That closed a lot of options. He didn't want to again be far from his family. He got his girlfriend pregnant, and their daughter was born. His mother still needed money. So, in the end, Anselmo Enríquez did not accept a scholarship to a four-year school. He went home to his mother's house and the graveyard shift at IBP.

What Anselmo wanted most was to coach high-school soccer and maybe succeed Padilla someday. Padilla encouraged this, but told him he needed a four-year degree. As the 2003 season began, Anselmo was getting older and had a daughter. The graveyard shift at the meat plant in Garden City became Anselmo's path of least resistance. Thus, the best soccer player southwest Kansas ever produced could be found at IBP, shipping boxes of beef until seven in the morning.

As Adam Hunter kept recruiting Latino players from the beef towns, he watched his best former players, whose All-Conference plaques adorned his wall, drop by the wayside. True, their lives weren't done yet, but things didn't look good. He had been unprepared for this part of coaching soccer in the new American heartland.

"Guillermo's down in Hot Springs, when he could be in college right now, in a dorm somewhere, possibly on a football team, or certainly somewhere playing for a school's soccer team, being their leading scorer," Hunter said. "Anselmo was All-Region, our leading scorer. He had chances to get out of here and go to school. He decided to go back to Garden and work in the plant. He knows soccer. He wants to coach. He doesn't want to be doing what he's doing, but he's doing it anyway, and I don't know why."

Alba Torres, however, had seen this so often that she was not surprised. She was Juan Torres's mother. For many years now, her life's project had been protecting Juan, her only child, from a similar fate.

Alba is a short, light-skinned woman with, where her son is concerned, a monumental capacity for work and sacrifice. Education was the point of being in America, Alba believed. She was one of eleven children growing up in a village in Chihuahua where her father had been the postman. Alba had left school as a child, but as an older girl went back to finish elementary school. She had even swallowed her pride at age nineteen and attended a junior high school for three years—with students six and seven years younger.

She divorced Juan's father when Juan was just an infant and raised her son alone. She often worked two jobs, leaving Juan with his aunts and uncles. Juan was born in Dodge City, but Alba had taken him back to her hometown in Chihuahua after her divorce. Eight years later, they visited her brother in Kansas. She saw Juan could get better schooling in the United States, so they stayed.

Over the years, Juan grew into a skilled soccer player. He was graduating after the 2003 fall semester, and Adam Hunter was offering him a soccer scholarship at Dodge City Community College. So for Alba, the decisions he'd make over the next few months were what she'd been working toward all her life.

"I don't want him to just do two years at a community college," she said. "I want him to get a four-year degree. I've always told him, 'I can't give you what you want, but you'll have it once you have an education.'"

The choices young Mexican men around her were making scared Alba. Mexican immigrants now made up almost half the population of Garden City. This, and the proximity to Mexico, kept the families around her emotionally in Mexico, she felt. They lived in the American heartland as Mexicans, returned home often, and therefore certain attitudes they brought with them didn't change.

Among the most harmful of these, Alba believed, was to minimize the importance of higher education. The way Alba saw it, the problem was that college required young people to be poor for a few years as they went to school. This was unthinkable to many immigrant kids. In Mexico, the United States was where people with no education were supposed to get rich. Millions of uneducated immigrants had been proving this for decades by returning to Mexico at Christmas laden with new clothes, cars, tennis shoes, stereos. The stories they told of the United States made more kids in these villages want to go north to test their mettle. These stories didn't often include the indignities immigrants endured as dishwashers, drywall hangers, and factory workers at the bottom of the U.S. economy. It didn't matter. They were living proof of the lesson Mexico had imparted to its poor for at least two generations: menial work in the United States was worth more than a profession at home.

The strange thing was how these attitudes were impervious to the American crucible of western Kansas. It was as if something had broken down. This region that had changed people so fundamentally for more than a century now had ceased to do so.

On one hand, these immigrant kids consumed what the United States was selling; they avidly ate at McDonald's and bought Ford Explorers when they got older. On the other, the Mexican enclave that formed in Garden City quarantined them from America's most liberating ideas. Immigrant families, Alba saw, clung to Mexican ways of thinking regarding issues as mundane as debt and banking and as transcendent as education, work, civic involvement, and what they dared hope for the future. Alba felt it ironic that these attitudes had been part of what had kept Mexico poor, which is what immigrants had left Mexico to escape.

Out on the High Plains of southwest Kansas, these enduring Mexican attitudes combined with the beef plants to create a mixture as hazardous as heroin. In beef plants, a young man without much schooling could earn up to thirteen dollars an hour. Turnover at the plants was high, so these jobs were easy to get. It was quick money and far more than he could make in Mexico. In southwest Kansas, these wages were enough for that young man to make car or house payments.

Once he had a car or house payment, though, that same young man couldn't stop working. For the beef plants were also the *only* place around where someone without much schooling could earn thirteen dollars an hour. The result was disturbing: some Mexican families had two generations working in the plants.

This was unheard of among Vietnamese meat-plant workers. Like Mexican immigrants, the Vietnamese who came to Garden City were poor. They had been peasant farmers with little education and came speaking no English. Yet second-generation Vietnamese were moving into higher rungs of the U.S. economy much faster than Mexicans.

The Vietnamese enclave was never as large, nor as continually replenished, as the Mexican. But Vietnamese immigrants had another distinct advantage over Mexicans, tough as it was: they came from farther away. They had to cut ties to Vietnam and move into America. Vietnamese parents used the meat plants to save money to leave meat-packing and start businesses in Houston or Atlanta, or buy fishing boats on the Gulf Coast. Meanwhile, they emphasized education. Almost all the Vietnamese children in Garden City went to college. They took student loans and combined them with family savings and scholarships to attend public universities far from family, sometimes in other states. This they did routinely. One thing they never did was join their parents at the beef plants.

At least Tri Dang had never seen this happen.

"I think it's just different expectations," he said, sitting one afternoon at a McDonald's. "My dad would slap me if I said I wanted to go into IBP."

Tri had come to the states with his family when he was nine. Tri's father had been an officer in the South Vietnamese Army. The Vietnamese government began expelling those who had worked or fought with the South Vietnamese government. The Dangs were allowed to leave in 1995. They flew from Vietnam to New York, and from there to Garden City, where IBP had a job for his father.

Now a senior, Tri had the best grades on the soccer team, was the shortest player—standing "five feet three on a good day"—and possessed an endearing and self-deprecating sense of humor.

"I'm not a Tri," he told Padilla once, "I'm a bush."

In Garden City, the Dangs found housing in a trailer park. Their neighbors were mostly Mexican immigrants who also worked at the meat plants.

"Walking home they'd make fun of you," Tri said. "There were a lot of fights. They'd say 'Chino, chino, japonés' (Chinaman, Chinaman, Japanese)."

In time, though, Tri learned a little English. The kids from the trailer park were in his ESL class. Pretty soon, he and the Mexican kids bonded in their status as immigrants. By his senior year, the number of Vietnamese students at school had dwindled to fifty or so. Tri's friends were mostly Mexicans. The taunting turned into good-natured ribbing, and the racial jokes were made now in fun.

At eighteen, Tri listened to rap music and spoke a hip-hop English with an accent, as did his Mexican friends. But their paths in life were diverging. This was not something that came up when they joked around.

Tri was taking calculus and writing classes at the local community college to prepare for college. He planned to move to Columbia, Tennessee, where his sister now lived, and study at Middle Tennessee State University. He could help his sister with the beauty salon she owned. His sister, his father, scholarships, and loans would pay for Tri's schooling at Central Tennessee.

Tri had always had an A average. School wasn't that hard, even when he didn't speak much English, and, anyway, his parents accepted nothing less. But Tri doubted any of his Mexican friends planned to attend college.

"The way they think, if you can't get an education and go higher, there's always IBP. They always got IBP to back them up," he said. "Some of the guys go to Dodge City Community College on soccer scholarships, but finally they end up at IBP or Wal-Mart."

Alba Torres saw that her nephews and other young Mexican men thought this way. So as Juan grew up, she went to great lengths to push him toward college. In the ninth grade, Juan saw friends dropping out of school to work and begin buying things. He wanted to do the same. Alba said no. Terrified that he would leave school, she enrolled in a class to study for her GED high-school equivalency exam—to show him that it could be done. For two hours a day she took GED classes, and at the end of a year, she earned her diploma. Juan stayed in school.

She wouldn't let him work part-time until his senior year. Alba knew mothers who couldn't wait for their sons to leave school so they could contribute to the family income. They criticized her for not letting her son work. But Alba had seen young men grow hooked on the short-term cash, buy cars, go into debt, marry, have children. In the end, their commitments kept them from returning to school.

One of these was her nephew, Álvaro Torres. Álvaro was the third great Garden City player Adam Hunter had coached; the third plaque on Hunter's wall was his. Álvaro was a handsome, intelligent young man. After high school, he accepted a scholarship at Dodge City Community College and was one of the team's stars. Then he hurt his knee before his second season. He dropped out of school and went to work at IBP. Eventually his knee recovered, and he could play. But by then Álvaro had three children with three different women and had to pay child support.

He found an easy job in the shipping department at IBP, where a cousin was manager. As Álvaro moved into the plant, it began to take up most of his time. IBP managers often asked workers to come in early and stay late. A worker couldn't plan much of a life beyond the plant. By 2003, school and soccer seemed distant memories to Álvaro, who saw his future increasingly bound up in his meat-plant job.

This drove his mother, Sylvia Trevino, nuts. Silvia had grown up in Garden City and was raised by her grandparents, who were from Mexico. In eleventh grade, Sylvia had dropped out of high school to support her grandparents, as they were getting old. Her working life began. She did many jobs, and then in 1982, she entered the Monfort meat plant. She hurt her back lifting boxes on the second day. A couple years later, cutting brisket with a dull knife, she hurt her hand. Neither pain disappeared through a decade of working at the plant.

Silvia married Alba's brother, Álvaro Torres Sr., whom she'd met through friends. He also found work at Monfort, working on the killing floor and developing over the years a variety of hand pains. As the years went by, they had three children.

"I've always wanted to go to school," Sylvia said, sitting in a recliner at the house she and her family share with Alva and Juan. "But you can't work at (a meat plant) and go to school. You can only do one."

Then one day she couldn't take it anymore. She entered a cosmetology program at Garden City Community College. Finishing that, she took the first job she could find, while saving money to open a beauty salon. This happened to be at the Head Start program for infants and toddlers.

Head Start proved to be Sylvia's calling. She was bilingual, and this made her invaluable to the agency. Sylvia never did develop much of a hair-cutting business. She threw herself into her new job, visiting immigrant families with toddlers, taking them to doctors when the kids were sick, urging the parents to educate themselves about health care.

When the Monfort plant burned down in 2000, Álvaro Torres Sr. got the push he needed. His hands now in constant pain, he left meat-packing and found work with the Garden City Street Department.

With great effort, two of the Torres-Trevino family had left the meat plants. Yet they watched in horror as their sons moved to the plants in their place. Álvaro was already at IBP. Their youngest son, Sergio, a high-school senior, wanted to work at IBP when he graduated in the spring.

This was a different Kansas these immigrant kids were growing up in. The America on display on the High Plains heartland of Kansas was no longer rail-thin; the Protestant work ethic of postponed gratification no longer seemed quite so powerful. Kids in the Mexican-immigrant enclave were often urged to take the quick money—the thirteen dollars an hour—and sacrifice the future for the present. Meanwhile, all around them was an America that seemed to be saying that that was the right thing to do.

How much money one's parents had was a central concern among kids at Garden City High School. The wealthy kids were white, and they were the one who received endless recognition, often for football. These kids had fancy new cars. White kids in class talked often of spending hundreds of dollars of their parents' money on clothes at The Buckles—Garden City's only young-people's upscale shopping option. Sylvia's son, Sergio, came home one day and told his mother of a girl who had blown the clutch in her car. The repair job cost three thousand dollars. She had the car fixed and at school the next day.

"The only thing they can see is the dollar signs," said Sylvia, of her sons and their friends. "They don't want to wait for the long term. They want fast money. They want something that's going to put nice clothes on their back, get them nice cars. As parents, we give them everything they need, but we can't give them the life-styles of the rich and famous. But when they get out of school, they want that right away.

"[Plus] they don't think they can do certain things. I think it's a fear of moving on, a fear of failure. Guillermo Tamayo's a prime example. It's fear that kept him where he's at. My son [Álvaro] is at IBP because they feel it's a necessity. But if him and his wife worked and found jobs somewhere else where they could both go to school, they could do it. Álvaro could work anywhere else. He's real good at computers, but [IBP] is where he wants to go because he wants the fast buck. . . . Once you get into the meat-packing plant, nothing matters as much as money: 'If I want something, I just buy it.' Leaving that is really hard."

As if in reaction to this, Sylvia had returned to school. Now forty, she was getting an AA degree in early-childhood development at Garden City Community College. As Sylvia struggled with homework each night, her children asked her why she worked so hard at it. She planned to get her bachelor's degree at Fort Hays State College in the same major. It might take five years to complete, but she didn't mind.

Alba, meanwhile, had been preparing herself to accept that one day her son would leave home for college. She began this conditioning in 2000. That year Juan received an invitation to play for a national soccer team of fourteen-year-olds and travel to Australia. With teenage melodrama, Juan let his mother know the trip was his life's dream. The thought would have tested any Mexican mother: to watch her son leave home alone to fly on an airplane halfway around the world; plus the trip cost four thousand dollars. Finally, though, Alba realized that her son might return with bigger ideas of life's possibilities.

To raise money, Alba sold enchiladas, tamales, and cakes to friends. The *Garden City Telegram* ran a story about Juan's Australian quest. Teachers and parents found clients for Alba's enchiladas. In the end, selling enchiladas wasn't enough, and her brother borrowed the rest of the money she needed from a bank.

The trip was a disaster. The coach who chaperoned the team turned out to be only twenty-one and liked to drink. Alba worried incessantly. Juan lost his luggage, and she had to send more money. The telephone charges—since he was calling home twice a day—amounted to a thousand dollars. In all, Alba laid out eight thousand dollars for Juan's trip to Australia; it took her two years to pay off the bank loan. Yet Alba got used to the idea that he would leave home some day. Plus, in Australia, Juan had to do his own laundry for the first time. Alba had spent her life making him breakfast and dinner and taking it to his room. That stopped after Australia.

With all this preparation behind her, Alba was alarmed when, as the 2003 fall semester began, Juan informed her that after graduating in December he planned to work at IBP to buy a car. He said he'd work until the 2004 fall semester began, then enroll at Dodge City Community College on the soccer scholarship Adam Hunter was offering him. But Alba was adamant. She insisted he enroll at the community college immediately after high school. As the season progressed, she secretly set about saving twenty-five hundred dollars so he could buy a car without working at the meat plant.

"I don't want him to leave school to go slaughter cows," she said.

"I've seen that they'll start liking the money and working and prefer that to studying. I'm afraid that if he goes to work, he won't go back to school."

Late in October, as the soccer season ended and the team headed into the playoffs, the issue of how Juan would spend the nine months after graduating still had not been settled between them.

❦

Garden City finished its 2003 season a glorious 15–1–1. The team's only misstep was to tie a mediocre Wichita Southeast High School toward the end of the year. A soccer buzz began that no one could remember before. Attendance topped a hundred people at every game. The bleachers were packed. On campus, the team began to get the special treatment reserved for football players—though this was not always a good thing.

Rey Ramírez was far behind in his statistics class, partly from missing school to travel far to away games. His teacher gave him a midterm A anyway.

"I'm not going to argue with it," Rey said, "but I haven't done nothing in the class.

"Last year, if I was walking down the hall, a teacher would have stopped me and asked me why I wasn't in class," he said. "But if I was a football player, it'd be, 'Hey, good luck on Friday.' Now if I'm wearing a soccer sweater, she'd say, 'Good luck on Thursday' or something, even though it's obvious I'm ditching a class. It's not good. It's sending a message to me that schoolwork is secondary and sports is first."

The team's success had created gleeful anticipation on campus about the upcoming playoffs. That anticipation reached another level when Garden City won its first soccer playoff game ever, barely sweating to beat Wichita North 5–1.

Now Garden City prepared to play a much tougher opponent: Maize High School—a white school from Wichita—for the Southwest Kansas Regional Championship.

The game was played in Garden City the day before Halloween, under an aluminum-gray sky, and accompanied by a mercilessly cold northern wind. Maize showed up tall and in red, white, and black uniforms. White soccer teams in Kansas adopt many of the traits of football teams. Maize players did organized drills before the game, and its coaches drew up plays on an erasable board. Garden City's warm-up, meanwhile, was ragged and desultory. As the team warmed up, some of the freshmen on the junior varsity team played squirrelly games of keep-away. Padilla put on a tape and for ten minutes, ranchero singer Vicente Fernández sang "El Rey" (The King), his classic hymn to Mexican machismo, over and over to a cold field of Latino soccer players and white players who probably didn't get the point.

The way soccer is played in the United States and Mexico reveals a lot about the two cultures. Americans have a more in-your-face style, using their strength and height, and tending to brashly blast the ball downfield into the opponent's side. Mexican soccer, on the other hand, is self-effacing, involving lots of quick passing and darting, indirect attempts at pushing the ball forward, as if the players are mortified at their own effrontery.

This describes the first minutes of the game between Maize and Garden City high schools. Maize tried to boom the ball downfield over the Garden City defense. Garden City packed Juan Torres and Luis Posada in around the defense. Later, Garden City players would acknowledge that Maize was the better team. Their players were stronger, taller, and faster. Maize players outjumped Garden City's and spent the first half breaking onto Garden City's side of the field.

Defense saved Garden City. With each breakaway, Maize ran into one of the Hernández boys, an unlikely pair of defensemen: Servando Hernández and Rudy Hernández, who are not related. Rudy had had his troubles in school, but, wanting to graduate and play soccer, was now going to class, making up what he'd missed, and his grades and interest in school were improving. Servando, one of the league's best defenders, had arrived a year ago from a small village in Guanajuato and still spoke no English.

Again and again, the Hernándezes repelled Maize attacks. When Maize players got through the Hernándezes, they collided with impenetrable Miguel Benítez in his lime green goalie shirt. Miguel is a big, thick kid, whose parents are from El Salvador. Miguel himself was born in Queens before his parents moved to Garden City. As the 2003 football team's kicker, he routinely kicked field goals of more than forty yards and was the only top college prospect the football team produced that year. As the soccer team's goalie, he dominated the game against Maize High School.

The goalie on a soccer team has a lot in common with the field-goal kicker on a football team. Both endeavors are solitary and essential to their teams. Neither one participates in the action for more than a few tense moments during the game. Both positions require nerve and the mental ability to ignore crowds and pressure.

This is what Miguel Benítez displayed against Maize. Maize players would streak down the field and rocket a shot at Garden City's goal that no one in the crowd believed would miss, only to have it freeze in Benítez's gloves. Over and over Miguel stopped the ball. He ran at Maize players to smother loose balls. Or he leaped, stretching his body lengthwise in the air in front of the goal to deflect a shot. The students on the sidelines would chant "Por-te-ro! Por-te-ro!"—Goalie! Goalie!—with each save.

As all this was going on, Garden City had trouble even getting off a shot at Maize's goal. So midway through the first half, Garden City began to boom the ball downfield as well, and the game changed. Now it was as if two tornadoes grappled. Up and down the field they went. Each team threw ferocious and desperate attacks at its opponent, who found just enough strength to blunt it.

Facing a superior opponent, Garden City players reached a higher level of play. They put on a sublime demonstration of feints, speed, no-look passes, and the footwork of tap dancers. As they raced down the field, at times they seemed to find a place similar to where jazz musicians go when they lose awareness of their instrument and technique and express perfectly what their minds imagine. Garden City's players twisted and faked and did three scissors in a row to leave a Maize defender behind.

Yet when they got shots, which was not often, they missed. Several times, Hugo Blanco broke away down the left flank, only to have a Maize defender deflect the ball out of bounds.

The timidity with which Garden City had started the season was gone. Players elbowed Maize opponents and slid magnificently to steal the ball. But in this, Maize players matched them, diving into the path of their Garden City opponents again and again. These tackles, performed with a combination of abandon and precision, became the metaphor for how both teams played the game. In a rugged ballet, bodies flipped and flew. Garden's midfielder, Carlos Reyes, tackling so often, seemed to spend the entire game on the ground.

Meanwhile, a stream of students, parents, and teachers moved through the gray, numbing cold to the bleachers to watch. By halftime, more than three hundred people were in the stands. Never had that many people shown up for a Garden City soccer game. The cold froze reporters' pens and dug deep into bone marrow. Children and grown men shivered in the wind, but the game was electric, so no one left. From afar, the bleachers seemed to undulate, as lines of young men hopped in place, bellowing with each attack, rooting on Rey Ramírez and Pablo López as they sped down the near side of the field, and chanting "Ru-dy! Ru-dy!" when Rudy Hernandez would blast a Maize ball away from the Garden City goal. Packs of girls shrieked and broke into chants of "Por-te-ro! Por-te-ro!" after each miraculous Benítez stop.

The game seemed to go on forever. Through the first half and then the second half, the game was scoreless, and so it remained as players ran and ran through one overtime period and then another, and a third, and, finally, a fourth. Neither team hit a wall of exhaustion; at least no player asked to be replaced. Yet neither team could score. Finally, after 110 minutes of soccer, playing time ended with the teams tied 0–0.

In Kansas high-school soccer, when two teams are tied when the game ends, they play an overtime. After the overtime, if they are still tied, they play another, and if the score doesn't change, a third overtime, and then a fourth. After the fourth overtime during the regular season, the game is officially tied. But when the game is a playoff game, and one team must move on and another must go home, then the matter is settled by a shoot-out.

Shoot-outs consist of each team taking turns firing penalty shots at the other's goalie. Each player tees up the ball and aims like a rifleman at the goal, the target, twelve yards away, with a jittery goalie standing between the shooter and jubilation. This tension is only released by a split second of joy or agony, which the crowd endures or enjoys only momentarily before it's the next player's turn and the ordeal begins again. If after five shots the teams are still tied, they continue on, battering each other in deliberate strikes to sudden death: when one team makes a shot and the other one misses.

So it came to this, a frigid shoot-out on the grass under the darkening sky. The crowd poured from the bleachers and streaked down the sidelines to be beside the field's east goal, gripping themselves and hopping in place from the cold. Young men bellowed bilingual cheers, "Let's go, Miguel. Es tuya. Es tuya! He's got nada." Wrapped in blankets, mothers shivered, covered their mouths, and looked about to cry.

During a shoot-out, the goalie's job reduces to guessing which way the opponent will fire and hoping to guess right. On the first ball of the shoot-out, and for the first time all day, Miguel Benítez guessed wrong. He dove left, the ball went straight and into the goal, and the Maize players jumped to their feet, jubilant. A second Maize shot went over the net. But Garden City missed its first two shots. With each shot, the crowd grimaced, stomped and kicked the grass, and doubled over in agony.

On Garden City's third ball, down 1–0, up came little David Villegas. David is a plucky ninth grader, born in Mexico City. He is also thin and one of the shortest players on the Garden City team. David's presence is impish, a look aided by a massive smile that winds around his face and reveals a mouth of big teeth. Murmurs swept the crowd, as people wondered what Padilla was thinking placing little David on the list of kickers. Still, David's presence is deceiving, for in practice he'd shown himself to be one of the team's fiercest penalty kickers. He put the ball down. He calmly backed up. Then he ran forward and shot a rocket into the net, tying the shootout at one goal apiece and sending the crowd into delirium.

The shoot-out now became a war of attrition. On the next ball, Maize scored, but Garden City kept pace with a score of its own. On the fifth ball, Maize shot wide of the goal, giving Garden City an opening. But Rudy Hernández, his legs shaking from the nerves and the fatigue that comes with almost two hours of soccer in the cutting cold, banged a ball over the goal. With each shot, the crowd reached another kind of frenzy. Maize put its sixth ball past Miguel again, and defeat loomed. But Juan Torres answered, tying the shoot-out at three goals apiece.

Then came the seventh ball. The Maize player lined it up, raced at it and kicked it hard, and directly into the hands of Miguel Benítez, where it froze. A Garden City goal would win it. The crowd went berserk, screaming, bellowing, pleading for the team to end it.

The game now rested on the foot of Elbin Palencia. Elbin is tall and thin—a likeable, soft-spoken fellow, whose parents are from El Salvador. He was born in Los Angeles. His parents split up when he was two, and his mother remarried. Elbin's mother and his stepfather had moved the family to Garden City from Los Angeles when he was in the seventh grade. His mother and stepfather worked on the cutting line at IBP. In the plant, his mother lost a lot of weight and often came home with her fingers frozen in a knife-gripped position. Seeing this made Elbin want something else for his life. He wanted to go to college and study architecture.

On the soccer field, Elbin's play sometimes reflected his demeanor. It was distracted at times, and many were the games when from the sidelines Padilla could be heard yelling "Palencia!!", which usually meant that Elbin had let a ball go, or failed to be aggressive enough.

But Elbin could kick, so Padilla put him on the shoot-out list. "It could have been somebody else, better than him," Padilla said. "But it was just him, him and the goalie, and that was it."

Night was closing in as Elbin stood there on the frigid field. He looked down and placed the ball on the ground. Before him the desperate Maize goalie waved his arms and hopped in place to keep limber. Brought to a fever, the crowd now pleaded with Elbin to put an end to it. Elbin backed up, stopped, said a little prayer, and ran at the ball.

The Maize goalie guessed correctly and dove to his right, but Elbin's kick was too hard, low, and toward the corner to be stopped. As Elbin Palencia's ball skipped into the net just under the goalie's outstretched arm, a frozen mass of students and teachers, children and parents, exploded in cries and tears, and raced onto the field. And from midfield, his teammates came running at Elbin, arms outstretched, like lovers too long apart.

Late the next night, Elbin's stepfather, Maurelio García, who'd raised him since he was two, died of a heart attack.

Five days later, Garden City was to play Wichita Heights High School to decide who would advance from western Kansas to the state soccer championships in Topeka.

Shortly before noon, an announcement over the high-school intercom called the team to a special meeting in the locker room with their coach. The players left class and met in the locker room. As they did, they heard another announcement, requiring all students to come to the big gym. So relegated had soccer been at Garden City High School that even after this announcement, some of the players still didn't realize what was about to happen.

In the locker room a few minutes later, they heard the band start up "Hail to the Buffalo." The team walked out, and before them sat the entire student body, packed to the rafters in the gym. For the next half hour, Garden City High held its first pep rally for the school's soccer team.

Pep rallies at Garden City High School, as in most high schools, amount to a secular mass. They consecrate what the school holds dearest. Up to then Garden City had reserved rallies for the annual anointing of the football and basketball teams. But things were different now. The football team hadn't had a good year since winning state in 1999. This soccer team, made up mostly of children of meat-plant workers, was the best thing Garden City had going.

Aware of what was now about to take place, the players stood dazzled and nervous and pumped with pride. They had sat in the stands of this gym and watched many pep rallies dedicated to the adoration of the football team. Here before them were the great hallmarks of high-school sports glory: cheerleaders, school band, teachers, and fellow students.

Hernán Macías's knees began shaking. Carlos Reyes's heart pounded, and butterflies were making him weak. He was almost sick and was not the only player hoping not to trip when he trotted out before the crowd. He looked at Juan Torres. Finally! they said to each other.

For the next fifteen minutes, a gym teacher named John Ford, with a voice made for monster-truck rallies, boomed out the players' names, taking five to ten seconds in the windup and delivery of each one: "Meeeguel Montohhhhyyya," "Loooooowwwwees Posaahhhda." The school had brought out the inflatable tunnel that the football team uses to run onto the field at home games. As his name was called, each soccer player now ran out through the tunnel and onto the basketball court, high-fiving teammates. The students packing the bleachers received each of them with a roar. Walking out through the tunnel, assistant coach Anselmo Enríquez remembered his years playing soccer for Garden City High School and thought, "We never got anything like this."

Ford continued priming the delirium, making up with energy what he lacked in the subtleties of Spanish pronunciation. With a machine-gun "r," he crowed "RRRaaay RaMIIIrez" and "RRRuuudy Hernaaandez." He continued on through the roster. The junior-class section stood and gave Carlos Reyes, a junior, an ovation when his name was called. "Elllbin PalENNcia," Ford announced, reminding the crowd that it was Elbin's goal that had beaten Maize a few days before. Elbin's stepfather was to be buried the next day, but there was no way Elbin was missing this. It just felt so great.

Ford finally crescendoed with "the man with the golden glove . . . Meeeguel Beniiitez" and ended by introducing Juan as "a great student athlete . . . Juan Torrrrrres. . . . Here they are, your regional champions and after next weekend, your state champions."

In her seat in the sophomore bleachers, Vanessa Ramírez was giddy. "It was like this excitement, that we are something in this world," she said later. "For once the whole school sees what we're doing. They see what we've accomplished."

Thus fired with optimism and giddy dreams of going to the state championship in Topeka, the Garden City High School soccer team took the field a few hours later.

The steely cold and low clouds remained from the week before. Another tall, white soccer team in red and black uniforms—Wichita Heights—had come early and was already well into its warm-ups when the Garden City players showed up.

Now, the full range of American sports symbols were laid before the team. Six cheerleaders, white and Asian girls all, arrived to urge the Buffaloes to "S-C-O-R-E, Score!" and again to "F-I-R-E, Fire up!" The bleachers filled with parents and students. Four white students showed up wearing no shirts in the painful cold. Each fellow had painted on his chest a different school initial: "G," "C," "H," and "S." The athletic trainer was there. The entire band and drum line came, too, and at half time they played "Brick House," the Commodores' 1970s disco hit. For the first time, the soccer team had what the football team had every Friday night.

The game shaped up at first as a replay of the Maize ordeal. To several players, it seemed that Heights wasn't as talented as Maize. Still, neither team gave an inch, neither team could score, and in the gray cold, they went up and down the field. The half ended scoreless.

It was twenty minutes into the second half when Garden City scored. Servando Hernández whistled a free kick from thirty yards out. The Wichita Heights goalie bobbled the ball, and it bounced before Luis Posada, who smacked it into the goal.

The stands roared, and the shirtless guys with the GCHS letters on their chest ran the school flag back and forth before the crowd.

At this point, Garden City fell back, and there was the slightest perceptible letting up. It seemed as if, ahead 1–0, the team didn't run as hard for loose balls. They stood a bit more, even though nineteen minutes remained.

This letup now stung them. Garden City defenders didn't get back to cover a Heights breakaway in time, leaving a Wichita Heights player alone with Miguel Benítez. The Heights player chipped a ball over Miguel's head to score.

Now tied 1–1, the game rocketed back and forth across the field. Wichita Heights, feeling the momentum was theirs, laid siege. The Garden City crowd pleaded with its players, chanting "Si Se Puede! Si Se Puede!" (Yes, We Can!). Girls began to pray for another goal. Yet after relenting a bit while ahead, Garden City had trouble digging up that extra vehemence once the game was again tied. Finally, a Heights player scored again.

In a Hollywood movie, the game would have gone on until Garden City tied it, then won it in overtime. Instead, time ran out two minutes after Wichita Heights scored for the second time.

Garden City's soccer season slammed to an end. The crowd deflated visibly. Players collapsed, pounding the cold grass. Others stood on the field with their heads down. The tricky footwork, the dazzling dribbles through three and four defenders, Miguel Benítez's miraculous saves. They had been so close, and so good.

Silence covered the field, broken only by the yelps of Wichita Heights players as they ran to their bus and left. Garden City's cheerleaders, band, and much of the white crowd trailed off for the parking lot. The players walked off the grass and slumped down around their bench on the far side of the field. Seeing this, Vanessa Ramírez and some of her friends broke through the fence built especially for this game to keep spectators off the field. Groups of Latino students began a slow pilgrimage to the far sidelines. There, they came to a stop in a semicircle around the team, as if to protect them. Vanessa began to cry. No one could think of anything to say, but no one wanted to leave, either. So they stood like that for a long time. Miguel Benítez looked out glumly at the field, comforted by his girlfriend. Carlos Reyes saw people crying and wondered if he should be crying, too.

They had gone further than any other soccer team at Garden City High School. Their success was the success of the Mexican and Salvadoran students whose parents worked in the plants. The Latino half of the student body stood a little taller around school each time the team won. Facing Maize, a better, stronger team from a big city, which trained all year long, they'd drawn strength from the hundreds of students and parents who cheered them, and hung in to win. Beyond that, the team had galvanized a part of the population of meat cutters and packers that the beef industry had drawn from La Piedad, Michoacán, and La Unión, El Salvador, to the High Plains of southwest Kansas.

To one side stood Alba Torres. "Well, it's sad," she said, "but they are regional champions."

Padilla gave a brief, dispirited speech, lauding the seniors, saying the team would be back next year. Still, the players had also come to hope for so much more from this year. It was heartbreaking to think that now it wasn't going to happen. Their parents and friends had planned trips to Topeka for the weekend championship tournament. The first pep rally Garden City High School ever held for soccer, for Mexican and Salvadoran immigrants, had been for them.

Juan Torres sat staring at the grass. "I can't imagine that this would have ended here," he told the *Garden City Telegram* later. "Nobody was prepared to have it end."

Seven months later, one bright Saturday afternoon in May 2004, the sun was again beginning its decline in the west over the flat plains of southwest Kansas as the 301 members of the 117th class of Garden City High School prepared to graduate.

Had a strong breeze not blown in from somewhere, the field at the high school stadium might have been deadeningly hot, as May afternoons can be on the High Plains. Two days before it had been so cold that school administrators had to prepare the basketball gymnasium as a fall-back venue, in the event of hail or rain.

As it was a sunny day, the ceremony was held on the school's stadium field, which, depending on your point of view, was now either the new soccer field or the new football field. The school had spent half a million dollars converting it from grass and football-only to an artificial turf that could handle soccer as well. White and yellow lines now traced the limits of both sports, creating a chaotic geometry across the emerald field. Football had made way for soccer in the cattle country of southwest

Kansas. At Garden City High School, the sport would now finally be played in the stadium under the lights. The field seemed a lot like the heartland nowadays: a place that had once been simple and homogenous was now a bit more complicated, maybe a bit more interesting.

Five Gonzálezes, five Nguyens, a Brookover, and an Irsik were in the graduating class. Up into the bleachers filed wizened grandmothers, toddlers, girls in heavy makeup, boys with Ramones T-shirts, and parents speaking Vietnamese, Spanish, and southern-accented English. They were from Zacatecas. They were from Da Nang. They were sunburned ranchers with baseball caps from Midwest Seed Genetics.

Students and administrators gave speeches expressing the clichés of graduation, though these were no less important for being clichés. They were about setting out in life, opportunity, about making choices, and about dreams and the importance of following them. This being Kansas, one student speaker urged his fellow graduates to have "a heart . . . a brain . . . and courage" and to remember, "there's no place like home."

As the sun was setting over a Garden City water tower, seniors filed across a stage on the field to receive their diplomas. John Ford, the teacher who had announced the soccer team's pep rally, was more subdued this time, but lapsed occasionally into his monster-truck voice when announcing the names.

He called the names of Hugo Blanco, Chuck Dodge, Armando González, and Miguel Benítez. Miguel, with his powerful leg, was not leaving to attend a university on a football scholarship, though he was a Division 1 prospect. He was staying to attend Garden City Community College. Miguel had fathered a son, and his girlfriend was only a junior.

Elbin Palencia had planned to move to Los Angeles. But after the death of his stepfather, he was staying to work to help his mother and attend Garden City Community College as well, hoping to take drafting classes, and one day to become an architect.

Tri Dang graduated with a 4.0 grade point average and Principal's Honors. He would leave soon for Middle Tennessee State University.

Rey Ramírez had accepted a soccer scholarship from Adam Hunter and would attend Dodge City Community College in the fall.

Alba Torres watched Juan receive his diploma. She was happy. "But it's not yet what I want," she said. "I'll be really happy when I see him with a diploma from a university. That's what I want."

Alba had been true to her plan and bought her son a car, a white Chevrolet Malibu, for six thousand dollars, so he wouldn't have to work in the meat plants. She took out a loan to buy it. As it turned out, Juan wasn't too interested in enlisting at IBP after all. It was hard work, and he liked his free time. He worked as a cook at the Lonestar Steakhouse in town.

Anselmo Enríquez and Álvaro Torres were still working at IBP. Álvaro and his wife had had a baby and bought a house. To Sylvia Trevino's great chagrin, her youngest son, Sergio, graduated from high school and two weeks later started work at IBP. Watching her sons sever their educations and rush to be fitted for the meat plant's corset made Sylvia ill, and more determined than ever to get her bachelor's degree in early child development.

"It started as a personal goal," she said. "It was something I had to have for myself. But I also want to show my children that I can do it, so you can do it."

A few weeks after the 2003 soccer season ended, the city officially named the field at Kenneth Henderson Middle School for the late Martín Esquivel. It was the first public facility in Garden City, or perhaps anywhere in southwest Kansas for that matter, named for one of the Mexican-immigrant meat-plant workers who extract the wealth from cattle and corn that sustains the region's economy.

Shortly before graduation, James Mireles was named principal of Garden City High School, becoming Kansas's first Hispanic high-school principal. Mireles, the son of a Mexican immigrant, was a school administrator and former football coach who spoke English with the accent of the Texas panhandle where he'd grown up. Like many of the Mexican Americans in Garden City, he spoke no Spanish, but Mireles got congratulatory e-mails from Latinos from across the state.

IBP had been bought by Tyson Foods and was called Tyson Fresh Meats, though everyone in Garden City called it IBP anyway. The Tyson purchase amounted to another consolidation of the U.S. meat industry. Based in Arkansas, Tyson now was the country's dominant producer of beef and pork, as well as chicken, and in dozens of small rural towns it ran plants of the kind Andy Anderson had devised. It was also one of the largest private-sector employers of Mexicans anywhere in the world.

Meanwhile, the boys' soccer team's success was still being felt on campus that spring. The girls' team had more than twice the player turnout than in its previous three years. Half the players were Latinas, many of them ESL students. Vanessa Ramírez was not among them. She was still fighting academic problems. But she had made the school's dance squad and was working to improve her grades so she could participate in it in the fall. The girls' team even won three games, which was more than it had won in the program's first three years combined.

Joaquín Padilla was expecting more boys to try out for soccer next fall.

Soccer in Garden City was facing some interesting challenges. One was whether the sport should leave the immigrant ghetto in which it resided. Padilla, the team, and the school will have to decide if they want soccer to be a racially diverse and consistently winning program or a segregated program designed to keep Latino kids in school. Doing both probably won't be possible. To be successful statewide, Garden City will have to beat the perennial winners: schools from Topeka, Kansas City, and Wichita, where players are predominantly white, tall, strong, and fast, and who train far more rigorously than Garden City. Without a few tall, strong white players of its own, Garden City may have trouble beating those teams. But that will require that Garden City make a prolonged effort to cultivate interest among white kids in the sport that Mexicans brought to town.

Like the Mexican enclave in America, soccer in Garden City will have to open itself to outside influences to fulfill its potential. In the same way that football shared its field and lights with soccer, Latino immigrants will have to share their sport and reach out to make white players who speak no Spanish feel comfortable on the team.

But that was for later. For now, the Garden City High School team had diverted the attention of a town obsessed with football. Immigrant kids had puffed with pride, and more than a sport emerged from the shadows on the High Plains.

A change occurred in the years that followed. Most of the players on the 2003 squad would go on to at least junior college. Several would go on to four-year colleges. They would look back and know the season, as Rey Ramírez put it, "opened the eyes of a lot of guys on the team, to let them dream a little bigger."

And nothing like that had ever before come out of a soccer season in southwest Kansas.

Chapter Nine

Delfino III

Alive in L.A.

As he installed flooring in houses and condominiums across Southern California, Lázaro Juárez thought often about how he wanted his house back home to look.

First, of course, he wanted plumbing that worked. He wanted a roof that didn't leak. He had to have a bathroom with a shower, a kitchen, a living room, and bedroom. His house was to be the second story on a house that his oldest son, Delfino, had built after only two years in the United States.

But what Lázaro Juárez wanted most was to install three lights in the ground below to shine up at his new abode at night so everyone could see it. He'd seen these kinds of lights on apartment buildings around Southern California.

"It will be like one of the condominiums here," he said, sitting one day in a one-bedroom house in the town of Maywood, a suburb of Los Angeles.

Lázaro Juárez spoke softly, and he was slow at times. He didn't know how to read or write. He had grown up in a shack with dirt floors. That was the most he'd ever given his family after he got married and began having children. His mother had had twenty-two children, only four of whom lived beyond infancy. His father and uncles had all been drunks. Lázaro had once been unable to go more than a week without a bender on the local hooch that left him drooling drunk. For fifteen years, he'd never failed to fail his wife and children, and his binges kept his family among the poorest in his rainy village of Xocotla, high on a mountain in the state of Veracruz.

But by now, he had spent eight months in Los Angeles and had traveled across the region putting in floors of wood slat or tile. He wasn't the best worker—it took him longer than it took the others to learn. But as he cut wooden slats and glued them across miles of gringo floors, Lázaro Juárez had come to a new point of view.

His daughter, Abigail, had called recently from the village. She was ashamed. She was fifteen years old, and all her friends were getting married, while she was still in school.

"First you have to study," he told her. "Every house I go to up here —and I've been to houses all over—has a computer. The children, the mother, the father, the old people—they all have them. I don't know how to write my name, but you're going to learn."

Indeed, one effect of the arrival of Delfino Juárez in the United States was the reinvention of his father. There were others.

Delfino landed in the United States worn and ragged from the desert.

But he found work quickly. Guadalupe Cocotle's brothers had come to the United States several months before and found jobs with a Mexican-immigrant flooring contractor named Porfirio Quiñónez. Quiñónez rented them his garage floor in his house in the small L.A. suburb of Bell.

Delfino joined them and began installing flooring for what seemed generally to work out to eight dollars an hour—though the amount Quiñónez paid them always varied week to week. For many weeks, Bell and the garage floor were all he knew of the United States. He spoke no English and didn't know how to drive. It seemed the contractor liked it that way.

After three months of this, Delfino walked one morning out of his confinement, down Pacific Avenue in Huntington Park, and into America.

Pacific Avenue is a lively strip of clothing stores, record shops, bridal boutiques, money-wiring services, and restaurants—all serving shoppers from the Latino-immigrant belt of suburbia southeast of Los Angeles. But as the southland has come to depend on illegal-immigrant labor, Pacific Avenue has also become a pit stop in the region's undocumented economy. Here the papers essential to working in the United States—green cards, state IDs, Social Security cards, and driver's licenses—are for sale as easily as they can be printed in the avenue's back shops.

That morning, immigrant men stood on every block whispering in Spanish as he passed: "Mica!" [green card], "Seguro! [Social Security]," "ID!" Within five minutes, Delfino had paid seventy dollars for a phony Social Security card and California ID. An hour later, he had them in his pocket as he asked around and found a bus that took him a few miles east. He got off and walked the few blocks to the garage floor where he slept.

This was the first bus he'd taken in the United States, and he remembered it later as an important moment. It introduced him to L.A. County's mass-transit system, limited though it is. He wanted to see more of California and didn't want to be like many folks from Mexico who never ventured far from the L.A. neighborhoods they knew. He began to study where buses could take him, and on the weekends he rode them to the beach in Santa Monica and into downtown Los Angeles.

Flooring, as it turned out, also showed him the world. At first, a driver would take him and other workers to jobs across Southern California. But several months after taking the bus that first time, he bought an old Toyota for eight hundred dollars. He learned to drive and mastered the freeways to get to jobs. After finishing in Santa Barbara, Big Bear, and Las Vegas, he would convince his friends they should stay the weekend.

Flooring, moreover, forced him to speak to clients. He gradually lost the fear of sounding foolish that keeps many Mexican immigrants from learning the language. He threw himself into speaking with each customer, stumbling along, until, within a year of crossing the desert, he spoke a serviceable English. He was paid more because of it. English also allowed him to arrange privately with clients to do jobs for them on Saturdays and Sundays for less than Quiñónez was charging them.

Flooring brought him into contact with Americans in a way afforded few immigrants, and so to him they lost a little of their mystique, and the country intimidated him a little less. He saw their children's photos, their televisions in every room, their dirty laundry, the liquor they drank, and the rings around their bathtubs. He floored the house of an occasional Border Patrol agent.

As he floored houses, America's new possibilities unfolded before him. He began to imagine businesses he could start upon his return to Xocotla. He might buy a taxi to haul people up and down the mountain, or maybe a sound system to rent out for parties, or maybe he'd buy hogs for fattening—though he knew nothing of raising hogs.

After six months of working six days a week and sleeping on Quiñónez's garage floor, Delfino and the others rented a house. It was a one-bedroom place in nearby Maywood, a tiny suburb originally built for GIs after World War II. Since the 1980s the town had become a Latino-immigrant enclave. Delfino's brother, Florentino, arrived in Maywood and learned the flooring trade, too.

By early 2004, Delfino was armed with the immigrant's tools of survival: phony papers, a car, a shared house, a job, some English.

It was then that his attention turned to other things. Back in Mexico, his family's eight-by-twelve-foot shack had been the most visible sign of its defenselessness and low social standing. The shack had dirt floors, leaked rain, and left them unprotected from the cold. A girl's family once refused Florentino's marriage proposal because that shack was all he could offer her.

Delfino began sending extra money home every month. His family bought him concrete blocks and stacked them in a corner of its small property. Then, in the middle of 2004, the family moved its shack to one side—it took only a few men to lift it. On the site where the shack once stood, Delfino built the first house in his village ever paid for with dollars.

It had one story, but from the roof rose rebar strong enough to support two more. It had an indoor toilet, a kitchen, and concrete floors. The house was fronted by two smoked-glass windows so wide and tall that it looked as if the house wore sunglasses.

"I wanted it to look good when you pass," Delfino said, "and to have a nice view."

In Xocotla, nothing like it had ever been built so quickly by a youth so poor.

A few months later, Florentino was working in Oxnard, a suburb of Los Angeles, when he spied a house with brick archways, large windows, and a planter in front. He called home and described it to his father and some construction workers. Soon, he was paying men in Xocotla to build him a replica of that house in Oxnard. It stands at the entrance to the village and has a tiled bathroom, a shower, and a hot-water heater.

All this helped change their father. He had stopped drinking and discovered Alcoholics Anonymous. He was now in his forties and tired of waking up in the pig muck. He also now had sons in the United States who were doing well. As they worked up north, he attended AA conventions in the port of Veracruz—the farthest he'd been from the village, other than Mexico City.

His sons could now send him money for construction materials and know he wouldn't spend it on booze. So within a year of Delfino's arrival in the United States, Lázaro was not only sober but supervising construction of first Delfino's house, and then Florentino's, in Xocotla.

Lázaro was proud that his children could trust him. He told anyone who would listen how happy he was that his sons had made something of themselves and changed the story of the Juárez family.

But the village was used to much slower change. The rise of the Juárez boys upset the way things had been up to then, and some folks took it badly.

One night while Delfino's house was being built, a young man named Carlos, a school friend of Delfino's, came to the house enraged and waving a machete. He threatened Delfino's mother, Adelina, saying that the Juárez family was now arrogant and pretending to have lots of money, while he had nothing. He vowed to tear down the house they were building.

Lázaro deflected the envy of townsfolk who watched the Juárez family rise from poverty along with those houses. The changes in him and his family especially upset his drinking buddies, to whom he suddenly seemed too high and mighty, what with his sons doing well in the states and Lázaro no longer drinking.

"People got mad," he said.

Lázaro had never been the object of anyone's envy. He found that he liked it. He kept building those houses, telling everyone that he'd build until his sons in America told him to stop.

For a time, the Juárez brothers were the village's largest employers—spending close to forty thousand dollars on labor and supplies. As Florentino's house went up, the family of the girl who'd refused his marriage proposal let it be known that they regretted their decision. When Delfino returned to Xocotla for a few months in late 2004, older men, who'd once laughed at his mohawked hair, came to him to borrow money.

"Now everyone says hello," said Delfino.

In the end, it was seeing the poorest kid in town put up a concrete house with plumbing and smoked-glass front windows that changed Xocotla.

Years before, Delfino's mohawk haircut sent kids streaming out of Xocotla for Mexico City. Now, his dollar-built house ignited the village's first exodus to the United States. By the time his father finished Delfino's house, young construction workers were paying coyotes like Diez to take them north. Many landed in Florida, Mississippi, and Ohio. Several of them went to Louisiana to rebuild bridges after Hurricanes Katrina and Rita.

The Maywood house, originally home to four guys, came to resemble a Gold Rush bunkhouse. Young men moved through it. Dirty dishes rose from the sink, and posters of naked women went up on the walls. The house was finally equipped with two bunk beds—one with a trundle bed—two sofas, and a mattress in the dining room. When those were taken, men slept on the floor.

By late 2005, one of them was Lázaro Juárez. Fortified by his sons' success and his own sobriety, Lázaro went north with twenty others from Xocotla in the fall of 2005. Up until the hour the group left, people were approaching the coyote asking if he could take them.

Delfino Juárez in front of the house he built with the dollars he earned in the United States. A second story is under construction.

At the Arizona border, the group was caught and deported. Many of the men had no funds to go on. They returned to Xocotla. But Lázaro stayed. He was caught crossing and was deported three more times. He slept at a warehouse the Mexican government provided for the new migrants. Down to his last fifty pesos, he called Maywood. His sons sent him money. Delfino gave him the immigrant's pep talk: "You have to keep at it. Eventually you'll cross." On his fifth attempt, Lázaro Juárez arrived in Maywood and began installing flooring, alongside his sons.

Víctor Gutiérrez, Xocotla's doctor, watched a change come over the village's young men. He noticed that while working in Mexico City, they wanted clothes, boots, a tape recorder.

"Now that they're going to the United States," he said, "they want to have houses, a truck, a complete stereo system, a telephone."

He urged the kids to stay in school, but they scoffed. With a few years in the United States they knew they could do better than if they stayed in Mexico and studied medicine, which none of them could afford to do anyway.

Gutiérrez knew they were right, but "it shouldn't be that way," he said. "Otherwise, the village will be ignorant and won't know anything but how to go work in the United States."

Also observing the Juárezes' advance was Rubén Morales, a fourteen-year-old from another of Xocotla's poorest families.

A thin boy with a toothy grin, Rubén was one of the few who wanted to stay in Mexico and study. His father had been an itinerant coffee and sugar-cane cutter, and the family moved frequently when Rubén was a toddler. Rubén taught himself letters before he was four and read his first book at seven. In time, his family settled in Xocotla, and Rubén was able to attend kindergarten. He loved it, and ever since then he'd relished school and took pride that, though poor, he got the best grades.

But as Rubén grew older, his parents kept having children. Now there were eleven people in the family, living in a two-room shack with dirt floors. They slept on four wood-slat beds with no mattresses. His father injured his back in Mexico City and couldn't work. Rubén couldn't afford books or the bus to attend high school in the county seat of Coscomatepec. He and his father had walked down the mountain to Coscomatepec to apply for scholarships. But the county president, solicitous of the family's support during his campaign, hadn't much time for them since taking office. So Rubén knew his ninth-grade year would be his last.

"It's like Mexico doesn't take me into account," he said, sitting on a chair in the family's cold shack one rainy morning.

"I want to become an important person, someone who stands out," he said and began to sob. "I want to study. I want to be an engineer."

But as that seemed unlikely, he monitored the progress of Delfino and Florentino in the United States, and as their houses went up, he, too, made plans to leave one day.

"My mother's afraid I'll get lost," he said. "But I think the risk is worth it."

Two years into his U.S. adventure, Delfino cut his left hand at a job in Oxnard. He lost movement of two fingers. His contractor, Porfirio Quiñónez, gave him money from time to time, but that dried up soon enough. Rather than sue, Delfino went home.

He came back to a village he'd done a lot to change. Parents were now used to their kids returning from Mexico City with green hair and Che Guevara, whoever he was, stenciled on their pants. Groups of men, meanwhile, were leaving for the United States every few months. Kids asked Delfino about his California years. He told them of the death march with Diez in the desert and of the houses he'd floored up north.

One thing Delfino didn't return to was Mexico City construction work. After working for $10 an hour, the idea of $170 a week seemed demeaning.

The Alameda had changed. The towering Sheraton Hotel was now complete. It had marble floors and black-glass windows. City leaders hoped it would spark redevelopment around the park. The hotel's basement was a parking lot and no longer home to the dozens of young construction workers who erected the hotel. They had moved on.

Part of the area's resurgence was the destruction of the parking lot across the street from the Sheraton on which Samuel Shapiro held the dance hall where Delfino learned to break dance. In its place was Puerta Alameda (Alameda Gateway)—a cube of six hundred condominiums, with elevators, hardwood floors, and fully equipped kitchens that faced the grand park and promised buyers an "entry into a new style of life."

Delfino preferred to settle into Xocotla and gamely attempted to find an acceptable life for himself and his family. He'd missed his wife, Edith, and was upset that his son, Axel, didn't know him when he returned.

"Up there in the United States, you live so fast. You go here, there, in a car," he said. "Here, I can spend the day walking. One day feels like a year. I'm never going to live again in a place that's not mine, I swear."

But Xocotla offered little to sustain him. The business ideas so full of potential when he was in the United States seemed unworkable now that he was back home. His money ran short. A virus swept through town, killing five children. So after several months, in June of 2006, he and three other men from the village took that same bus with the movies playing to Sonora and walked across the line and into the Arizona desert again.

And there, trekking out of Mexico through the saguaros and the cholla cactus, is where we leave Delfino Juárez.

With him went his gumption and chutzpah—the precious commodities that bleed out of Mexico every day at its border with the United States.

I'd met him four years before, while he was break dancing at a dance hall near the Alameda. He was short and from the hills. But while other kids at the dance hall would mutter and look timidly at the ground, he raised his chin and spoke clearly to a tall American twice his age.

He had supported his family from age twelve in the muck of the big city, battling his family's poverty and his father's alcoholism, and attempting an adolescence all the while. For this, his little brothers and sister revered him like a monument. He remained cheerful, generous, ever hopeful for his country's embrace, and hid his disappointment when it never came.

He was mortified that he couldn't offer me a place to stay the first time I visited Xocotla. His family's shack was too mean and crowded, he felt. So he found a family with a better house and swallowed his pride while I stayed with them. His father appeared in the shack drunk while I ate dinner with the family and shamed him further.

But then he went north. He built his own place with dollars and proudly offered me a room when I visited again. Older men were deferential, and his father, by then, was sober and producing for the family in the United States.

Delfino's journey is about what Mexican immigrants seek—a house, respect, protection, an end to humiliation—and about how personalities and desire change places as much as do economic forces.

"I don't want to be rich," Delfino said the last time I saw him. "I just don't want to have to leave to work."

Mexico has an anthem, an army, and a constitution, but it will be half a country until it can fulfill Delfino's dream.

Epilogue

Leaving Mexico

One morning in October of 1999, Oklahoma law enforcement officers swept through neighborhoods in Oklahoma City and the towns of Oakley, Binger, and Thomas in the west-central part of the state.

Concluding a ten-month undercover investigation of a Mexican drug ring, officers arrested sixteen people that day; eight more people were indicted in absentia; agents confiscated ten thousand pounds of marijuana and twenty-three hundred pounds of cocaine.

The bust was the largest in Oklahoma history. Yet what made it truly distinctive was that, though the dealers arrested were Mexicans, the drugs and the network the agents dismantled were part of a ring organized by traditional German Mennonites from the state of Chihuahua in northern Mexico. The case itself hinged on an informant who also was a German Mennonite from Mexico and would soon be dead.

The state narcotics agent who ran the investigation—a genial fellow named Jesse Diaz—told me the story of that drug bust a few years later.

Diaz told me the quantities of drugs smuggled into the United States by this Mennonite ring were huge. Agents convinced a Mexican national they'd arrested who was highly placed in the Mennonite ring to work for them. The informant took Diaz and the other agents on a tour of cities where the ring was sending its drugs. They ended up driving to Nashville, parts of Wyoming and West Virginia, Chicago, Denver, and Kansas City—all where one German Mennonite smuggling ring sold truckloads of drugs.

"It's a lot of dope," Diaz said.

I'd been spending a lot of time in southwest Kansas. Hundreds of Mennonite families from Chihuahua worked on the feedlots that fatten cattle for the beef-packing plants in Garden City, Liberal, and Dodge City. Mennonite couples pushed carts down the aisles of the Wal-Marts and ate at the Mexican restaurants that, like them, came to southwest Kansas with the beef industry. They were gaunt German peasants, resembling the pioneers to the American heartland of an earlier century—only they came from Latin America, ate tacos, and spoke Spanish better than English, and spoke their obscure Low German dialect best of all.

In southwest Kansas, I met a traditional German Mennonite from Mexico named Heinrich. He was a sturdy, rosy-cheeked man of thirty-seven, with wispy sandy-blond hair. He ran the first Alcoholics Anonymous meeting for German Mennonites in a small town in southwest Kansas. Every Saturday night, out on a lonesome county road in a mobile home filled with rugged Mennonite farmhands, Heinrich would lead the meeting with a Low German description of his descent into hell.

As a child growing up in a Mennonite settlement in northern Chihuahua, Heinrich attended a one-room schoolhouse where teachers taught as they had since they'd left their Prussian homeland two centuries before. He did his lessons in chalk on black slates and barely learned to read and write.

As a teenager, he was forbidden from listening to music, from playing sports, from dancing. Drinking was also forbidden, he said, but alcoholism by this time had quietly become a problem in the settlements. Four of Heinrich's uncles had died of diseases related to alcoholism. Soon Heinrich was a drunk, too.

In the mid-1990s, Heinrich, along with other Mennonites, discovered cocaine. It was so prevalent that Mennonite dealers would deliver it to his house. On weekends, Heinrich and his friends would prowl the red-light district of the nearby Mexican town of Cuauhtémoc, snorting coke and using prostitutes. To his inebriation went all Heinrich's money. His friends were addicts. He owed dealers ten thousand dollars.

One day, he told his wife, "If I keep doing this I'm going to die pretty soon. If somebody stops by today, I'm not home." After hiding from his addict friends for a week, he headed for a fresh start on the high plains

An Old Colony Mennonite one-room schoolhouse near Cuauhtémoc, Chihuahua.

of southwest Kansas. He found work as an electrician. His wife and children followed.

Diaz's and Heinrich's stories startled me. I knew what most people in Mexico know about Old World German Mennonites. They'd lived for decades in cloistered colonies, primarily in the state of Chihuahua near the city of Cuauhtémoc, which is four hours south of El Paso, Texas. They didn't mix with others and thus remained fair-skinned, blond-haired, and blue-eyed people. Many of the men still wore straw hats and tight blue overalls; the women usually wore bonnets and ankle-length dresses. They were skillful dairy farmers. I'd seen the men, in their overalls and straw hats, selling cheese at intersections in Ciudad Juárez and near my apartment in Mexico City.

They were doctrinal cousins to the Amish. I assumed they led simple, biblical lives, rejecting pride. Naturally, my question, then, was this: how did they become drunks, cokeheads, and drug runners?

I went to the town of Cuauhtémoc, Chihuahua, to answer it. It seems now a strange thing to have done—go all that way to answer one question. But the beauty of freelance writing is that your editorial decisions are your own. So when a story strikes you as strange or surprising, you might as well go do it. Hunches like this had been luring me around Mexico for a decade. I was hypnotized by stories that submerged me in worlds I knew nothing about. It's what makes journalism less a job and more an enthralling way to live.

This story turned out to be the last one I'd do in Mexico. Yet by the time it was over, I couldn't say I'd gotten to know Mennonites well. I don't speak Low German, and few of them spoke strong Spanish or English. I felt as if I'd watched them through a fog. It's not the way I like to report, but in the end the editorial decision wasn't my own after all.

❋

Before I begin my last Mexican story, I should say that not all—not nearly a majority of—Mennonites in Chihuahua are alcoholics or drug addicts. I should also point out, however, that their leaders don't dare study how large the problem really is.

Let me say, too, that most Mennonites in the world are modern and are not Old World traditionalists anymore. Modern Mennonites, in fact, tend to pity their Old World cousins, to the point even of sending missionaries to lift them from their darkness. Most Mennonites are integrated into their societies, which is, I think, closer to the real point of early Mennonism.

Mennonism grew from Martin Luther's reformation of the Roman Catholic Church in the mid-1500s. Like other Protestant denominations, Mennonism was a reaction to the church's religious monopoly in which arid tradition trumped spirituality and priests paid lip service to piety, while violating God's laws in private. Mennonism grew to emphasize pacifism, humility, and applying the Bible to daily life.

Yet in time, as Mennonites were persecuted across Europe, some of them decided they were God's chosen people. Their faith came to involve less the teachings of Jesus Christ and more the separation from the sinful world, the preservation of Low German, and an agrarian way of life. Only nonassimilation with the world would guarantee a heavenly reward. Over the centuries, Old Colony Mennonites, as they came to be known, held to their isolation and traveled the globe to escape the world.

In 1789, they left Germany for Russia at the invitation of Catherine the Great, who coveted their agricultural expertise for the then-desolate Ukraine. She let them live apart and unmolested. They fled Russia a century later when Catherine's promises did not outlive her. Some Old Colony Mennonites moved to Paraguay, where their ancestors remain.

Others traveled to the Canadian wilderness of Saskatchewan and Manitoba. But after World War I, anti-German sentiment convulsed Canada. Authorities forced Mennonites to join the army and attend English-only schools. Some of them did so. Other families fled.

Mexican Pres. Álvaro Obregón, also coveting productive agriculture and wanting to colonize a barren northern region, invited Mennonites to live autonomously on the high desert in the Bustillos Valley of Chihuahua. Some 7,000 Mennonites came to Mexico in 1922. They bought land; dug wells; grew oats, wheat, and milo; fed it to their cows; and produced Mennonite cheese with the milk. They implanted cutting-edge agriculture in northern Mexico. Cuauhtémoc was a hamlet of a few houses when they arrived. The town became a prosperous agricultural hub of 125,000 people, and the place where Mennonites went to shop. It has a large number of banks for a Mexican town, thanks to Mennonite prosperity and trustworthiness.

Yet by the end of the twentieth century, Mennonite peasant life was in crisis. Scarce credit, drought, cheap imported cheese, and their own overpopulation buffeted them. Large Mennonite farms bought out smaller ones.

"Before, you could do well with three to five cows, two hogs, thirty to fifty hens, and that was enough. You could support a family of eight with that," one Mennonite shopowner told me. "Now you need a lot of cows and really good cows. You need to be rich to do it."

Many German Mennonites from Chihuahua entered the global workforce. Like Heinrich, they emigrated illegally to work as farmhands in

Texas, Kansas, Iowa, and Oklahoma. A good many of them, too, turned to alcohol, and some of them to using and smuggling drugs.

※

In its natural state, the Bustillos Valley in the highlands of northern Chihuahua is a desert of powdery soil the color of dishwater. Rainfall is so rare that only mean-looking shrubs survive naturally. If untended, the land quickly develops a pocked, forbidding look. One testament to Mennonite industriousness is that most of this arid valley is today carpeted with immaculate fields of emerald green, separated by wide country roads that are perfectly straight.

Running through the valley north of Cuauhtémoc (pronounced Kwow-TAY-mock) is a straight-line highway that doesn't veer for twenty-two miles until it arrives at the town of Rubio. Off of this highway are the numbered Mennonite settlements, or *campos*: Campo 2, Campo 4, Campo 6.5, Campo 19, Campo 22, and others. Each campo is a village of a dozen or more flat gray houses, occasionally a one-room schoolhouse, a dairy cooperative, a store, or a farm-mechanics shop. Today, many homesteads are overgrown with weeds, their owners residing in the United States or Canada.

I arrived there in May 2004. To travel among these campos, I rented a car for the first time in Mexico. I'd never owned a car in Mexico; I'd almost never driven in the country. To save money when traveling, I'd taken buses and taxis or walked wherever I went. Because the Mennonite campos are far from Cuauhtémoc, and taxis scarce, I broke with tradition.

The town's lone rental agency had only one car available at a price I could afford. It was a gold Chevy Luv, an economy car, the smallest Chevrolet. For the next week I drove it through the Mennonite campos, talking to God's chosen people about their substance abuse.

Police Commandant Manuel Enríquez warned me about that twenty-two-mile highway. Mennonites hadn't learned to drive the cars and trucks with which they'd replaced their horses and buggies. Mennonites were madmen behind the wheel. They drove at hair-raising speeds, gunning the gas, then jamming the brakes, changing lanes, or pulling onto the highway when the urge seized them.

"Every week we find Mennonites getting drunk, using drugs, and driving vehicles in the scariest way," Enríquez told me when I visited his office. "Mennonites usually are very respectful. They've always accepted the ticket and gone on their way. But lately we've found that they see a patrol car and try to escape. Then when you stop them, they fight the officers."

I found seven Alcoholics Anonymous groups operating in the Mennonite settlements. Many more groups would have formed by now, I was told, had not some pastors labeled AA a cult to be avoided. Moreover, Mennonite authorities had just opened the first drug and alcohol rehabilitation center in North America to exclusively treat German-speaking Mennonites. It had sixty beds.

"We have the image of people who are honorable, humble, and simple," said Juan Loewen, a bishop of the thirteen-thousand-member Manitoba Reinlander Old Mennonite Church, told me one day when I visited him at home. "Often we're not."

The older folks I talked to lamented that things had gotten so bad. They offered a variety of explanations, which usually began with the story of the rubber tractor tires, for that, they believed, was when things began heading in the wrong direction.

❖

Old Colony Mennonite life contained a series of prohibitions intended to enforce humility and keep the world at bay.

In the 1940s, as rubber became available, Mennonite leaders prohibited rubber tires on tractors. Heavenly salvation was achieved only with arduous work on earth, so rubber tires were forbidden because they made plowing easy. In time, though, tires grew cheap. Mennonite farmers began buying them. The pastors excommunicated the first farmers to do this, but they couldn't excommunicate everybody. So in the early 1960s, as more farmers equipped their wheels with rubber tires, church leaders lifted the prohibition. Instead, they forbad cars and trucks, which were becoming more common in rural Mexico.

A generation later, too many families were replacing their horses and buggies with cars and trucks for church leaders to excommunicate everyone. So cars and trucks were allowed, too.

Rubber tires and motor vehicles brought the world closer. Mennonites began buying what it offered. In time, religious prohibitions served only to be flouted. At church, families would listen to pastors denounce, say, the radio as not God's way. At home, fathers would listen to small radios hidden under their beds. Over the years, Mennonite pastors waged and lost fights against electricity, the telephone, the radio, and modern clothes. Television is the current battlefront. "Many people have them in secret," said Bishop Loewen. "We're going to lose that battle, too."

Still, Old Colony Mennonites clung to other traditions that both weakened them and defied common sense. They spoke Low German, for example. Only the men learned any Spanish, though they lived in Mexico. Their children attended one-room schoolhouses where they wrote on black slates as their parents had, were taught with methods two centuries old, and consequently learned very little. Marrying their own, they corrupted the bloodline.

("Mennonites have more deformation of the cornea," an optometrist told me. "It has to do with reproducing within the same bloodline. With Mexicans, finding an optical prescription is easy; it takes five minutes. But you spend half an hour trying to find the correct prescription for Mennonites.")

Old Colony Mennonite pastors also kept the centuries-old tradition of preaching in High German—the language spoken in Germany. But neither the ministers nor their congregations speak High German well. The result: pastors preach clumsily in a language they haven't mastered, and their congregations don't fully understand. The Bible, too, is written only in High German. Mennonite pastors, who can't read well in any language, don't seem to have grasped the book. Bishop Loewen startled me once by asking, uncertain, if Egypt was where the Israelites were exiled.

Mennonite girls walking to look for some friends on Sunday afternoon.

Prohibitions took the place of gospel. To youths, much was forbidden. This included drugs and alcohol, of course, but also sports, dancing, music, fancy clothes, even running and yelling. Pastors could ban the healthiest activities—music and sports, for example. Kids couldn't practice these without attracting attention and bringing a visit from the elders. But alcohol could be imbibed privately. So while church leaders kept their people from playing baseball or the accordion, men and boys snuck into town to buy booze and get plastered.

"[Alcohol] became seen more when we accepted modern life," said Jacobo Fehr, a conservative Mennonite leader. "When people had buggies, it would take them two hours to get to a store. Now it takes them fifteen minutes [in a car]."

Sundays became less the Lord's Day and more a weekly chance to get wasted. By the early 1990s, young people were drinking in public. A curious Mennonite version of cruising evolved and can be seen Sunday afternoons. Old Colony young men drive their pickups wildly along unpaved country roads, looking for groups of friends to get drunk or high with. (Mennonite authorities make kids pick up one bag of trash for every burnout they do in their trucks—one reason why Mennonite roads are so clean.) By 6:00 PM, the roads empty as youths, drunk or sober, return to milk the family cows.

In the 1970s, a schism, a localized Reformation of sorts, took place. A small group of Mennonites rejected the old ways. They opted out of the one-room schoolhouses in favor of modern education for their children and a more relevant Christianity. They were ostracized and excommunicated. Those modernists today have prosperous industries and educated children, though they are still a minority.

Most Old Colonists in Chihuahua entered the twenty-first century with one foot in the nineteenth. They drove pickup trucks and had telephones, yet had attended one-room schoolhouses and couldn't read or write well. They were fluent only in a language few people understood and had been sheltered from the world most of their lives. Like Indians who had no biological defenses against European smallpox, Mennonites' isolation made them defenseless before the world's most pernicious offerings. As farms began to falter in the early 1990s, alcoholism skyrocketed in these families.

Because Mennonite settlements happened to lie on a major drug corridor into the United States, it wasn't surprising that cocaine came next.

❈

The man who acquainted these communities with drug smuggling was a Mennonite mechanic and farmer named Abraham Harms.

Harms and his sons were migrant workers. They lived in Campo 6.5, but they migrated every year to the town of Leamington, in Ontario, Canada, where they picked tomatoes for a nearby Heinz ketchup factory.

Harms fell in with bad folks in Leamington. He had connections to people who could get Chihuahua mountain-grown marijuana. About the mid-1980s, he began taking loads of weed north to Leamington. He proved adept at fashioning hollow-walled trucks. In time, the Harms family would be known for devising hiding places in hollowed-out sofas, carburetors, drive shafts, and gas tanks, as well. At the border in El Paso,

U.S. Customs agents waved through the quaint peasants.

In 1988, Harms was arrested in an undercover investigation in Ontario, making him and another man the first Old Colony German Mennonites busted for drugs in North America. Released on bail, Harms fled to Cuauhtémoc. In 1996, while still a fugitive, he died in a car crash. Not long after that, his career as a smuggler was immortalized in a corrido—or ballad—by a local band, Banda Joven.

"El Corrido de Abraham" goes:

> "I'm tired of being poor,"
> Abraham said to his sons.
> "I'm going to the U.S.
> To sell a few kilos." . . .
> God took Abraham away
> But his sons remained.

Indeed, his five sons diversified the family smuggling operation. Police believe that this included buying cocaine from the Colombian cartels and distributing it to other points in the United States. Some of that cocaine stayed in the Mennonite campos, where by the end of the 1990s, hundreds of people were addicted.

(One Harms brother, John, bought himself a career as a film actor, starring in several narco shoot-'em-ups that he produced. The films are popular rentals at area video stores. In one movie, he suffocates a man by jamming his face into a pile of cocaine.)

I spoke with Mark Loop, whose position as a police officer in Leamington, Ontario, through these years has made him the continent's leading expert on Mennonite drug smugglers. Loop believed the ring to be the largest importer of marijuana into Canada but had trouble getting anyone else interested in Mennonite drug smugglers.

"What I've seen since 1988 is that it went from a guy selling a couple hundred pounds of marijuana, to guys who sell hundreds of thousands of kilos of marijuana and cocaine all over the United States and Canada," Loop said. "[The Harms] are the inventors of the Mennonite mob. That's the original family. They're involved in homicides and everything else."

Seeing the Harms' success, other Mennonites began to smuggle marijuana and, in time, cocaine. Desperate farmers began asking the smuggler families for the chance to drive a load north. By trafficking drugs, many Mennonites survived the vicissitudes of cheese prices, droughts, and unattainable bank credit. Some families stopped farming altogether to devote themselves to drug running.

U.S. Customs got wise. In El Paso, agents searched Mennonite vehicles. Dozens of Old Colony Mennonites are now in prison in Texas, as well as in Chihuahua and Canada, for running drugs.

Meanwhile, the Harms and others set up legitimate businesses on the Cuauhtémoc-Rubio highway that launder money and undercut the prices of the lawful businesses, angering law-abiding Mennonites. Enrique Harms built himself a house in Campo 107, which he bulletproofed by reinforcing it with thirty tons of 1 1/2-inch steel plating.

One place the Harms began sending their drugs was Oklahoma, as police discovered in 1999 when they stopped a Mennonite named Abraham Weibe for drunken driving.

The son of an abusive father, Abraham Weibe had a drinking problem, no education, and few prospects when he left the Cuauhtémoc settlements sometime in the mid-1990s looking for a new life in Oklahoma. In Oklahoma, things went about as well for Weibe as they had in Chihuahua. He was often jobless and drank a lot.

Drunk one night, he drove through the town of Thomas, a couple hours west of Oklahoma City. Thomas police Chief Ronnie Jackson pulled him over. This was Weibe's third offense. He could lose his license. As soon as Jackson appeared at his car window, Weibe began talking about huge quantities of drugs, more than anyone in the area had ever seen, and how he could make Jackson's career.

Not knowing what to think, Jackson called Jesse Diaz, an agent with the Oklahoma Bureau of Narcotics (OBN) in Oklahoma City. Diaz is a muscular fellow, the son of Mexican immigrants, who speaks English with a mellifluous accent that combines elements of Mexico and the American South. As he drove to Thomas, Diaz expected little from the encounter he was about to have with this strange Mennonite.

"But he told us names, locations," Diaz said. "Once he started telling me things as indicators that I know from doing other cases, I thought, 'OK, this guy's not lying.' We had no idea Mennonites were involved in drug smuggling. There was a whole lot of interest once Mennonites were involved. It helped sell [the operation] to our bosses."

The Oklahoma Bureau of Narcotics put Weibe on their payroll. He thought himself clever; narcotics agents found him reliable. Abraham Weibe had likely done nothing in his life as well as he worked undercover for the OBN.

The agents set up Weibe in an old farmhouse outside Thomas, surveilling it around the clock and tapping his phones. Weibe would receive truckloads of marijuana from the Harms organization in Cuauhtémoc every week. The quantities and frequency of the deliveries were, as Weibe had promised, unlike anything Oklahoma drug agents had seen. Weibe's job within the drug ring was to divide the dope shipments into smaller packages, then deliver them where directed around Oklahoma City.

"For ninety days, I felt like I never slept," said Diaz. "I felt like I was operating on caffeine the whole time. At 3:00 AM, they'd call him and say, 'Hey, get the dope ready.' You'd have to scramble agents out of bed."

Off Weibe would drive in a car full of drugs, with agents tailing him and noting the addresses where he delivered it. In Oklahoma City, the exchanges would take place at 6:00 AM, which the Harms organization knew was when the police department changes shifts.

"We were letting marijuana hit the streets," Diaz said. "If it were a different drug, that wouldn't have happened. But we had to understand the scope of everybody involved."

The case changed Oklahoma law enforcement's conception of how drugs were distributed in their state. The conventional idea was that drugs came to the cities first, then were distributed across Oklahoma. It startled law enforcement that Oklahoma's farming heartland, the repository of the state's healthiest values, was where the drugs landed first, and that it originated from German-speaking Mennonite peasants in Mexico, whom agents assumed embodied the best of those rural values.

From wiretaps, agents learned the name, and heard the voice, of Enrique Harms, oldest son of Abraham Harms, who ran the operation from Cuauhtémoc. Through Abraham Weibe, the agents came to understand how the Harms operation used the Mexican and Mennonite diaspora across the United States to move its dope. Agents discovered that Oklahoma and Texas—particularly a large Mennonite colony near the west Texas town of Seminole—were storehouses for the ring's narcotics before they were shipped elsewhere.

The Weibe case is now Oklahoma legend. Diaz and the other agents on the case received a commendation from the director of the FBI, and Diaz has spoken about the case at law enforcement seminars around the state. Oklahoma authorities indicted Enrique Harms, though he still lives near Cuauhtémoc.

Not long after those arrests, Abraham Weibe inexplicably announced he was returning home. Diaz urged him not to go. It was suicide. The Harms knew he had informed.

But not long after Diaz paid him for the last time, Abraham Weibe reappeared in Cuauhtémoc. Two weeks later, he went to Ciudad Juárez with a man who called and was interested in buying a truck he owned. No one has seen Abraham Weibe since. Another informant months later told Diaz that Mennonite smugglers in Cuauhtémoc tortured Weibe in a room for two weeks and dumped his body in a lake.

"I think he was hoping they would be compassionate," Diaz said.

I went to Cuauhtémoc not hoping for compassion but certainly without thinking too deeply about what questions I could ask, and of whom.

I'd written about the narco culture in Mexico, but never about drug smuggling itself. I felt the topic was well covered, and I didn't have a big publication backing me up, so I'd avoided the topic. Maybe for this reason, I'd traveled all over Mexico alone without much trouble, and that had made me complacent.

During my stay in the Mennonite territory, I visited their new drug and alcohol rehabilitation clinic. Clinic directors didn't allow visitors. They did suggest, though, that I speak with a fellow who'd recently completed the program and owned a barbecue restaurant out on the highway. Coincidentally, his name was also Enrique Harms.

I dropped by the restaurant a couple days later. This Enrique Harms was small and thin, with the ferret's pinched face. Sure enough, he told me, he'd had a hundred-dollar-a-day cocaine habit before entering the clinic. He was done with it now, though. During our conversation, I mentioned how curious it was that he had the same name as the well-known Mennonite drug capo. The Harms brothers were his cousins, he said, but he had nothing to do with them anymore.

For some reason, I believed this. I never asked myself how a peasant who'd recently given up a cocaine habit could have so quickly saved enough to open a restaurant. I left and set about my story, which I felt would have less to do with Mennonite drug smugglers than with Mennonite society in collapse.

A few days later, I went to his restaurant for lunch. The food was good. The restaurant was also conveniently located along the highway. So the next day, I returned. Harms saw me but pretended not to.

The next day, I was planning to leave town. I'd been in the region for more than a week. I had several interviews that morning. My travels took me near the restaurant for a third day in a row. So I went there again for a quick lunch.

No sooner had I sat down than Enrique Harms II abruptly sat down at my table and asked why I was still in town. I told him I was going to one of the reformed Mennonite schools, then to a couple interviews before leaving that night for Mexico City.

He interrupted me to say that, oh, by the way, he had spoken with the mother of the other Enrique Harms, the Mennonite narco. She said that he'd gone to California. As it happened, I knew this was untrue. Harms lived in a house along the highway. But I no longer cared. My story was to be about Mennonite society, not its narcos. Still, I said nothing. He left, and I finished eating.

Then as I walked to my car, he appeared by my side.

"Hey, let me take your picture," he said.

I raised an eyebrow and declined. He insisted. I declined again and got irritated. He was getting on my nerves. I turned on him. I told him I didn't believe Enrique Harms had left for California, as he said. I told him that I'd like to speak to his cousin, if his cousin wanted to talk. Foolishly, I gave this ferret-faced ex-cokehead my card for the second time.

Driving off, I realized I'd made a huge mistake. Sure enough, ten miles later, on the way to the school, a purple Dodge Stratus appeared in my rearview mirror. It had smoked windows, no plates, and it was following me.

In my ten years in Mexico, drug smugglers had never followed me before. I'd never imagined that the first to do so would be German Mennonites. So, along with a clarifying terror, a hallucinatory surreality accompanied me down that highway in my gold Chevy Luv.

I did a quick interview at the school, but I was rattled. When I left the school, the purple, unlicensed Dodge Stratus was parked next to mine, its motor running. I turned around and went back inside the school. The Stratus peeled away. From the back of my mind came a mental picture of the parking lot at Enrique Harms II's barbecue restaurant, and in it was a car of this color.

The school administrators told me the highway was the only way out of there. So with no choice, I drove off down the highway to Cuauhtémoc.

As I approached town, I realized another car was following me: a white Stratus this time, smoked windows, no plates. This was serious now. What could I do to lose them? I tried to remember reruns of *Rockford Files* or *Miami Vice* and how those guys ditched cars that were following them. I tried a few lame diversionary tactics. I took a quick turn down one street and parked outside a business, but I had no idea how many Mennonites were looking for me. Plus, they knew the town, and I had the only gold Chevy Luv around. They could see me coming a mile away.

Realizing how pathetic were my attempts to lose them, I got back on the main boulevard. The white Stratus was there again. It followed me through town, pretending to pull in for gas when I pulled over once, then leaving the station after me when I moved on.

I drove to my motel, which I'd left that morning. From a pay phone, I called a couple people to cancel interviews. I pondered my options. They were few. I sure didn't want to spend another night anywhere in Chihuahua. So I headed out of town, aiming for Chihuahua City and a plane to take me away from all this.

As I left town, I saw in my rearview mirror that a large, forest-green pickup truck was now on my tail. Smoked windows. No plates. I stopped at a red light. The pickup came up fast in an open lane beside me. The driver pulled to a stop next to me and leaned out of his cab. He was a German Mennonite. He was not sunburned—which was rare, since many Mennonites worked in the sun all day. His short-cropped blond hair was nicely coiffed, in a way most farmers couldn't afford. He was in his thirties. Another fellow sat in the passenger's seat.

The driver grinned, not caring if I saw his face, wanting me to see it. There, from his truck beside my gold Chevy Luv, he pulled out a digital camera and began taking my picture. He grinned at me the whole time.

Thoroughly rattled now, I raised my hand in front of my face. The light turned green. The cars in front of me moved on. I sped away and into the driveway of the nearest business—a Volkswagen dealership. The pickup truck pulled over and watched me go. At the dealership, I terrified the showroom clerk on duty by telling him to call the police because narco-Mennonites were after me. He did so and began hyperventilating.

I stood in the showroom, imagining all the ways I could die. I'd been foolish and blithe. I had no cell phone—I never could afford one and never needed one until now. I'd relied on public phones and the phone cards they accepted. Even the money on my phone card was almost gone.

The vehicles following me had no licenses plates. How was that possible without police complicity? Chihuahua, moreover, is the playground of the Juárez drug cartel. Jesse Diaz thought the Harms organization was affiliated with the cartel or paid it a tax to run their drugs up through Juárez. I'd heard that Enrique Harms, the capo, was connected to the governor of Chihuahua.

I had no large newspaper or company backing me up. The *Los Angeles Times* had just hired me, but the job didn't start for six weeks. I didn't think they'd appreciate a cry for help before I was even on the payroll. Finally, I had sixty miles to go to catch a plane, on a highway on which I'd be easy to follow.

No Old Colony Mennonites with Uzis appeared as the minutes ticked by. The Volkswagen clerk urged me to leave. I stayed. Finally, two police officers arrived. After listening to my now-garbled Spanish, they escorted me to police headquarters.

A reporter in a situation like this knows to get Mexico City involved. I called my dear colleague, Lynne Walker, from Copley News Service in Mexico City. She called the U.S. embassy, other correspondents, and President Fox's spokesman. As I sat in the police chief's office, Fox's spokesman called to assure the chief that higher-ups in Mexico City were watching the situation.

Two officers—one driving my gold Chevy Luv, the other driving me in a large pickup truck, and both with AK-47s at their sides—sped me the sixty miles to the Chihuahua Airport. I flew to Mexico City where I spent an anxious night in a hotel. A "lawyer," name of Martínez, called my apartment that night asking for me. The tenant didn't know where I was.

In anticipation of taking the *Los Angeles Times* job, I'd planned to spend a week moving out of my apartment in Mexico City. Instead, I flew to the United States the next day. Three weeks later, I returned quietly to Mexico City, packed, and left in two days.

What happened to me was minor. Worse happens to Mexican journalists, who are more vulnerable than I. Still, it was scary enough: chased out by drug-smuggling, semi-inbred, Old Colony German Mennonites, one of whose brothers was a bad-movie actor, all of whom had received their education in a one-room schoolhouse and were a generation removed from the horse and buggy, but who now ruled the roads of Cuauhtémoc, Chihuahua, with a fleet of shiny, unlicensed, cocaine-acquired vehicles with smoked-glass windows.

I don't think I could have invented an ending like that. After ten beautifully surreal years, it seemed a fitting way to leave Mexico.

So I did.

Story Updates

Delfino Juárez

DELFINO CROSSED THE DESERT again and made it to Phoenix. Heading to Los Angeles, he was caught up in a Border Patrol roadblock and deported.

He'd already paid the coyote for the trip. So, his money nearly gone, he took a bus down the Baja peninsula to the Cabo San Lucas tourist resort for Americans, where his wife's father and brothers were working construction. There he remains and may for some time. In Cabo San Lucas, there's work, at slightly better pay than in Mexico City, the weather is beautiful. He's working on houses for Americans, but now it's in his country. Two months after arriving, he sent for Edith and their son, Axel, and they live together again.

Florentino and Lázaro Juárez still live in the Maywood house and install flooring across Southern California. Lázaro struggles some with alcohol, but remains, for the most part, sober.

When last heard from, Diez was continuing his "work" of bringing people from Veracruz across the Arizona border.

Many of the people he's brought are from Xocotla, for the exodus has not diminished. On the contrary, Xocotla is on its way to becoming yet another Mexican village of empty houses, one which belongs to Delfino Juárez.

The Tomato King

In 2004, Andrés Bermúdez ran again for mayor of Jerez, Zacatecas. He ran with the center-right National Action Party (PAN), won again, and this time his election was not annulled.

Midway through his three-year term, however, Bermúdez had achieved few of the changes he hoped an immigrant could bring to Mexico.

311

"His administration was a disaster due to his own lack of preparation," said Zacatecas immigration scholar Rodolfo García, "but also because of the consistent attacks on him by the PRD and the PRI. Yet with all his errors, his magnetic personality keeps on having an impact on campesinos."

In the 2006 federal elections, the PAN made him its candidate for congress. Bermúdez won again. As of this writing, the Tomato King was about to become federal congressman from the state of Zacatecas.

The Saga of South Gate

In November 2006, a federal judge sentenced Albert Robles to ten years in prison.

"There are different levels of hoodwinking," a teary-eyed Robles told Judge Stephen Wilson, pleading for mercy, "but I didn't think hoodwinking was a crime. During that period I decided not to be a very good man every day. But I did not decide to be a criminal."

That didn't convince Wilson, who said, as he pronounced sentence, that Robles had preyed on city finances and South Gate residents themselves. He called Robles a "puppetmaster."

The city of South Gate, however, recovered rapidly from the Robles years and the brink of bankruptcy.

Courts ordered lawyers to return a portion of the money the Robles crew had given away. Motivational speaker Tony Robbins returned forty-five thousand dollars of the city's money Robles had used to buy himself a platinum membership in the speaker's organization. Police busied themselves retrieving the badges the Robles crew had given away.

Xochilt Ruvalcaba and Maria Benavides have disappeared from local politics.

Henry Gonzalez remains on the city council. A year after the recall, Hector de la Torre won a seat in the California state assembly. Bill De Witt ran for, and won, the city council seat De la Torre vacated.

A dark spot in the city's rebound came when Rudy Navarro, the treasurer who defeated Robles in 2003, admitted he'd lied in claiming he'd finished college degrees in finance and political science.

Doyle and Chuy Wrap Juárez in Velvet

Chuy Morán never could make a go of velvet painting in Juárez a second time. Within a year of trying again, he gave it up and moved back to Rosarito Beach, in Baja California, where he remains today. But the change did him good. He found work painting houses—and sometimes the murals within them. In his spare time, he paints for himself—on canvas.

In 2004, Doyle Harden retired from Chico Arts. He gave the company to his employees and wife to run and took a tax write-off. He lives in El Paso, though he sold his desert ranch, where he and the painters had chased jackrabbits on three-wheelers, to the city of El Paso, which coveted the ranch's water rights.

"I bought a forty-five-foot travel trailer. I'm just kicking back, relaxing, and traveling," he said. "I kind of forgot the business life."

Meanwhile, merchants along the Avenida Juárez tourist strip, where in 1964 Doyle Harden discovered his life's work, report that they rarely sell a velvet painting anymore.

Tijuana Opera

Sadly, in 2006, Enrique Fuentes closed his café after five years. The costs of running it were draining his pocketbook. One Saturday in July, he auctioned off much of the thrift-store decor with which he'd furnished the café—among them the sixty-inch Magnavox with the red velvet curtains.

Yet before he did, he helped stage the third annual opera street festival, which packed people again onto Fifth Street in Colonia Libertad.

Having caught the music-promotion bug, Enrique continues to organize recitals in restaurants and halls around Tijuana. And to his delight, he was soon to appear in his second Ópera de Tijuana production—*Rigoletto*—this time as a singer.

In the years after *Pagliacci*, La Ópera de Tijuana went on to present *Don Pasquale* and *Romeo and Juliet*, as well as scenes from several other operas. It has also formed a permanent chorus.

Mercedes Quiñónez, meanwhile, continues to study music, volunteer at La Ópera de Tijuana, and is happy to be, at fifty-four, Tijuana's premier soprano.

Atolinga

Two men and one woman were convicted of Raúl Briseño's murder and robbery, which they'd done to get money for drugs. They were sentenced to lengthy prison terms.

The Briseño family remains in the restaurant business, as does Chon Salinas. He has not yet brought himself to sell the California-style ranch house in Atolinga.

According to a 2000–2005 Zacatecas survey, forty-two of the state's fifty-seven municipios—similar to counties—had lost population.

A Soccer Season in Southwest Kansas

The 2003 soccer season indeed opened the horizons of Latino students at Garden City High school.

As of this writing, five guys from the team—Rudy Hernández, Servando Hernández, Hugo Blanco, Pablo López, and Elbin Palencia—were attending Dodge City Community College and playing soccer.

Rey Ramírez is now studying school administration at Wichita State University, hoping to become a principal some day.

Juan Torres, to his mother's delight, was about to begin at a four-year private college—McPherson—three hours northeast of Garden City, with a scholarship to study to be an elementary-school teacher.

Making the dance team helped Vanessa Ramírez get a dance scholarship at Garden City Community College. As of this writing, she is also planning to go out for the school's soccer team—as GCCC finally added men's and women's soccer. She hopes to study radiology or education administration at a four-year school some day. Her parents' attitude toward her education has not changed.

Joaquín Padilla remains the school's soccer coach. In 2006, the Garden City High School's girls' soccer team was the first soccer team, men or women, to go undefeated in league play. They lost in the playoff's quarter-finals.

A headline in the *Garden City Telegram* recently read:

HAIL, RAIN PELT AREA

HEAT WAVE ON THE WAY

Epilogue: Leaving Mexico

Jesse Diaz continues his work at the Oklahoma Bureau of Narcotics.

So, too, police believe, does Enrique Harms continue to smuggle drugs into the United States from the Mennonite colonies near Cuauhtémoc, Chihuahua.

Old Colony Mennonites can still be seen on street corners in Juárez and Mexico City, wearing tight overalls, straw hats, and selling cheese among the cars at stoplights.

I assume the problems of drug abuse and alcoholism still afflict the Old Colony Mennonites of northern Chihuahua. But I haven't been back there since then, so I wouldn't know for sure.

Acknowledgments

AFTER MY FIRST BOOK was published in 2001, people at my speaking engagements at various universities asked me how I came to tell stories.

I think this is how:

When I was four, my father and mother, my younger brother, Nate, and I drove from Cambridge, Massachusetts, to Claremont, California, and what is now known as Claremont McKenna College, where my father was to take a job as professor of literature.

Along the way, my father, as he drove, began telling me the adventures of Odysseus from Homer's *Odyssey*. As I was four, I'd forget Odysseus's name from time to time; he became "the guy who begins with the letter O." But I found the stories addicting and pestered my dad for more, even at times kicking the back of the front seat of our old brown Buick station wagon.

As we drove through what I remember as Arizona and New Mexico, my dad kept telling me the stories of Odysseus and the Cyclops, the Sirens, and others.

When you grow up hearing great stories, you probably end up loving to tell them.

My father, Ricardo, retired from CMC a few years ago, having written five books and about to publish another. I thank him and love him for all he's given me.

During the reporting and writing of this book, he and his wonderful wife, Roberta Johnson, a professor and author herself of four books about Spanish literature, gave me encouragement and a place to sleep on my sojourns into the Mexican diaspora in Los Angeles, while listening nightly to the latest wacky story from South Gate.

My mother, Lolly, and my brother, Nate, died in 1979, and I miss them still.

My younger brothers, Ben and Josh, and I have new additions to our family: my sisters-in-law, Marion and Michelle; my nieces Laurel, Sarah, and Cecilia; my nephew Nathaniel and my niece Sophia; and now my sweet wife, Sheila Tully.

Again, I would like to say "Hey" to my lifelong friends from Claremont High School. Claremont in the 1970s was a great place to grow up—a town with enough order to allow for freedom, full of guitar players and keggers in orange groves.

I'd like to say "Howdy" to my equally dear friends from U.C. Berkeley's student coop, Barrington Hall—now defunct. When I was at Berkeley, Barrington was the best place to live—a three-story forum for exploration, perfect for punk-rock shows and great all-night parties.

I have had several great editors in nineteen years in journalism. Sam Enríquez, who brought me from Mexico to the *Los Angeles Times* in 2004, is probably the best I've worked with. My thanks, too, to the folks at University of New Mexico Press, particularly to David Holtby, and now to Clark Whitehorn, for so enthusiastically accepting my work. Members of my wife's book group—Laura Field, Becki Lindley, Melanie Harris, and Darcy Moore—read chapters of this book and provided wonderful comments.

Delfino Juárez and his family welcomed me to their home several times. I thank them, and the people of Xocotla, for their great generosity.

Two people I've not mentioned in this book helped me understand immigrant Mexico. Luisa Moreno, Jaripo's pharmacist, and Guadalupe Ramos—director of the Lázaro Cárdenas Center for Studies of the Revolution, in Jiquilpan, Michoacán—were always welcoming. Their insights into immigrant reality were like going to school.

Above all, I'd like to thank for their stories the Mexican immigrants I've met in a dozen years of writing about the greatest movement of people from one country to another in our time.

In ending, I'd like to introduce the world to our wondrous little daughter, Caroline Kateland—born just weeks ago, as I write—whom I hope will be daring, story-loving, and choose, as her father did, the thing she loves for her life's work.